Mirror Talk

Susanna Egan

The University of North Carolina Press

Chapel Hill and London

Genres

of Crisis in

Contemporary

Autobiography

© 1999

The University of North Carolina Press

All rights reserved

Designed by Richard Hendel

Set in Carter-Cone Galliard by Keystone Typesetting, Inc.

Manufactured in the United States of America

The paper in this book meets the guidelines for permanence

and durability of the Committee on Production Guidelines for

Book Longevity of the Council on Library Resources.

Library of Congress Cataloging-in-Publication Data

Egan, Susanna, 1942–

Mirror talk: genres of crisis in contemporary autobiography /

Susanna Egan.

   p.   cm.

Includes bibliographical references (p.   ) and index.

ISBN 0-8078-2499-2 (alk. paper). —

ISBN 0-8078-4782-8 (pbk.: alk. paper)

1. Autobiography. I. Title.

CT25.E25   1999

920 — dc21   99-17970

        CIP

03 02 01 00 99   5 4 3 2 1

For my mother

Contents

Acknowledgments

The Social Sciences and Humanities Research Council of Canada has provided significant support for this work, as has the Killam Foundation, which enabled me to take a sabbatical. I am grateful to both.

Portions of this book have appeared in the following journals:

"Breytenbach's *Mouroir*: The Novel as Autobiography." *Journal of Narrative Technique* 18 (Spring 1988): 89–104.

"From the Inside Out: *Lily Briscoe a Self-Portrait: An Autobiography by Mary Meigs.*" *Prose Studies* 14 (September 1991): 37–55.

"Lies, Damned Lies, and Autobiography: Hemingway's Treatment of Fitzgerald in *A Moveable Feast.*" *a/b: Auto/Biography Studies* 9 (Spring 1994): 64–82.

"*The Book of Jessica*: The Healing Circle of a Woman's Autobiography." *Canadian Literature* 144 (Spring 1995): 10–26.

"Encounters in Camera: Autobiography as Interaction." *Modern Fiction Studies* 40 (February 1995): 593–618.

I have revised and adapted these articles as the book evolved and am grateful to these journals and to their reviewers for housing my work in process and encouraging me to improve it.

I also acknowledge permission to use extracts from comic books that have facilitated discussion of the genres of autobiography. I am grateful to use extracts from *Doonesbury*, copyright © 1993 and 1995 by G. B. Trudeau, reprinted with permission of Universal Press Syndicate, all rights reserved; extract from *Maus II: A Survivor's Tale* by Art Spiegelman, copyright © 1973, 1980, 1981, 1982, 1983, 1984, 1985, 1986 by Art Spiegelman, reprinted by permission of Pantheon Books, a division of Random House, Inc.; extract from *Our Cancer Year* by Harvey Pekar and Joyce Brabner, copyright © 1994, art by Frank Stack, reprinted by permission of Four Walls Eight Windows.

This book has been a long time in the making, and many people have helped me along the way. I am grateful to the research assistants who have found my materials, organized my notes, read and edited my writing, and contributed suggestions and information from their own areas of expertise: Titilope Adepitan, Julie Archer, Roberta Birks, Rosemary Croft, Elizabeth Emond, Marian Gracias, Nancy Pagh, and Leslie Williams. Students, graduate and undergraduate, have suggested books, songs, and films, and have read many of the texts considered here in ways that challenged and helped my thinking. Among these, Greg Beckman, Dylan Dix, and Adam Lund went to some trouble to find materials for me. Many people have been generous with their own work in process; I have profited from manuscripts by Blanca Chester, G. Thomas Couser, Peter Dickinson, Valerie Dudoward, Marilyn Iwama, Jennifer Lawn, Sharon Meneely, Roger Porter, Dorothy Seaton, Julie Walchli, and Penny van Toorn. Many have read sections of this book, contributed their expertise, and scolded, criticized, and praised in generous doses: Timothy Dow Adams, G. Thomas Couser, Paul John Eakin, Margery Fee, Wendy Sue Hesford, John Hulcoop, Arnold Krupat, Mary Meigs, Nancy K. Miller, Maureen Ryan, Judy Segal, Risa Sodi, Sandra Tomc, and Penny van Toorn. I am grateful to Peter Friedman, Louise Hager, Jim Lane, and Sarah Kennedy for very particular help with film. I have profited from conversations with James Banham, Marguerite Chiarenza, Vera Rosenbluth, and Jonathan Wisenthal. Andrew Busza, Jane Flick, Sneja Gunew, and Jerry Wasserman have helped me with materials. Roberta Kremer and the staff at the Vancouver Holocaust Centre have been most helpful for my work on Primo Levi. I am especially grateful for the fierce editorial attention of two former graduate students, now distinguished colleagues, Janice Fiamengo and Gabriele Helms, and for the extraordinary resources of Eva-Marie Kröller, who has repeatedly over the years known exactly what I needed to know before I knew it myself, dropped off books and articles, and cut her *New York Times* to ribbons for my benefit. At the University of North Carolina Press, I have received valuable guidance and encouragement from external readers and am grateful for the patience, skill, and support of Sian Hunter, Pam Upton, and Ian Finseth. Without the constant loving-kindness of Kieran Egan, patient critic and computer whiz, I could not be smiling at the end of the day.

Mirror Talk

Facing Off

Genres of Life and Death

In the beginning was a review essay by James Olney in the Spring 1986 edition of the *Southern Review*. In its comprehensive title, "Autobiography, Theory, Criticism, Instances," this edition of the *Southern Review* acknowledges both the mix of genres contained in the journal and the curious and inescapable ways in which readers of these genres are also and simultaneously their writers. In his essay, furthermore, titled "(Auto)biography," Olney makes a new claim: not just that an element of the autobiographical directs a biographer's choice of subject but, more radical and of far-reaching consequences, that "the finest biographies — *as the very condition of their being the finest biographies* — always and invariably reveal clear and compelling traces (and often much more than mere traces) of autobiography" (429). Olney's appreciation of this genre mix, elaborated with discussion of three particular texts,[1] opens discussion outward in three specific ways: first, he foregrounds the biographer as the reader of a life whose own life, in turn, is available for reading in the written "life"; second, he suggests that the "authorial 'I' . . . draws biography across the vague, wavering, and indistinct line that separates history from literature," thus endorsing the reader as writer while liberating autobiography from the constraints of verifiable data; and third, he suggests that "the encounter of two lives . . . produces the biography that is in its nature a work of art or of literature" (429). Olney clearly values the timbre of personal urgency that such encounter generates, but I read this qualitative judgment also to mean not some canonical "best" but, rather, the most effective matching of genre to the needs of the original situation. Since

1986, the poetics of autobiography have certainly increased and multiplied in numerous directions, but I pick up here on that complex "encounter of two lives" for my own starting point.

The tension that Olney notes between narrator and subject replicates between two people the tension that theorists have long noted within the relationships of author, narrator, and protagonist as one person. The very claim on an audience already splits the internal and external manifestations of the writing self. Shirley Neuman puts it this way: "[T]he imaginative act is double: the autobiographer imagines both himself and a reader he hopes to convince of his experience. We might, therefore, restate the paradox of veracity thus: in order to make his reader believe in the truth of an experience so subjective that the autobiographer alone can attest to its veracity, he will in some sense treat that experience as if he were examining it from outside himself, as if he were a biographer" (1981, 320). Connecting this observation to Stephen Spender's "great problem of autobiography," Neuman explores strategies of "distancing the self in autobiography." She quotes Spender's formulation of "the great problem" as follows: "An autobiographer is really writing the story of two lives: his life as it appears to himself, from his own position, when he looks out at the world from behind his eye-sockets; and his life as it appears from the outside in the minds of others; a view which tends to become in part his own view of himself also, since he is influenced by the opinion of those others" (317). Neuman then reads the autobiographies of Wyndham Lewis and Hal Porter through the lens, so to speak, of Spender's "double vision" in order to unravel what she calls "the paradox of alterity" (318). This essay, "The Observer Observed," examines both the heightened self-consciousness of these particular autobiographers and the rhetorical strategies with which they move between the speaker and the one spoken, between inside and outside perception.

Spender's sense of the self as constituted in part by the perception of others provides a twist to Olney's (auto)biography: the encounter of two lives may also impact upon both. What happens if Rodger Kamenetz, for example, meditating on his mother's last illness and death in *Terra Infirma*, were engaged in a dialogue in which his mother responded, if his perception of her were corrected, so to speak, by her perception of him? One result, surely, would be an increased degree of apparent authenticity established, paradoxically, by the very instability that such externalized doubling would create. Precisely because no single "authorial 'I'" would control perception, the ironic reader would be more fully implicated in the text than before. Because the perceptions being established would destabilize each other, they would also confirm each other. Spender's doubled self, when doubled outward between two people, would tackle head on the problem of "truth" that has dogged our conceptions of autobiography from the beginning.[2]

The narrator's ability to remember or be truthful generated considerable speculation in the early days of autobiography theory. Such problems were laid to rest in part with a recognition of the relevance of fiction to the kinds of truth that autobiography could tell,[3] and in part because of a sharpened focus on autobiography as a literary or illocutionary "act."[4] This deflection of attention from product to process has also been important for the discussions that follow. Whereas Roy Pascal did not think he could "evade the conclusion that the supreme task of autobiography is not fulfilled in modern autobiography" (160), later theorists, focusing on the activity or process and the necessarily fictive nature of writing, have altered our conceptions of "the supreme task" and revealed the rich lodes of contemporary work. Contrary to Pascal's expectations, significant numbers of recent autobiographical works foreground the processes and present time of their own construction. Downplaying even the narrative formations of identity that Eakin examines (1999), many forfeit historical depth for immediacy of experience and personal doubling of vision for interpersonal exchanges. One curious result is that "I" speak and am spoken in exchanges that authenticate presence, but only in the fragile moment.

The kind of (auto)biography to which Olney was drawing attention has certainly proliferated, and many such works will figure in the present discussion. Writing frequently becomes a matter not only of intense involvement of narrator with subject or of self-recognition in terms of the imagined perceptions of others, but also of co-respondence, in which two or more voices encounter one another, or interact. Similarly, critics and theorists have begun to insert themselves more willingly into their discussions of autobiography, first replacing critical authority with a relativist stance that acknowledges limited and particular perspective, and then often moving toward fuller participation in the autobiographical venture.[5] I propose first to identify some of the critical elements that generate and condition much contemporary autobiography, then to trace that "encounter of two lives" between reader and writer of life and of "life," repeated both outside and inside the text — an encounter that I describe, somewhat problematically, as "mirror talk" — and finally to expand that notion of interaction into discussion of the genres of autobiography. The chapters that follow explore genres in two particular ways: first, as malleable and responsive to particular life crises, and second, for the interactive elements inherent in their composition. Finally, as interaction between people and among genres makes dialogism a recurring feature of many contemporary autobiographies, I shall focus briefly on mirror talk as dialogical.

CONTEMPORARY ELEMENTS:
THE POLITICS OF CRISIS AND THE BODY

Olney's suggestion that encounter is particularly creative has led me not only to explore varieties of encounter and of creativity but also, by virtue of the readings that followed this lead, to acknowledge Jean Starobinski's point that crisis is seminal for autobiography. What Starobinski actually wrote was, "[O]ne would hardly have sufficient motive to write an autobiography had not some radical change occurred in his life" (78). More recently, Anthony Paul Kerby developed the point that "[m]uch of our own narrating can be usefully seen as driven by some . . . conflict, tension, or crisis in our own lives" (63). I cannot think of a single autobiographer discussed in the following pages for whose text crisis is not key. Whereas Starobinski, however, was working with the Gusdorfian model of the autobiographer, a Western man of single and coherent identity embedded in the Christian-humanist tradition, I have focused on the contemporary phenomenon of "writing engendered by a crisis that is not yet resolved" (1987, 24).

The urgent present tense of this writing is particularly significant for its contestatory or resistant strategies that untrammel the subject from discursive helplessness. Paul Smith's work is illuminating here. He finds that current conceptions of the subject have produced a purely theoretical subject removed from political and ethical realities and sets out to discern a new subject. For example, he finds the subject subjected to ideological interpellation inappropriate for the conception or practice of resistance and suggests we need to "dis-cern," or release, the subject because "each of us necessarily negotiates the power of specific ideologies by means of our own personal history" (37). Discussing autobiography, Smith deplores de Man's refusal of a meeting between "I" and "me," subject and object, except by the illusion of the mirror, calling this brand of deconstruction moral and political blindness. It ignores the "cerned" and complete individual; the autobiographical "I" is de facto a third-person pronoun, he suggests, "supposedly having full objective possession of that which it views" (105). It guarantees its own knowledge by means of its learning and experience. For Smith's "dis-cerned" subject, as for subjects responding to one another in un-resolved, present-tense crisis, the personal is political and assumes agency.

In practical terms, crisis is an unstable condition seeking change. In some cases, the genre itself creates the crisis, as with variations on documentary film or in drama, where the genre in which people have chosen to work reifies the human encounter. In other cases, as in that of diaspora, crisis has become a permanent state, a balancing act re-enacted in the text. And in others, crisis takes the form of disaster, as with time at Auschwitz or diagnosis of terminal illness. The genres of life and of death, in other words, evolve from "in the middest," to use Frank Kermode's term (1966, 8), close encounters of intensely creative kinds. Significantly, because the crisis in each case is current and con-tinuing, it seems to emphasize memory rather less than future pos-sibility, narratives of identity rather less than the presence of a survivor. In narrative terms, David Carr describes "retention" and "protention" as both part of a present field of occurrence, so that knowledge of the past and anticipation of the future determine present understanding. Enjoying minimal control over narrative teleology, such crisis writing often seeks to affect the politics of its environment. ("[P]resent and past," David Carr writes, "are experienced as a function of what will be" [29].) Narrative protention and political change form a propulsive triangle with personal transformation, which figures largely in many of the texts to be considered here.⁶

Another distinctive feature of contemporary concern has been the foregrounding and emphatic presence of the body. I use the word "presence" deliberately because the body resists current cultural no-tions that the self is constituted entirely in language and in text. In part, some resolution of the body-mind dualism results from a cultural para-digm shift that revalorizes the body as a significant component of iden-tity. Elizabeth Grosz suggests that Western philosophy has been estab-lished on a foundation of profound somatophobia (5) and borrows from Lacan the image of the Möbius strip in order to describe embod-ied subjectivity/psychical corporality:

> The Möbius strip has the advantage of showing the inflection of mind into body and body into mind, the ways in which, through a kind of twisting or inversion, one side becomes another. This model also provides a way of problematizing and rethinking the relations between the inside and the outside of the subject, its psychical inte-rior and its corporeal exterior, by showing not their fundamental

identity or reducibility but the torsion of the one into the other. (xii)

This model, furthermore, depends on the interaction, not the opposition, of the psychic and the physical. It depends also on the recognition of an embodied self as both part of and distinct from the world around one, as having both center and limits, coherence and threats of dissolution that take bodily form. Paul Ricoeur, for example, writes of "the absolutely irreducible signification of one's own body," suggesting that its dual status, as a fragment of one's experience of the world and as one's own, enables it to provide "the limiting reference point of the world" (54).

As a limiting reference point of the world, the body retains its boundaries with difficulty. Grosz draws on Julia Kristeva's theories of "abjection," which describe the ways in which the body may spill over into its surrounding world — bodily wastes producing fearsome evidence of sexual difference or, more generally, anticipating the ultimate dissolution of the body in death. Indeed, the permeability of the body challenges notions of autonomy or entity. Women's autobiographical theory in particular takes up the body as a source of knowledge (see Sidonie Smith 1993; Neuman 1989), but so do those for whom physical disability threatens the very sense of self.[7] Oliver Sacks has written extensively on body image and identity, and Eakin draws on his work to explore the role of the body in autobiographical conceptions of the self (1992, 184–90). In particular, Eakin details the lacunae that gape in one's experience of identity when neurological disorders damage one's sense of "self," suggesting the role of the body in creating that sense and the cataclysmic effects of bodily damage. Elaine Scarry writes of the body as the center of experience: "It is only when the body is comfortable, when it has ceased to be an obsessive object of perception and concern, that consciousness develops other objects" (39). Autothanatographers experience their deathward dissolution as physical transformations that alter their sense both of who they are and of what matters about their lives. They tend on the whole to be more preoccupied with rendering the impact of death on life than with giving birth to the author of the text.

For the autobiographer, this body (itself, of course, already inscribed by all the variables of its cultural production) represents also the ground from which personal inscribing begins. Steering between the Scylla of disembodied, universalizing narratives and the Charybdis of reductive essentialism, contemporary autobiographers seem concerned with exercising textual construction in such a way as to posit pre-, post-, and extra-textual selves.[8] Certainly, the physical self grounds such issues as gender, color, and sexuality that are central to the cultural constructions manifest or resisted in the text. Certainly, too, the crises that generate autobiography may begin with the body; suffering, illness, and death go to work on the body and determine its narratives. Not least, when two or more subjects work out their (auto)biographies together, they do not do so as talking heads or lambent souls; intersubjective recognitions are both more whole and more present than their solipsistic predecessors. Not only the hand that writes but also the body that needs, wants, hurts, inherits, disgusts, and so on, "figures" in the text. For contemporary genres of autobiography, furthermore, the body provides maps of experience, presences for the camera, metaphors for the material production of the artifacts of life construction. Finally, the unresolved crisis embroiling the physical identity of the autobiographer figures as crisis to some extent because it lacks literary precedent or canonicity, or pushes the limits of what can be represented.

MIRROR TALK

Mirror talk begins as the encounter of two lives in which the biographer is also an autobiographer. Very commonly, the (auto)biographer is the child or the partner of the biographical subject, a relationship in which (auto)biographical identity is significantly shaped by the processes of exploratory mirroring. Blake Morrison, for example, uses his father's final illness and his death to explore the bonds that knit him to this impossible man and concludes, very much his father's son, by wearing his father's clothes to the funeral. Or Philip Roth, jockeying for position in relation to his father, exposing his father's illiteracy and incontinence, paradoxically exposes his own likeness to his father and his need for recognition.[9] Such "reflections" within a text repeat processes common in lived experience, where one person is formed in relation to another, often but not always by genetic inheritance as well as by proximity in life.

Parallels between text and life become even closer when both subjects are involved in the preparation of the text. Narration then takes the form of dialogue; it becomes interactive, and (auto)biographical identification becomes reciprocal, adaptive, corrective, affirmative, as is also common in life among people who are close to each other. Such collaborations seem far less concerned with mimesis, however, than with authenticating the processes of discovery and re-cognition. These autobiographies, in other words, do not reflect life so much as they reflect (upon) their own processes of making meaning out of life. Anticipating discussion of the specular, I suggest Gertrude Stein as deliberate and exemplary in the matter of convoluted self-reflection; not only does *The Autobiography of Alice B. Toklas* play games with the author/subject connection and include numerous discussions of the effects of art upon life, but studiously posed photographs also develop such reflection. I am thinking of Stein in her armchair facing left (hair short) underneath Picasso's portrait of her facing right (hair piled up in a crown); and of Toklas and Stein on either side of their fireplace, facing out like ornamental cats or dogs.

One feature of such collaborative work is the likeness it can bear to spontaneous revelation in an immediate situation. Techniques vary widely, but manner and tone tend to the demotic, the daily, the interrupted. The very foregrounding or authenticating of process becomes one way to invite recognition of the autobiographical subject/s; they may be sophisticated, even ironic narrators, but they really were here — dealing with this problem or having this conversation. Ironically, because these works foreground the strategies of their own composition, this sense of immediacy provides a simultaneous illusion of unmediated reality. Autobiographers who, within one text, are both subject and object of speech and regard, becoming in turn self and other for each other, play out the politics of lived experience as a realistic trope for exploring, defining, and expressing just who they are.

Dialogue, after all, is one mode of "realizing" identities to which "attention must be paid," of positing the self as both respectful of and distinct from other selves. The significance of dialogue (of many possible kinds) for autobiography is its manifestation of what Jessica Benjamin has called "intersubjectivity." "The intersubjective view maintains that the individual grows in and through the relationship to other subjects" (19–20). The mirror metaphor can be problematic precisely because it does not acknowledge the freestanding nature of the other.[10] The intersubjective perspective, on the other hand, identifies "the need for *mutual* recognition, the necessity of recognizing as well as being recognized by the other — this is what so many theories of the self have missed. The idea of mutual recognition . . . implies that we actually have a need to recognize the other as a separate person who is like us yet distinct" (23). The reader of autobiography reacts to both likeness and distinctness, and so do the dual subjects reacting to each other within the text.

The "real presence," furthermore, of speaker or writer is confirmed by the responsiveness of each to the other and by the fact that their dialogue is comprehensible only in terms of the involvement of both. If the ontological self, as author/autobiographer and as object of reference, has been theorized out of existence, it is forced into reappearance by interacting with another.[11] The point I am making here connects with two current strands of important theorizing: on the one hand, responses to the problems that deconstruction has posed to autobiography studies and, on the other, the significant feminist rethinking of autobiographical identity since the late seventies.[12] Eakin, for example, has been working on what he calls "the relational life," and he suggests that "*all* identity" is "relational" (1998, 63). Writing on "death memoirs," Nancy K. Miller suggests that "the self of autobiography may well be neither simply autonomous and separate . . . nor terminally fragmented and dispersed. . . . Rather, through their relations to the other, these are subjects as doubled *out* as split within" (1992b, 13). The other, she adds in a footnote, "provides the map of the self" (14). Eakin and Miller are both concerned with relaxing the gender divide between "his" and "hers" in our understanding of autobiography, recognizing in the process that we can fruitfully reread traditional texts for elements of cross-dressing not recognized before. Miller suggests that "perhaps the 'I' of an autonomous and separate self is autobiography's deepest fiction of 'masculine' truth" (1992b, 13). Eakin suggests that feminist distinctions between women's lives and men's say more about past reading of autobiography than about lives or texts: "All selfhood . . . is relational despite differences that fall out along gender lines" (1998, 67). Once again, reading and writing are both implicated in their cultural moments, which add another dimension to relationality; the cultural moment for reading and for writing makes significant new components visible and comprehensible to the autobiographical imagination.

If women's reading of women's writing first enabled reading of relational selves, and if women's studies of female psychological development also suggested relationship, in contrast to separation, as a developmental model,[13] these specific, gendered contributions have certainly been supported by theorists in other areas. Narratologists, for instance, elaborate on some of the ways in which mirror talk need not involve two participants within the text but may manifest itself as a function of the narrative. Ross Chambers, writing of the politics of oppositionality and the power of literature to alter desire, discusses the power relations between narrator and narratee and concludes: "As an activity of mediation, reading — as the production of a text-reader relation in which each component functions as the other's other — demonstrates that the production of identity is relational and systemic and that, as a consequence of this systematicity, its outcome is change" (249). (I associate this "change" with what I have called the forward-looking political focus of works that cannot reach narrative closure, with Paul Smith's enabled subject and with Carr's narrative "protention" that helps to make sense of the present moment.) Ironically, even as the multiple participants of the text acknowledge both the textuality of their production and the specificity and limitations of its particular cultural moment, such textual production represents life precisely if only because narrative protention, personal transformation, or political change, rather than conclusion (as in fiction), is the desired, even necessary end.

Where Chambers discusses the production of identity as relational, Carr discusses the continuous process of composing and revising personal and communal autobiography for constantly evolving meaning and the very events of such storytelling as necessarily intersubjective; we co-author ourselves with others in our social roles (84).[14] Similarly, Richard Terdiman, who describes culture as the field of struggle (33), builds his discussion of "discourse/counter-discourse" on narrative tensions. *"Language presupposes difference.* It exists only within a differential world, a world of conflicts and oppositions" (15). The social roles in which a teller requires a listener to arrive at a communal story are also political roles in which conflict, opposition, and alliances create interactive tensions comparable and indeed parallel to those between (auto)biographical individuals. Narrative theory therefore overlaps with and finds support in relatively recent developments in anthropology.

Issues of class, "race" (an unstable term), gender, and ethnicity necessarily contribute to the interactions between people and between the cultural systems from which they write. Long-standing assumptions that binary divisions favored the metropolis over the colonies, the white man over the black, the man over the woman, and the anthropologist over the native informant (or, indeed, the biographer over the object of study) have given way before recognition of relative perspectives. So Clifford Geertz has been influential in calling for us to see ourselves as others see us. Anthony P. Cohen develops two ideas pertinent to interactive autobiography: first, in order to recognize anthropological perspectives and assumptions, "the inevitable starting point for my interpretation of another's selfhood is my own self" (3); and second, "For the anthropologist to give others back their selfhood is to contribute modestly to the decolonisation of the human subject"

(192). Many of the autobiographies discussed in the following chapters elaborate on the resistance of the colonized to the controls others have exercised over their stories; they talk back, not to implode the margins upon the center but to decentralize the telling of their lives.

Among revisionist anthropologists, Michael M. J. Fischer has made specific contributions to the study of autobiography. Introducing three distinct autobiographical voices, he calls them

> compositions of identity, dialogic relations with alterities and triangulations of post(modern) sensibilities: Autobiographical voices are often thought of as deeply singular attempts to inscribe individual identity (1st voice). They are, however, not only mosaic compositions but may often be structured through processes of mirroring and dialogic relations with cross-historical and cross-cultural others and thus may resonate with various sorts of double voicings (2nd voice). In modern times mediation by collective rational and rationalizing endeavors such as the sciences, which themselves depend upon explicit triangulations among multiple perspectival positionings and understandings, is increasingly important (3rd voice). (79)

Fischer works from the premise that "autobiography seems particularly useful as a vehicle of access for anthropological investigation" (83) and achieves, in the process, an understanding of autobiography as composed of many genres and constituted by means of dialogic or mirroring encounters.

Because I am engaged by encounters between people, and by the enactment of such encounters in shifting and original genres, the mirror talk of my title derives rather less directly from Lacan than might be supposed—though readers more familiar with his work than I am may identify opportunities for illumination that I have missed. I cannot, of course, discount the impact of Lacan's thinking on my own in general terms. James Mellard, for example, quotes a phrase from Ragland-Sullivan that is most apropos for my current thesis. He refers to Lacan's notion, given the primacy of language over experience, of "the intersubjective and, *therefore*, intertextual nature of our 'selves'" (45, emphasis added). My choice, however, of the mirror as a metaphor depends on a combination of reflexive practices in autobiography, both problems and solutions. For example, autobiographers have always wrestled with the split between subject and object, between writing and written selves, seeing the very act of autobiography as present "reflection" upon the past. Contemporary autobiographers, furthermore, who seem to stake no claim for a unified or coherent identity, seek no illusions of coherence from the reflections available to them. Their texts display fragmentation, incoherence, even dissolution. The mirroring process in these cases comes to no more than moment-by-moment confirmation of another subject or of generic means for articulating the crisis of the moment. The mirror of my title is more constructive than reflective of the self. It foregrounds interaction between people, among genres, and between writers and readers of autobiography.

The problems attaching to such relatively simple interaction does find confirmation, however, in Lacanian thinking. Malcolm Bowie, for example, clarifies Lacan's distinction between the ego, developed from the mirror stage, and the subject, who might choose to function as an autobiographer: "Whereas the ego, first glimpsed at the mirror stage, is the reified product of successive imaginary identifications and is cherished as the stable or would-be stable seat of personal 'identity,' the subject is no *thing* at all and can be grasped only as a set of tensions, or mutations, or dialectical upheavals within a continuous, intentional, future-directed process" (131). Breytenbach's *Mouroir*, discussed below, plays with the impossibility of seeing the self or even enabling the self to be seen. It also introduces the text as the medium for speculation and death as the elusive but quite certain discovery. Repeatedly, other writers resort to the mirror as a metaphor — for revelation as for disappearance — reminding the reader of the scopic drive that implicates us in the desires of the text. Mirror as metaphor shares unlikely company with photography and film,[15] with mapping, and with the visual arts that posit space and vision as suitable for articulation of the self.

GENRES OF LIFE AND DEATH

If Breytenbach's title, *Mouroir*, conflates the concepts of self-reflection and death, or self-discovery in confrontation with death, it also describes life writing as a death sentence. This ultimate, or foundational, relationship of life with death has always been important to autobiography, but the writing of unresolved crisis implicates death or some subordinate form of unwelcome resolution in every full stop. The text that concentrates on presence in the present moment, insisting on confirmation and resisting resolution, is using strategies that may be new in autobiography. The genres that best articulate the resistance of the living to death do not simply defer this inevitability but also suggest the means whereby other "inevitabilities" may be countered — such as hierarchies among genres themselves, or among races or cultures or peoples. Resistant strategies that untrammel the subject from discursive helplessness subvert established verities and need to be identified.

The question for me, then, is this: what are these strategies? How do autobiographers co-opt and adapt the genres that express this fraught moment of in-between? How do they spell out their intersubjective or their relational selves?[16] And what happens to our sense of autobiography when we see the soloist involved in duets or chamber music? One immediate effect, on which Eakin has worked extensively, is the embedding of that self in its culture; the individual becomes securely positioned in time and context. Another effect, running parallel with these discoveries and not therefore strictly an effect, is the increasing claim to be heard and recognized by voices either marginalized or silenced under old dispensations. If subjectivity and alterity can take turns within one text, with neither one disappearing as a subject, then dialogues between cultural and political margins and centers also become possible within the text. Indeed, not only possible, but necessary. With the result that the center, as center, ceases to be a fixed or stable point of reference. Another implication that I need to elaborate is the destabilizing of written narrative as a primary mode for autobiography. Not only is dialogue frequently oral, in origin at least, but the exercise of interaction and the foregrounding of the processes of mutual recognition also invite dialogue in generic terms, among genres, within genres, and from genres beyond the traditional autobiographical canon.

Indeed, the very term "autobiography," suggesting a specific or definable genre, has proved problematic for a number of theorists for quite a while. Olney, who first expanded the term to mean both more and other than a verifiable historical narrative, describes autobiography as slippery and finds "no way to bring [it] to heel as a literary genre with its own proper form, terminology, and observances" (1980, 4). Feminist theorists, however, have taken issue with the assumptions attaching to early definitions of autobiography as a genre. So Sidonie Smith, exploring women's writing as marginalized for too long, concludes that "'[a]utobiography' no longer makes sense culturally. Its structural, rhetorical, and imagistic rigidities have been fractured by the heteroglossic possibilities inherent in new ideologies of selfhood" (1987, 174–75). These heteroglossic possibilities, I suggest, emerge quite clearly in varieties of mirror talk. Smith's description of women's needs to develop "a complex double-voicedness, a fragile heteroglossia of [their] own" (50), coincides with Chambers's observation that the oppositional, always on the weaker side in power relations, is therefore prone to improvisation.[17] Again, this observation describes the genre-blending so common in varieties of mirror talk, particularly for confrontation between opposing forces. Caren Kaplan has written about the powerful elisions, co-optations, and experiments that constitute the cultural margins that have been transforming the practices of autobiography: "As counterlaw, or *out-law*, such productions often break most obvious rules of genre. Locating out-law genres enables a deconstruction of the 'master' genres" (119). Kaplan writes about what she identifies as "transnational feminist subjects," but Leigh Gilmore is indignant that the "law of genre which defines much of traditional autobiography studies has been formulated in such a way as to exclude or make supplemental a discussion of gender" (1994a, 21). "In short," she concludes, "the law of genre creates outlaws" (21–22). Reconfiguring autobiographical identity in relation to discourse rather than to the real, Gilmore then suggests that the "mark of autobiography indicates a disruption in genre, an eruption or interruption of self-representation in genres in which it has not been previously legitimated" (1994b, 7). What has happened, I suggest, outlines a remarkable series of interactions between autobiographers and their readers. Whereas Gilmore's "autobiographics" identifies women's writing in particular as transgressive of received genre descriptions, I suggest that those very descriptions were always malleable, open to new suggestions, new input, so to speak, from the autobiographer. What is remarkable about the (notably plural) genres of autobiography is that they go on expanding, responsive to the politics of lived experience and of that culture-constructing to which both texts and critics contribute.

I tend therefore to think we are politically and theoretically short-sighted when we quarrel with a term as comprehensive and as flexible as "autobiography." I recognize that each alternative term has been introduced either as a form of resistance to the exclusionary practices of traditional humanism, and part of a valuable reshaping of the field, or in what I think of as a mistaken understanding that this or that curious item that has caught our attention does not really belong. With the field of autobiography studies radically reshaped over the past twenty years, my concern now is that we reach for the new horizons not as separate or contested territories but as significant features of the landscape, protecting ourselves from anxiety about what does or does not belong by acknowledging the flexibility of a word that admits so many variations.

Consider the range: Domna Stanton's "autogynography," for example, raises the question whether women's writing is inherently different from men's and moves attention from the text to the circumstances of its originating life — a move that other "minorities" have been eager to adopt, and a move that is significant to those who write in crisis. Gilmore defines "autobiographics" as "those changing elements of the contradictory discourses and practices of truth and identity"; avoiding "the terminal questions of genre," she asks, "Where is the autobiographical? What constitutes its representation?" (1994a, 13). H. Porter Abbott coins "autography" as an umbrella term that includes the reader's response; distinguishing autobiography from both fiction and fact, Abbott suggests that an autographical reading asks of the text, "How does this reveal the author? It is to set oneself analytically apart from the author in a project that often succeeds in spite of him" (613). When Jeanne Perreault uses the term autography, she "invites the reader to reconsider the imbrications of subjectivity, textuality, and community" (2). Autography is different from autobiography because it "makes the writing itself an aspect of the selfhood the writer experiences and brings into being" (3–4). Audre Lorde's "biomythography" (1982) is specific to her own need both to trace an "imaginary homeland" for herself and to present its map to her successors. Distinguishing genres like essay or meditation from retrospective narrative, Michel Beaujour referred to "autoportrait." Françoise Lionnet describes Zora Neale Hurston's works as autoethnography (1989, 97–129). Identifying illness narratives as crucial to autobiography, G. Thomas Couser coins the term "autopathography" (1991, 65); similarly, focusing on relations with a dying parent, Miller's coinage is "autothanatography" (1994, 12). Specific terminology — and these terms are just samplings — is valuable for specificity of focus and serves well to recalibrate assumptions or exclusions. These terms, however, do not suggest that autobiography itself is an outmoded or unusable term, but rather that this genre, like Whitman's amazing self, contains multitudes.

If we have worked ourselves free from past exclusions, surely we can allow the humanist, Gusdorfian model an honorable place in the history of autobiography studies and be wary of creating new procrustean beds with new exclusionary language. We can use the traditional term as an originary composite that allows us to identify its numerous subgenres not as in rebellion against but as authentically of the same genre. In short, returning to Olney again, genres are not isolable but organic, transformative among themselves: "Autobiography, like the life it mirrors, refuses to stay still long enough for the genre critic to fit it out with the necessary rules, laws, contracts, and pacts; it refuses, simply, to be a literary genre like any other" (1980, 24–25).[18] My own instinct is to reject the mirror metaphor in this instance as presupposing a passive mimesis and to suggest instead that experience generates appropriate modes of representation. Just as theorists moved rapidly from the seventies on to include a range of genres in their discussion, and just as they quickly ceased to ask whether we could trace the boundaries between history and fiction and began asking instead just how fiction serves the purposes of history, so the question now is not what we may allow but what it is that autobiographers are doing in times that keep on changing. As Eakin reminds us, attending not only to particular autobiographies but also to a wealth of theory from several disciplines, "[T]he autobiographical act [is] performed . . . in strenuous engagement with the pressures that life in culture entails" (1992, 71).

In their wonderful collection of essays entitled *Getting a Life*, Sidonie Smith and Julia Watson and their contributors explore the genres of autobiography in which we all engage daily — the medical file or the professional C.V., television talk shows, vicissitudes of family life, or losing one's wallet and the whole "identity" that it contains. What they call "backyard ethnography" (16) has its "uses," as their subtitle indicates; it foregrounds the cultural workings of self-invention and dignifies the humble and the various modes of identification that place us within our circumstances. Technological developments, of course, increase both the range and the variety with which ordinary components of everyday living can become matters of record, interaction, and self-construction. Amateur use of the video camera, for example, alters the role of film in autobiography, not only because more people participate but also because professional filmmakers find new value in the immediacy signified by home-movie techniques (see discussions of Tom Joslin and Jim Lane in Chapter 3). Similarly, the Internet now hosts a plethora of sites for the personal situation, the reactions it provokes, and the communities it builds. The CD-ROM invites participation in the processes of life-production; I am thinking, for example, of the CD-ROM that accompanies Art Spiegelman's *Maus*. Having produced an (auto)biography so powerful that the role of comics in autobiography must now be assured, Spiegelman added both process and audiovisual components to the generic dimensions in which it could be received.[19]

The genres of autobiography on which I shall focus are not at all backyard ethnography. For the most part, they depend on established forms of literature and other art forms. But they do quite frequently contain or suggest these kinds of common experiences and daily gestures both as the material products of living that need to be considered (like the information on a death certificate) and as the common production of a community creating the cultural signs that bear witness to a life. Because these gestures result from particular crises, they can go unremarked in the wider encounter that constructs the autobiography. So we should notice references to forms or photographs or maps; these are often metaphors but do not escape their role as material constituents of the lives under construction. Increasingly, we are asked to imagine many dimensions to imag-ining a life, the kaleidoscope of possibility standing still not at the end of any text but only when we as readers cease to attend.

One vast and symbolic cultural production, for example, is the NAMES Project AIDS quilt. The quilt is useful for discussion of mirror talk because it evolves as continuous process, situates personal concerns in the political domain, and relies upon or invents strategies that have proved enabling for contemporary autobiographers. Beginning with a life and a death, increasing in scope to encompass the tens of thousands of lives lost to the AIDS epidemic and the lives bereft by it, the AIDS quilt epitomizes many of the qualities of contemporary autobiographies that are more limited in scope.[20] Quilting, of course, is a traditionally female and frequently communal activity. It involves the patching together by hand of scraps of fabric, which form a new, variegated whole. Yet the individual scraps can still be identified by those who know this man's shirt or that child's jumper; family scraps become memorabilia reworked for that most intimate of comforts, warmth in bed. For a gathering of quilters, furthermore, the work itself provides times and rhythms for gossip, storytelling, community business. For women, their historic struggle to exchange the needle for the pen was a matter of seeking public responsibilities and recognition but not necessarily finer methods of making histories. Quiltmaking continues to provide, for men and women now, (auto)biographical opportunities that are therapeutic, explanatory, and political in nature. The breast cancer quilt, for example, responds to this female epidemic. Judy Elsley also lists the works of the Boise Peace Quilters, which honor particular individuals and the political issues they have embraced.

In a chapter from *Quilts as Text(iles)*, Elsley compares the AIDS quilt to the novel as a dialogic genre, calling the project "[o]pen-ended, protean, populist, cultural critique" (45). It exists, of course, in a continuous state of change. It represents aspects of individual experience (frequently containing, beyond the name, often a photograph, but also belongings, material extensions of the body, or representations of individual behaviors, qualities, characteristics). It contains, of course, the voices of its many makers. "Heteroglossia works at every level of the NAMES Project: the individual quilt blocks, the layers of fabric, the different makers, and the audience create a continuous polylogue that does not privilege any one component. The author/maker, in particular, is toppled as king of creation. . . . The reader/audience becomes an active participant in the novel/quilt, changing the text and changed by it in a complex and continual interplay" (46–47). The author/maker in this case is not only the traditional (auto)biographer but specifically the person being commemorated in any given panel. No longer in control of this manifestation of his or her life, the autobiographer becomes one of the many voices of self-invention and construction. As one panel is combined with thousands of others, it becomes part of a map of distinct but related lives and deaths.

Even while the quilt involves a larger and larger community, involving its visitors, too, both as physical parts of the pattern and as contributors to blank panels, it also expresses most poignantly the individual, the intimate, the emotional components of each life. It involves many simultaneous dimensions of plural (auto)biography, functioning also as potentially infinite process, each individual panel contextualized by its neighbors, just as the names are read out in oral performance embedded in their context of hundreds and thousands. Scarry writes of the impact of the individual on the imagination, particularly in a mass catastrophe, when she writes about symbolic aspects of war or torture (60). So the individual faces of AIDS become vivid components in a visual display, and the individual names part of a politically charged litany for support and for change.

This memorial has been compared to the Vietnam War Memorial in Washington, but is also an extended version of the family album or the community graveyard—material evidence of personal value made available for public representation. Like Holocaust museums in various cities, or like the Resistance museum in Oslo, for instance, it combines the dimensions and purposes of architecture with visual display, oral "presence," and the artifacts that serve metonymically to reproduce lives and times that are past. Furthermore, Epstein and Friedman's Oscar-winning documentary film, *Common Threads—Tales from the Quilt*, brings the quilt, which already travels in sections into the public spaces of large cities, into the private home through the intimacy of television viewing. Focusing on a hemophiliac child, a drug-using heterosexual (who infects his wife), a gay father, and two gay partners of men who have already died of AIDS, the film projects a variety of situations and of narrators. These private lives interact in the film with the public and political concerns about the epidemic and with government's failure to respond, forcefully indicating once again the context in which the individual lives and suffers and dies, affecting the lives and the deaths of others. Intersections between people in sickness and grief, between the politics of government and of passionate lobby groups, and between modes of involvement and participation implicate the "reader" at every turn, ensuring one further and continuing dimension to all such interaction.

In an interview with Ariel Dorfman on the television program "Literati" (20 February 1997), the Canadian poet and novelist Michael Ondaatje talks about language as necessarily polluted and art as mongrel, altered by other people, like jazz, leaving spaces for its readers. His own autobiographical work, *Running in the Family* (see Chapter 4), bears curious comparison with the AIDS quilt, with its various generic components and episodes intersecting like individual panels. So does Trinh T. Minh-ha's film *Surname Viet Given Name Nam* (also discussed in Chapter 4). These are open-ended compositions of the individual in specific cultural contexts, in terms of other people and intersecting media or genres, "'a bit of a hodge-podge,'" as one panelist describes her panel (Elsley, 47). This hodgepodge describes the accidental or ad hoc nature of much (auto)biographical composition; like a potluck meal, it contains surprises for everyone involved. The solitary artist, then, like Ondaatje, incorporates these random and various elements into a work over which he may be presumed to have control, suggesting by means of his artifice the pressures of contingent experience.

Each genre in which an autobiographer chooses to work poses its own problems and advantages, all of them, it seems to me, raising questions about the representation of subjectivity and of multiple perspectives. Film and photography, for example, open possibilities for grounding a viewer's experience in a life before and beyond the text (viewers tend to believe in the prior existence of that which is photographed, to resist the possibility of absolute fiction), but it raises questions simultaneously about the subjectivity-in-representation of that life (because that which is manifest is the object of the camera eye and often of a photographer other than the apparently originating subject). Derek Jarman's *Blue* provides a curious reversal of this expectation. The AIDS patient suffering from damage to the retina produces a film in which no images appear at all but only the color blue; blue, he suggests, may be an open door to the soul, evidence of his walking behind the sky. But the sound effects of voices, music, bells, clocks, punctuate a narrative of loss, anger, and increasing limitation. Blue, as one watches the screen on which nothing else happens, becomes the perspective of the man without vision, holding the self together in a world composed largely of sound. Blue, indeed, represents the subjective position that envelops the viewer in its frustration (I have to sit here and *watch* this?) and horror. More common than Jarman's device is the paradox whereby film may address issues of referentiality but presumably at the expense of subjectivity. This paradox opens a number of questions that I explore in Chapters 3, 4, and 6: first, by addressing the assumptions that feed into such a paradox, and then by examining the possibility that film may enable autobiographers to define and represent subjectivity not as singular or solipsistic but as multiple and as revealed in relationship.

For Roland Barthes, the relationship between photographer and subject is death-dealing. Despite his desire to read the photograph as the perfect analogon of the living presence, Barthes describes the portrait-photograph as "a closed field of forces. . . . In front of the lens, I am at the same time: the one I think I am, the one I want others to think I am, the one the photographer thinks I am, and the one he makes use of to exhibit his art" (1981, 13). The sensation of inauthenticity "(comparable to certain nightmares)" suffered by the subject explains "that very subtle moment when, to tell the truth, I am neither subject nor object but the subject who feels he is becoming an object: I then experience a micro-version of death (of parenthesis): I am truly becoming a specter" (13–14). Barthes's suggestion that the photograph "is literally an emanation of the referent" (80) associates photography closely with autobiography, which has also been read until very recently as somehow unmediated truth; Lorraine York discusses the grounds these two art forms share in her work on a number of Canadian writers (1988) and in an extended essay on Timothy Findley (1994). She identifies the "seemingly unmediated relationship between signifier and signified," which Linda Hutcheon has described as the major photographic code, as "also the major autobiographical code" (1994, 647; Hutcheon, 45). Both photography and written text depend on the quondam presence of the subject and enact that presence by means of distinct but related codes.[21]

One effect of the relationship between words and photographs is their ability to fix and to release each other in representation of the flux of experience. So the written caption limits speculation on the picture, and the picture specifies the subject of language. Jo Spence uses this combination to position herself within the culture that constructs her. David Young spoofs the combination with his collection of stories ("all the characters were closely shadowed by real people when they entered this book" [Author's Note, n.p.]) combined with Jim Lang's collec-

tion of self-portraits. None of the texts to be discussed here is a photographic autobiography, but a number of them contain or refer to
photographs, and the role of the photograph cannot be underestimated even when it does not predominate. Where Harvey Pekar on
occasion inserts a photographed head on a cartoon body, Shirley Geok-
lin Lim (1996) assembles a formal album at the center of her book.
Maxine Hong Kingston (1975 and 1977) refers to pictures that she
does not provide, relying on language alone to summon up the con-
notations of lost or faded images. Ondaatje, on the other hand, captions his dark and puzzling pictures, which function as visual metaphors embedded in language. Book covers, too, produce versions of
the author/s, compelling faces and images of relationship that have
held and entranced me as I work with their apparently dominant choice
of language. The spectator and the reader re-enact the response to each
other of photographs and captions. Uses of space and image corre-
spond with the visually linear activity of reading, such co-respondence
or mirror talk repeatedly extending and surprising the reader's response, or participation. Whereas, in John Berger's phrase, the visible
world was once "arranged for the spectator as the universe was once
thought to be arranged for God" (16), the contemporary autobiographer who uses visual images knows that "God" exists in more than one
place, at more than one time, and in more than one genre.[22]

Every occasion for mixing genres demonstrates how distinctive sign
systems can intersect and merge to signify meanings at which neither
one could arrive alone. Spiegelman's *Maus*, for example, elaborates on
the interactions between drawing and language, present and past, father and son, narrator and privileged interpreter, who is also narrator
fully implicated in the meanings of the original story and of its retelling,
and so on. Vladek is a survivor of the Holocaust. His son, Art, a comics
artist, has been asking about his parents' wartime experiences, longing
for his mother's diary, which his father has destroyed, raising more
questions than his father can recognize or respond to, and receiving
clues about his father's character and his parents' relationship that his
father has no notion he is divulging. The sequence reproduced here
cannot convey the full complexity of this work, but demonstrates some
of the particular opportunities Spiegelman can take with (auto)biogra-
phy in the comics genre.[23]

"What about *your* side of the family?" Art asks his father, Vladek
(1991, 116). They sit side by side as in a formal interview. Not visible at
their feet is a clutter of old photographs that Vladek had thought he
had lost.[24] Vladek has been identifying them, telling their stories, his

words on occasion only to be guessed at because overlaid by the pictures to which they refer. Now the two men on the sofa give way to the father alone, framed into discrete comic-book sections, telling of the death of every member of his family except his little brother now in Israel (no longer little, of course, but, as the photograph indicates, large and married). The survivor's postwar photograph itself is represented as another comics drawing. Framed and captioned but slipping from the comics frame, this "snapshot" is all that remains. The absence of the others cries out through the empty frames that overlay the solitary Vladek: "From the rest of my family, it's *nothing* left, not even a snapshot." The visual and the verbal components of the comics format interact with each other. The visual impact of seeing through spaces that are meant to be filled reinforces the words—Vladek's Yiddish-inflected English distinguishing him from his American son. The balloons, furthermore, integrate this oral language into the visual field as they move farther and farther away from the head. In one reading, they emerge in the end from the foot, the empty box, the mess on the floor. In another reading, the voice fades as it wanders through painful memories, the large and lonely figure very moving in its loss. But the perspective is Art's, and the third reading disturbs without effacing the first two. Already, in the next frame, Art is down on the floor, assembling the photographs, which explains his view of the shoe and the box. And Vladek's selfishness and bigotry will surface again in a relationship the son continues to find very difficult.[25]

DIALOGISM IN CONTEMPORARY AUTOBIOGRAPHIES

Beginning this discussion of personal and generic encounters, I suggested that dialogism is a recurring feature of contemporary autobiographies. Much of what I have said will already have supported this observation. Interactions among people and among genres are not simply dialogues because they involve pluralities but are often also dialogic—in terms of their dynamic and reciprocal relations between text and context; their revelation of the *difference* between self and other; the contestatory nature of many of these relationships; the frequent recognition and destabilizing of power relations; the common move toward decentered heterogeneity; the omnivorous use of genres to subvert or destabilize each other; and, perhaps most important, the recognition that human beings exist within a hierarchy of languages or ideological discourses. Dialogism provides a sliding scale between the monologic and the polyphonic, and not all of the problems or all of the texts to be considered here will be dialogic in the same way or to the same degree. What is curious, however, is to see varieties of dialogism at play in a genre that has traditionally been very little given to irony or instability and rather prone to monologism.[26]

I am, of course, by no means the first to observe this trend in contemporary autobiography. Indeed, I wonder whether it has not been inevitable that poststructuralists should embrace dialogism. Certainly, autobiographies that adopt postmodern and postcolonial procedures provide ideal materials for analysis of dialogic principles at work. Betty Bergland, for example, writes about postmodernism and the autobiographical subject in terms of Bakhtin's chronotope, the concept of temporal and spatial positioning that Bakhtin suggests determines our image of the human being. Most significantly for the present discussion, Bergland concludes: "Because autobiography has acquired power in the culture to legitimate certain subject positions, autobiographical studies can be a site from which to not only challenge essentialist notions of the human being, but also to examine the effect of discourses on subjects, both those that seem to guarantee prevailing social relations and those that critique them. Autobiographical studies might also therefore provide a site for cultural critique and social change" (162). In the same volume, *Autobiography and Postmodernism*, Kirsten Wasson explores the voices of allegiance and of protest in Mary Antin's *The Promised Land*, describing as she does so "a geography of conversion"; Antin's linguistic tensions reveal a resistant discomfort with Americanization expressed in terms of "the text's dialogized landscape" (169). In both these examples, resistance is key to the possibility of change.

Most attention to dialogism in autobiography has come from feminists and theorists of "minority" literatures. In a paper titled "Importing difference," Neuman examines feminist writing in Canada which foregrounds "difference from the dominant discourse while speaking within that discourse," a "double discursivity," which, in Canada, "is sometimes encoded as bilingualism" (1986, 402). Sidonie Smith draws on Bakhtin's concept of the dialogic imagination in order to define a woman's autobiography as written from the margins of patriarchal discourse, engaging in an anxious dialogue with her reader in order to identify and justify herself: "Often, projecting multiple readers with multiple sets of expectations, she responds in a complex double-voicedness, a fragile heteroglossia of her own, which calls for charged dramatic exchanges and narrative strategies" (1987, 50). Later, she refers to this double-voicing as "a kind of double helix of the imagination" (190). In a special issue of *a/b* on illness, disability, and life writing, Helen M. Buss "read[s] for the doubled discourse" in American women's autobiography. Arnold Krupat has referred to the collective identity of Native Americans as dialogic (1989, 133), and Hertha D. Wong, analyzing the complex histories inherent in Plains Indians' names, argues that "if what Bakhtin suggests is true, the 'I' in any culture is inherently polyvocal and the construction of an individual subject is always a collaborative social activity" (215). Polyphony informs Lionnet's definitions and discussions of the practice of *métissage*, or braiding of cultural and linguistic pluralities.[27] Juxtaposing white text and black voice, Henry Louis Gates dialogizes "signification" itself. "Bakhtin's metaphor of double-voiced discourse, figured most literally in representational sculptures of Esu and implied in the Signifying Monkey's function as the rhetoric of a vernacular literature, comes to bear in black texts through the trope of the Talking Book. . . . [M]aking the white written text speak with a black voice is the initial mode of inscription of the metaphor of the double-voiced" (1988, 131). Whereas Native cultures have traditionally constructed the self in relation to other selves, and where women, or, in these examples, a black writer, have had to insert their different voices into the hegemonic languages of white patriarchy, many of the autobiographies to be discussed here demonstrate the need of that white patriarchy also to write itself out of a range of disabling margins. The politics of the periphery, I suggest, becomes significant for strategies of self-presentation for several reasons: first, I have already suggested that unresolved crisis is de-centering, and that autobiographers resist whatever forces threaten their personal agency; second, the circumstances that de-center any life find clearest articulation in terms of an-Other; and third, just as the double vision to which Spender refers affects both seer and seen, so double voicing affects both the one who speaks and the one who listens. Listening, as performative dialogism, will be important to the discussions that follow.

Whether alone or in company, in one genre or in several, the contemporary autobiographer turns with great frequency to double voicing, double vision, or that fluid and encompassing activity both personal and generic that I am calling mirror talk. Not privileging one perspective over another, but transforming the narcissistic by means of the corrective lens of the other, developing linguistic strategies that enable plural voices and that contain the oral and the written within each other, these autobiographers begin from positions that are politically weak and from those that are privileged, and are transformed by the process. One of the most interesting discussions I have heard is not (at this point) available in print: Roger J. Porter presented a paper called "Self and Other Is One Flesh: Double Voicing in Recent Autobiographical Writing" at an autobiography conference held at the University of Gröningen in The Netherlands in November 1996. Porter examined three kinds of double voicing: Natalie Sarraute's internal self-reflexivity in *Childhood*; Ronald Fraser's series of interactions with others in *In Search of a Past*; and Howard and Arthur Waskow's collaboration in *Becoming Brothers*. Porter concludes that each of these works "is something akin to meta-autobiography, in which we perceive the decisions that necessarily precede most self-writing but which normally get suppressed in the telling" (14). Whether the process of self-analysis is internal or an element of external mirroring, Porter suggests that the strategies of double-voiced autobiography reflect the struggles and experimentation with which autobiographers search for satisfactory modes of self-representation. Porter has put "in a nutshell" (so to speak) my central reason for engagement with the discussions that follow.

Chapter 2, "Literary Pyrotechnics: Finding the Subject among the Smoke and Mirrors," examines some of the literary tropes that professional writers have used to produce "mirror talk" in autobiography. Rereading Hemingway's notorious ill treatment of Scott Fitzgerald, I suggest that Hemingway in fact positions the two of them, as men and as artists, as mutually reflective. Mary Meigs, anxious to name herself lesbian, angles her self-perception and the perceptions others have of her through literature and art so that her own self-statement becomes multiply intertextual. Breyten Breytenbach produces his own non-existence during his extended imprisonment in South Africa by a sustained sleight of hand that eludes self-identification even as it posits extreme danger. All three extend and transform the familiar genres in which they work in order to establish both the precarious sense they have of their own subject positions and the means by which they might become "realized" to themselves and to their readers.

To explore the genres that are significant to contemporary modes of autobiography, Chapter 3, "Speculation in the Auditorium," focuses on film and drama. Reading gives way to "speculation," which relies on space, vision, oral discourses, and the role and position of the "audience." I look at documentary interview as interactive autobiography—Apted's *35 Up*, Lundman and Mitchell's *Talk 16* and *Talk 19*—and at the autobiographies that emerge from the fictive framework of Scott's *The Company of Strangers*. Film and drama are necessarily interactive, and their codes contribute to the experience of making autobiography and to the kinds of fiction on which autobiography can draw. Furthermore, as the play *Jessica*, in particular, takes appropriation as part of its subject matter, mirror talk can be seen to be both collaborative and contestatory.

The Book of Jessica, which provides an extended negotiation and rehearsal for the play *Jessica*, positions the white actor, Linda Griffiths, to "play" the Métis activist and writer, Maria Campbell. This encounter, in which the Métis challenges the white woman for center stage, introduces many of the issues of Chapter 4. "Dialogues of Diaspora" discusses Trinh T. Minh-ha's film, *Surname Viet Given Name Nam,* the collaborative work of Clark Blaise and Bharati Mukherjee, *Days* *and Nights in Calcutta,* and a series of single-author autobiographical works: Richard Rodriguez's *Hunger of Memory,* Audre Lorde's *Zami,* Shirley Geok-lin Lim's *Among the White Moon Faces,* Maxine Hong Kingston's *The Woman Warrior,* and Michael Ondaatje's *Running in the Family.* In every case, self-construction depends upon creating new spaces between languages, cultures, and places that are impossible to regain or achieve, and the present accommodation, which transforms the place of transplantation. These liminal spaces present creative, highly politicized opportunities for self-construction in mirror talk.

Chapter 5 concentrates on the work of one author and one situation. "Refractions of Mirror Talk" examines Primo Levi's writings about his time at Auschwitz. I focus here on language as it constitutes incompatible realities, on the one hand quite literally spelling out extinction both physical and semantic and, on the other, repositioning the self in terms of self-conscious multiplicity. Levi is particularly rewarding because he is so conscious of language as self-constructing and so alert to the implications of plural languages and the stories they contain. The interaction of unassimilable languages in Levi's texts provides an extreme example of an experience common in diasporic autobiographies, of the untranslatability of language — in this case equivalent to the extent to which experience exceeds its possible representations. (Scarry, for example, points to the impossibility even of irony when "[b]eside the horrible central fact, there are no peripheral facts, no relation between periphery and center, no irony, because in every direction there is only irony" [330 n. 11].)

Finally, in Chapter 6, I raise the question that has challenged me for a long time now. If Carr's sense of "protention" is correct, if anticipating future time affects one's understanding of the present, how do people who are terminally ill think "autobiographically"? What meaning can they make out of their immediate and critical circumstances? I explore these questions in works representing a number of genres: Tom Joslin's film *Silverlake Life: The View from Here;* Audre Lorde's mixed-genre *The Cancer Journals* and *a burst of light;* Harvey Pekar, Joyce Brabner, and Art Stack's comic book, *Our Cancer Year;* the collaborative work by Sandra Butler and Barbara Rosenblum, *Cancer in Two Voices;* and the brief filmed interview with Dennis Potter, *Seeing the*

Blossom. The role of genre is important both for the opportunities it provides for self-narration under duress and for the creativity with which these autobiographers present themselves within the relationships that sustain and enable them *in extremis*. Repeatedly, but perhaps never more forcefully than here, I find that particular genres, so identified because they invite particular expectations, are transformed by the needs of autobiographers in immediate and unresolved crisis. In so many cases, the autobiographical issues are what Chambers has called "obscene," that is, off the stage of culture. Witnessing, he suggests, brings such events and experiences from offstage to onstage precisely by means of genre adaptation (1996).

As one reader wittily reminded me, "[L]ife writing can't help being a form of death watch." Certainly, issues that are foregrounded and explicit in the writings of the terminally ill inform all aspects of mirror talk in varying degrees. Instability in the living moment is originary for every kind and dimension of crisis. Instability in perspective, narration, medium, or author-ity becomes not merely appropriate for expression of lived experience but also, ironically, a process that is convincing because it feels stable or real. The genres that eschew traditional realism and challenge secure knowledge become the means for moments of reality and knowing. Like water, they show us the movement of wind. I suggest, therefore, that my final chapter on death could well be a first chapter, that the problems I engage are circular.

Anyone who has worked in autobiography studies knows that the theorist, too, is autobiographical, engaged in personal encounters that expose at the very least our deepest curiosities and needs. As a white, heterosexual academic, working inside the walls of multiple privilege, I am distinctly other to many of the voices in this text and have no capacity or wish to speak for them. All of these explorations, however, have been for me a matter of very personal engagement. In theory, with care and with luck, my encounters as reader will be encounters and not appropriations. For me, the most significant transformation has been to listen without pushing for resolution. The dance of dialogic discourses proves most illuminating when accepted quite simply as process.

2 Literary Pyrotechnics

Finding the Subject among the Smoke and Mirrors

MODERNISM AND MIRROR TALK

Gone are the days when the autobiographer was born on such and such a date to such and such parents and told a story that moved forward from clearly historical beginnings to comprehensible narrative conclusions. If other people figured extensively in such writing, especially famous other people, the work faced outward and was known as a memoir. If introspection figured largely, then the autobiography was valued for its psychological, intellectual, or spiritual qualities. Either way, readers have tended to assume a certain transparency from the open text to the person of the subject and narrator. Only as artists in all media began to replace realism with experiments in perception, apprehension, and process did serious questions arise about the manner of representing the autobiographical subject in the text. Although I suspect one can read backward in time and find degrees of self-consciousness about process and the obfuscations of life-in-art in traditional autobiographies,[1] I am tracing the beginning of frequent experiment with self-representation to the beginnings of modernism. Marcel Proust represented the subject as unstable because defined by the sensory associations that connect the passing moment with memory and with desire. James Joyce uprooted the artist from his defining place and culture. Virginia Woolf developed varieties of impressionism in language that approximated the abstractions of paint and music. Gertrude Stein played games with ventriloquisms. These four alone, but of course not alone, altered the capacities of language to mediate between pre-textual and textual lives, simultaneously transfiguring recognition of both as imagined and constructed in language. Significantly, all four were attentive to somatic experience in their writing, suggesting not so much the disappearance of a physical subject as altered modes of artistic perception. All four, furthermore, blend the languages of visual art and music into the repertoire of writing to extend the imaginative and referential capacities of writing and of reading.

The autobiographers under discussion in this chapter are also artists — not writers by happenstance, in other words, but writers who have dedicated themselves to what Chaucer called the craft so long to learn. They are also the students of modernism both in particular and in general ways. In *A Moveable Feast*, Hemingway plays fast and loose with the the nature of reality, fact, and truth, creating multiple perspectives that undermine the possibility of an insistently monologic voice. Mary Meigs, beginning as a visual artist, has written four autobiographies in which her readings of literature and art provide the analytic and explanatory tools for her own life writing. Whereas Hemingway needs to establish himself as a writer whose skills and success do not depend on, are indeed separate from, the kindness or support of others, Meigs needs to identify herself as a lesbian despite the constraints of a repressive and homophobic environment and in response to unflattering perceptions that others have of her. In both cases, taking control of the story involves simultaneously embedding that story in the cultural context and materials to which it belongs. In terms of realism, this embedding involves people and places, conversations and occasions, as well as particular books and paintings that could all be documented. In terms of modernist representation, this embedding provides a language of referential and explanatory power well beyond the capacity of fact. With both Hemingway and Meigs, literary references in particular create an illusion of a hall of mirrors as one text responds to another text and as one writer includes another writer in texts that cannot be self-contained or provide any singular reflection. And Breyten Breytenbach, the Afrikaans poet who spent years in prison as an anti-apartheid activist, has taken sleight of hand in unprecedented directions, producing in his autobiographical novel, *Mouroir*, a work of absurdist surrealism in which the autobiographer is missing, has disappeared, along with any chance that his original context can find, explain, or recover him.

Writing in distinct contexts and at different stages of modernist experimentation, Hemingway, Meigs, and Breytenbach can usefully demonstrate both the inadequacy of traditional realism for twentieth-century autobiographers and the pressure of their lived experience to evolve new and convincing forms of expression. In each case, the creative tension between experience and expression is manifest in the varieties of mirror talk that we could call realism in modernist dress. When realism will no longer serve, when the living subject is trapped in cultural and linguistic constructions, more liable to be determined by outside forces than by any reliable sense of self, these writers experiment with literary tropes that enable some version of that original being to insist on recognition. In short, I propose to explore in this chapter some of the literary strategies that establish autobiographical subjects as present and "real" despite the smoke-and-mirrors illusion that they might not be real or true at all.

LIES, DAMNED LIES, AND AUTOBIOGRAPHY: HEMINGWAY'S TREATMENT OF FITZGERALD IN *A MOVEABLE FEAST*[2]

In terms of traditional realism or focus, Hemingway certainly disappointed his first reader. Mary Hemingway expressed her concern as she typed out sections of *A Moveable Feast*. She had thought the work was going to be autobiography but it contained so little of Ernest. He told her it was autobiography by reflection, bounced off the wall, so to speak, as in *jai alai*, the Basque version of handball. Certainly, he uses his character sketches to his own advantage. His industry, for example, reflects off Gertrude Stein's indolence. (She, of course, was the one who thought it took a lot of time to be a genius because one had to sit around so much doing nothing.) Critics tend to look at these sketches as something of a "literary morgue" (Brenner, 40). They are in places very nasty indeed, but I think Hemingway is doing something far more subtle than merely telling nasty stories about dead friends or making himself look good in contrast to artists less apparently disciplined or dedicated than himself.[3] With both style and content, he establishes the aesthetic conditions in terms of which we are to read *A Moveable Feast*. The spare, selective language that makes its own reality draws attention to the young writer learning his craft and to the writing process as his consistent subject matter. As autobiography, this use of language draws attention to the relationship between experience and art, to the lived life and its translation onto paper.

For these reasons, Hemingway's use of Scott Fitzgerald in this text, though clearly problematic, is profoundly significant as part of the creation of the young Hemingway. With close reference to some manuscript variations and to some unpublished materials that enable us to trace the development of *A Moveable Feast*, I would like to explore the ways in which Hemingway plays this remarkable game of *jai alai* in autobiography to create a relationship between himself and Fitzgerald that is simultaneously a completed production, the recognizable presence of the two men in the finished text, and a continuous process whereby such recognizable presences discover themselves. We may not believe what we read because, as I hope to show, the text unfolds as a series of lies, but we may not discredit it either. These lies have little to do with matters of verifiable fact or slander but are, rather, crucial to the process of a narrative in which two writers are participant; the deflected shots are deflected for both players.[4]

From beginning to end in *A Moveable Feast*, uncertainty about event, perspective, and understanding draws attention to the activity of narration, to the process of art, and to its problematic relation to varying perceptions of reality. Hemingway's genius for creating the impression of objective reality and simultaneous emotional response to that reality may persuade the reader to assign a more literal value to facts in his writing than his use of them justifies. From the preface to the end of this short book, Hemingway plays with angles of perception on almost every given fact. As an autobiographer, for whom facts may fairly be assumed to have a truth value, Hemingway is an early cubist; we recognize what he shows us but are startled by the tenuous nature of material that he seems to suggest is momentarily solid.

Referring to Cézanne (an important influence on Hemingway) in her work on literary modernism, Judith Ryan describes the effect of empiricist psychology on the arts in general and on cubism in particular. Cézanne's "famous apples seem about to roll off the table," she writes, "because they are seen from several vantage-points at once: the collision between these various perspectives creates the effect of precariousness" (93). Hemingway learned from Cézanne the necessity of creating affective meaning by means of what one could call geometrical dimensions within but beyond the factual statement. The information is precarious because it is multiple, contradictory, and in continuous motion. It exists, furthermore, in a tension between the achieved solidity of fact and the continuously explicit striving for that achievement, between product and process, between life and life writing, between life and death. With the "true simple declarative sentence," Hemingway worked for synesthesia, for the visual, aural, tactile quality of the living moment. Repeatedly he described the writer, the real writer, as one who could recreate experience so clearly and comprehensively as to make it the reader's own. Paradoxically and simultaneously, he worked to make that visceral moment, like all lived moments, ephemeral by means of and despite its entrapment in the permanence of a finite art form.

Continuing her discussion of Cézanne's influence, Ryan describes Rilke as writing poems "in which the object was no longer viewed from a single point of view. Extended sequences of similes that express the mind's inability to grasp the object other than approximately and through constructs essentially foreign to it are arranged as if in facets, like the various planes of Cézanne's paintings. In this, Rilke almost anticipates the cubist approach of 'walking around the object' or turning it in the mind's eye" (93). Hemingway seems less concerned with walking around the object, in this case his relationship with Fitzgerald, than with exploring the uncertainty of any truth, the invalidity of any single perspective. "Early (analytic) cubist pictures," Ryan continues, "use this technique of representing the intentionality of the subject-object relationship to great effect" (93). Hemingway uses elements of autobiography, himself and Fitzgerald, meetings and conversations between them, both as convincing data and as volatile impressions from uncertain, because unsustained and contradictory, perspectives. Arnold Gingrich vouches for the "convincing data" element when he describes this portrait of Fitzgerald as the best "ever done in print, for as I read there Scott stood alive again, at his inimitably exasperating best and worst. It simply *is* Scott to the last breath and the least bat of an eyelash" (quoted in Wickes, 28). Affective meaning results, however, not from the realistic portrait nor from the anxious relations between the two men nor from the malice of intent that has been so frequently noted, but from the tension between event and possible interpretation, between questionable fact and dual narration or plural fiction.

For example, Hemingway's preface to *A Moveable Feast* concludes with the brief, problematic paragraph: "If the reader prefers, this book may be regarded as fiction. But there is always the chance that such a book of fiction may throw some light on what has been written as fact." His manuscript notes indicate just how problematic this paragraph really is. He made numerous false starts with variations and painful explanations. He wishes to apologize to his first wife, Hadley: "She is the heroine of the stories and I hope she understands." Or he is afraid to hurt her and his second wife, Pauline, or the children. Or he has left out too many people. "The worst part of it is that you cannot publish it after you are dead because people will still sue even though you change the names and call it all fiction as it is." He does develop the role of the waiter at the Lilas and changes his name in succeeding drafts from Henri to Andre to the Jean who appears in a story about Evan Shipman that clearly "just growed" like Topsy and needed a whole section of its own. But Hemingway's fiction is always cannibalistic of life and he seems to have had little anxiety about disguise. Fitzgerald, for example, had to suggest that Hemingway alter the names of the living people in his first novel, *The Sun Also Rises*. If they were nobodies, Fitzgerald told him, their names served no purpose. If they were somebodies, Hemingway was taking cheap shots (Bruccoli, 46). In *A Moveable Feast*, however, Stein and Ford and Pound and Fitzgerald are not only recognizable but also appear very much *in propria persona*; for explicit autobiography they serve very little purpose unless their identities are clear. The question then becomes what purpose they serve in this form of fiction.

Hemingway's manuscripts make it possible to trace his progress with this text, from early pen-and-pencil work with words, phrases, and whole sections crossed out (sometimes in such a way as to preclude any chance of their being read), to typescripts with pen-and-pencil emendations, deletions, and additions. Corrections at this stage are often technical and involve correspondence with the typist. They also provide evidence of Hemingway's difficulties with the systematic focusing of a passage. Apart from his repeated initial tendency to spill personal anxieties onto the page, Hemingway is sensitive to numerous corrective gazes and concerned with what Neuman has called "the paradox of alterity" (1981, 318). As he struggles from draft to draft, he worries about the particular narrating center of self and the lights and shadows that fall there, the perspective he is taking that necessarily controls the perspectives of others. This anxiety in the process of writing, so evident in the manuscripts, highlights the balancing act of the final version.

Hemingway may be fighting his personal demons, he may be anxious about lawsuits, and he may be wrestling with the generic ambiguities of autobiography. Certainly he is camouflaging his own intentions, destabilizing Lejeune's "pacte autobiographique" (1989), feigning resistance, perhaps, to what Stone has called "the autobiographical occasion" (20). But he is also establishing the aesthetic that determines reader response. This possibly libelous rendition of people and events from his past is centrally a series of essays about composition, its subject being an apprentice writer laboring to master his art and still lacking the authority of a single novel. Given the explicitly

referential value of the place and the people in the text, this is, furthermore, preeminently a book about self-composition. These opening sentences describe the uncertainty of the whole enterprise, the
dialogue-in-process between life and art, the tentative claim on some
version of truth. The manuscript evidence of struggle and revision
provides an important way into the final aesthetic effect. It reveals most
obviously the damned hard writing that goes into easy reading. But it
also demonstrates the process by which Hemingway the artist, writing
constantly from hard-lived experience, stripped the ego from his most
explicit autobiography. To say this is not to deny the ego that he created, the persona that he wrote into existence, but I am referring here
to the ego that explains and justifies and apologizes, even to a significant extent the ego that tells the story, that locks readers into one
perspective to create one authoritative version of truth.

Philippe Lejeune suggests that pre-texts, presumably like these manuscript versions and unpublished ingredients for *A Moveable Feast*,
serve to reveal contradictions in facts and changes of meanings or purposes for fiction. Describing seven very different versions of Georges
Perec's childhood memories as extensions of the autobiographical act,
Lejeune asks: "Might not studies in genesis offer fresh possibilities to
deal with such thorny questions as the relationship between self and
language, between art and truth?" (1991, 2). Truth does not mean
verifiable fact. Indeed, Lejeune's short paper zeroes in on Perec's bizarre fiction which he describes as the writer's only means for explicit
treatment of his mother's death at Auschwitz. Truth may even incorporate what Timothy Dow Adams (1990) has so persuasively described
as the strategy of lying. Adams describes the kind of generic ambiguity
that Hemingway spells out as a main reason why autobiographers have
been accused of lying; they seem to be doing one thing when in fact
they are doing another.

One is reminded of Hemingway's fire-eater in Lyon who "also bent
coins which he held in his toothless jaws with his thumb and forefinger." He becomes an analogue for the autobiographer. "He said
there was no money in eating fire nor in feats of strength with fingers
and jaws in Lyon. False fire-eaters had ruined the *métier* and would
continue to ruin it wherever they were allowed to practice. He had
been eating fire all evening, he said, and did not have enough money on
him to eat anything else that night." Notably, the fire-eater offers to
help the young writer from his fund of stories, "some of them more
horrible and incredible than anything that had ever been written." Better still, the two of them could go "to the country of the Blue Sultan

where [they] could get stories such as no man had ever heard," of "battles, executions, tortures, violations, fearful customs, unbelievable practices, debaucheries; anything [Hemingway] needed" (158–59). Without commenting on the implicit contrast here between fiction and "contingent reality," Hemingway in fact needs to get back to his hotel. He does not, in other words, take the fantastic, the exotic, or the bizarre as his medium, but only the storyteller himself, struggling to make ends meet, the master of strength and deception, who may be upstaged by false practitioners.

The final printed version of the Hemingway / Fitzgerald trip to Lyon to collect the Fitzgeralds' car involves multiple misunderstandings between the two men. It seems to focus on Fitzgerald's problems with drink, with writing, and with Zelda. It culminates in Hemingway's admiration for *The Great Gatsby*. It is, furthermore, the end product of significant cutting and revision. In the unpublished manuscripts for *A Moveable Feast*, two whole sections concentrate on Fitzgerald. One, fairly slapdash and set not in Paris but in the States, is clearly connected to the Lyon trip. The other is more crafted, less likely to be based on lived experience, and offensive for its manipulation of real people in what I suspect is pure fantasy. Through these two unpublished sections, and through the manuscript versions of the first Fitzgerald section of *A Moveable Feast*, one can trace the development in the text from fairly straight narrative representation of presumably remembered events to the delicate balancing act that I am identifying as Hemingway's autobiographical trademark, from Lejeune's "thorny questions," in other words, to Adams's "sleight of hand."

The first unpublished episode that relates to chapter 17 of *A Moveable Feast* is labeled "Fitzgerald / Football Game." It describes a post-Paris experience that includes Pauline, the second Mrs. Hemingway, Scott and Zelda, and Mike Strater. It outlines the train journey to Philadelphia after a football game and then the car ride from Philadelphia to the Fitzgeralds' house outside Wilmington. This is a pencil manuscript containing minor emendations, cuts, and revisions. The date of this game between Princeton and Dartmouth is left blank, but the year that Fitzgerald and Strater had met at Princeton is given as 1922. Zelda is described as being in one of her "fits" of perfect ladyhood, and these "fits" are revised to "periods." Transitions improve with revision; Zelda, in a period of perfect ladyhood, is sitting ("quietly" is inserted) with Pauline. Originally, Zelda and Scott then get into the car. In revision, Hemingway stays with the train ride and says that Zelda, sitting quietly with Pauline, is "paying no attention to Scott's behavior." Scott's behavior is the issue throughout. He has stayed sober during the game but begins bothering people on the train by asking them questions ("startling" and "what might be shocking" are crossed out). Strater and Hemingway steer him away from potential trouble but he begins to out-maneuver them. Only one confrontation is fully developed. Scott finds a Princeton supporter reading a medical book. "Scott took the book from him in a courtly way saying 'Do you mind Sir?' glanced at it and returned it with a bow saying in a voice pitched for all that part of the car, 'Ernest I have found a clap doctor!'" Strater and Hemingway try to get him away and apologize to the student, who tries to ignore the situation. Scott persists: "You are a clap doctor aren't you?" and "There's nothing to be ashamed of about being a clap doctor," and "'A clap doctor,' Scott said. . . . 'Physician heal thyself.'"

Whether Mike Strater could have vouched for this episode as based on fact or not, the writing is essentially reportage. The dowser is not at work here divining water underground. Nor is the poet with his genius for saying several things at once. Fitzgerald's drunkenness, hypochondria, and sexual anxieties are merely items here, dependent for their interest value on the fact that they are about Fitzgerald. As the writing of the relationship develops, however, these items become complex features of Fitzgerald's character. In *A Moveable Feast*, they are closely woven into the drama of the relationship with Hemingway, and are significant as part of Hemingway's exploration of life writing.

After the train ride comes a car ride that also includes features that become important to the whole warp and woof of the printed text. The Fitzgeralds have imported a Parisian taxi driver to be their chauffeur. As the drinking starts in the car, the chauffeur speaks to Hemingway in French, which Fitzgerald does not understand. The chauffeur worries about the car overheating, and it emerges that Fitzgerald will not allow him to put oil in the car because this is not some worthless French car. Clearly understanding the gist of the dialogue, Fitzgerald says: "Philippe has some sort of fixation that you have to put oil in this car all the time like that ridiculous Renault we drove up from Lyon that time. . . . He makes Zelda nervous with that silly oil chatter. . . . He's a good fellow and absolutely loyal but he knows nothing about american motors." The "ridiculous Renault" that figures in *A Moveable Feast* has had its top removed after some damage. "Zelda had ordered it cut away and refused to have it replaced" (161). The garage man in Lyon, another version of Philippe, explains to Hemingway that "the car needed new piston rings and had evidently been run without sufficient oil and water. He showed me how it had heated up and burned the paint off the motor" (162). He has not been allowed to replace the top and feels that "'[o]ne has an obligation to a vehicle. . . . Try and make Monsieur be serious,' he said pleadingly. 'At least about the vehicle.'" In the published text, the rain that has forced the Fitzgeralds to leave their car in Lyon threatens to prevent Fitzgerald and Hemingway from getting it to Paris. In the manuscript episode after the football game, Zelda and Scott start quarreling during what the car's condition already makes a "nightmare ride" because they cannot agree on the road home. "Zelda claimed the turn off was much further on and Scott said we had passed it. They argued and quarrelled until Zelda went to sleep momentarily while the chauffeur drove slowly on. Then Scott told the driver to turn around and while he was napping too the chauffeur made the turn offx" (see note 2).

Again, this is merely incident. It suggests Hemingway's frustration, his sense of Fitzgerald's incompetence in practical matters, his own alertness and comparative sobriety, and the Fitzgeralds' unpredictability and self-destructive helplessness. But it lacks affective power and does not build meaning. In *A Moveable Feast* the car ride locks the two writers into an inescapable liaison both practical and perceptual; they depend upon each other for detailed management of a shared journey and they undertake parallel activities of interpreting experience and transforming it into narrative. Their ride together spells out the hazards of the writer's life, specifically the hazards of transforming life into fiction. In the final version, furthermore, Hemingway's perception of Fitzgerald's weaknesses is balanced by his perception also of Fitzgerald's great talent.

The other manuscript episode that involves Fitzgerald is headed "After Chapter 17," that is, after the Lyon trip. Much of it is lightly crossed through but it remains entirely clear to read. It consists essentially of a long dialogue between Hemingway and Bumby, to whom he refers as "My first son." As Bumby is the only son to appear in *A Moveable Feast*, this episode must have been written long after it is supposed to have taken place. Essentially, the tiny Bumby, aged between three and six — much information is elided at the opening of this episode — after sitting quietly in the cafe while his father works, discusses the lessons he has learned from Tonton, husband of their *femme-de-ménage*. "He has taught me much," says the young Bumby. "'I admire him very muchx' I said. 'He admires you toox He says you have a very difficult metierx Tell me Papa is it difficult to write?' 'Sometimes.' 'Tonton says it is very difficult and I must always respect it.'" In further conversation, it emerges that Monsieur Fitzgerald is sick because he drinks too much and cannot work. "'Does he not respect his metier?'" Bumby asks. "'Madame his wife does not respect it or she is envious of it.' 'He should scold her,'" replies Bumby, who, also under the influence of Tonton, has described a quarrel between his parents in terms of mother being bad and papa scolding her. The young Bumby, however, goes beyond parroting Tonton to taking it upon himself to reform Fitzgerald. At lunch, when the two men order Perrier, Bumby asks for a demi-blonde. He explains to his father afterward: "'Tonton says that a man should first learn to control himself. . . . I thought I could make an example.'" This episode, which includes discussion of the war, of Fitzgerald's interest in but ignorance of the war, and of the honorable wounds that men bear from war, works through some patronizing attitudes to a mostly absent Fitzgerald. "'Poor Monsieur Fitzgerald,' Bumby saidx 'He was very nice today to remain sober and not molest youx Will everything be all right with him Papa?' 'I hope so,' I saidx 'But he has very grave problemsx It seems to me that he has almost insurr-mountable [*sic*] problems as a writerx' 'I am sure that he will surmount them,' Bumby saidx 'He was so very nice today and so reasonablex'"

Out of the mouths of babes and sucklings do indeed come words that their parents should never have used in their presence. Certainly little Bumby must have been exposed to the pre-dawn visits of riotous Fitzgeralds. But the tone of this dialogue and the ingredients for discussion suggest a premature and unfortunate attempt to craft the relationship with Fitzgerald into fiction. Although many have expressed shock and outrage at the cruel picture of Fitzgerald that emerges from *A Moveable Feast*, these unfinished and unpublished versions indicate the nature of the ingredients with which Hemingway wanted to work and the extent to which he reworked his narrative stance. The final version still shows Fitzgerald drunk and sick and dominated by a wife who does not respect his *métier*, but it also develops the further dimensions whereby both writers make use of experience and in which the roles of mentor and disciple are strangely interchangeable.

Even the first draft of chapter 17 of *A Moveable Feast* is significantly more sophisticated than these unpublished episodes. This chapter outlines the meeting of the two men and Fitzgerald's avowed admiration for Hemingway's work.[5] It includes Fitzgerald's search for information by means of aggressive questioning, Fitzgerald's inability to hold his drink, their agreement to travel down to Lyon together in order to pick up the car that the Fitzgeralds had been forced by bad weather to leave there, Hemingway's expectations of pleasure and profit from the trip, the mismanagement of the entire outing, Fitzgerald's drunkenness and hysterical hypochondria, and Hemingway's conclusion that *The Great Gatsby*, inside its misleadingly tasteless dust jacket, is a remarkably fine book. This small point about the dust jacket, with the eyes of Doctor T. J. Eckleburg on the Long Island billboard, suggests the multiple levels on which Hemingway's now densely packed narrative can convey multiple meanings.[6] These eyes are offensive and removable. Hemingway takes off the jacket to read the book.

Misled by the garish cover, he is astonished by the book itself and determines that he should be Scott's friend no matter how preposterously Scott behaves. Hemingway cuts the word "preposterously" from the final version, but it is there for all three drafts. By the end of the chapter, in other words, Hemingway clarifies two key points: the bond between the two men is between two writers who admire each other's work, and valuable work redeems the man whose hold on reality is tenuous. Indeed, this chapter demonstrates the ways in which writing adjusts, interprets, and reformulates the factual into the fictive, a process that destabilizes or makes necessarily tenuous the reality from which it works. In his happy reunion with Hadley after the traumatic journey, the narrator is aware that happiness is also tenuous. The parallels between the two marriages begin early in the chapter with Fitzgerald's question about whether the Hemingways had slept together before marriage and end with the danger to Scott's writing posed by Zelda. (Fitzgerald's incredulity that Hemingway cannot remember whether he and Hadley had slept together develops the ironic parallelism between the two men as both husbands and writers; what Fitzgerald reads literally as a memory lapse can be read more effectively as Hemingway's refusal to answer such direct and personal questions.) Hemingway agrees to the Lyon expedition with enthusiasm because he hopes to learn much from this successful, older writer, but he comes home disappointed, saying he has learned only about the novels of Michael Arlen;[7] he incorporates into the narrative without comment, however, his more significant lesson in the processes whereby art and life interact. Indeed, this interaction, this implicit examination of the process of autobiography, dominates the chapter. By comparison, Fitzgerald's behavior becomes incidental; it provides only some raw material from which the two writers can work toward their separate perceptions of reality.

Reality is the central issue in the final version, and the reality of the text is created by a web of lies that destabilizes credibility in the original pre-textual reality. This relationship between textual and external realities is central, of course, to autobiography, which, however else it may be defined, is a referential genre (see Eakin 1992). When Hemingway begins, however, with a series of minor incidents that all turn out to be untrue depending on who looks at them, he is surely calling into question the notion that truth is possible; he is allowing Fitzgerald's truth to share the center of the story with his own; and he is, paradoxically, being true to the relationship in which simultaneous versions of experience cannot be the same. Again, this focus is the result of revision. An early typescript begins: "The first time I ever met Scott Fitzgerald was in a bar called the Dingo which was on the right hand side of the rue Delambre as it cuts through from the Boulevard Montparnasse to the Boulevard Edgar Quinet." He begins, in other words, by allowing the streets of Paris to distract him from his real focus and runs the danger of allowing his intimacy with Paris to take center stage. "In those days," he continues, "many people had no idea that the rue Delambre reached the Boulevard Edgar Quinet. They only knew that it went as far as the Dingo." (This paragraph appears on the verso of a cable draft dated late May 1958.)

Hemingway's refocusing for the published version takes the narrative not only straight to Fitzgerald but also, of equal importance, to the issues of relative perspective. "The first time I ever met Scott Fitzgerald a very strange thing happened," he begins. "Many strange things happened with Scott but this one I was never able to forget" (149). He describes Scott coming into the Dingo bar where Hemingway is sitting "with some completely worthless characters." Scott introduces himself and proceeds to praise Hemingway's writing in an extended speech. Embarrassed, Hemingway pays attention to the speaker. Bruccoli points out that Dunc Chaplin, the Princeton pitcher who comes into the Dingo with Fitzgerald, and who is the unofficial witness for what follows, was not in Paris or even in Europe that year. "But Chaplin," writes Bruccoli, "is carefully identified as part of the sense of exact recall Hemingway develops in these memoirs. As the scene is set up, it has to be Chaplin. One wrong detail undermines the whole thing: all of it has to be right" (3). Bruccoli calls this error problematic because Hemingway is the only source for some of the most frequently repeated anecdotes about Fitzgerald. What for Bruccoli seems a problem of truth value, however, is surely central to Hemingway's modernist agenda in which many-layered "lies" describe the problems that writer and reader share in securing the truth.

The text continues with the three men drinking champagne "with, I think, some of the worthless characters." Hemingway notices that Fitzgerald wears Brooks Brothers clothes, "a white shirt with a buttoned-

down collar and a Guard's tie" (150). Bruccoli suggests that Hemingway is here questioning Fitzgerald's taste in ties, but the textual value of
this tie is surely far more important than the personal; it serves at the
very beginning of this chapter to focus the lens through which the
whole chapter is to be read. This Guard's tie is, in fact, a "college-
looking tie" in the first draft. When it becomes a Guard's tie, it signifies
a garment that Fitzgerald has no right to wear.[8] Hemingway thinks he
ought to tell Fitzgerald about the tie "because they did have British in
Paris and one might come into the Dingo — there were two there at the
time — but then I thought the hell with it" (150). The early revision
from a "college-looking tie" to a Guard's tie indicates attention to this
scene; the British in Paris would not worry about the one but might
about the other. Parenthesizing dashes set off the casual observation
that there were two British in the bar at the time. Deciding not to raise
the issue, "the hell with it," Hemingway relegates this scene to his internal drama as he listens to Fitzgerald's speech of praise. Fitzgerald is then
overcome with alcohol poisoning and passes out quite dramatically.

The apparent focus of this scene has been first on Fitzgerald's strange
behavior in praising Hemingway so extensively to his face, and then on
his response to alcohol. When they meet a few days later, however, and
Hemingway expresses regret for what had happened at the Dingo,
Fitzgerald does not know what he is talking about. " 'There was nothing wrong with me at the Dingo,' " he says. " 'I simply got tired of those
absolutely bloody British you were with and went home' " (152). So
dramatic has been Fitzgerald's departure from the bar in Hemingway's
version that one can only assume that Fitzgerald has forgotten or has
never known or does not wish to deal with reality. But then it is Hemingway's turn to be strange. He denies the presence of any British, apart
from the bartender. When Fitzgerald persists, Hemingway assumes
that he had gone back to the Dingo later or had gone at another
time. Then, abruptly, he continues: "No, I remembered, there had
been two British there. It was true. I remembered who they were. They
had been there all right" (153). Fitzgerald then specifies: " 'That girl
with the phony title who was so rude and that silly drunk with her.
They said they were friends of yours.' " " 'They are,' " Hemingway admits. This is the man who had been drinking with some unidentified
but "completely worthless characters," who later acknowledges as an
afterthought that there were two British in the bar, as if they were not
part of the group, and who then denies that there were any British in
the bar. He now acknowledges that the girl with the phony title is very
rude sometimes. The first draft includes crossed-out versions at this

stage of the possibilities that there were some British in the bar and that the narrator may not have noticed them. This problematic presence of some British in the bar has clearly been reworked at each stage; Hemingway's confident narrative about the strange thing that happened when he first met Fitzgerald becomes itself the strange thing, as what happened becomes uncertain and even contradictory. These people (Duff Twysden and Pat Guthrie, who were perhaps even then in the process of being transformed into the leading characters of *The Sun Also Rises*) emerge from the shadows in Fitzgerald's perception of the evening and turn out to be not only there, perhaps, somewhere, but very specifically there as Hemingway's friends and drinking companions and, Hemingway admits, as capable of behaving like the "absolutely bloody British" that might bore Fitzgerald. When Hemingway then thinks to ask whether they were rude about Fitzgerald's tie, Fitzgerald cannot think why they might have been and says he was wearing " 'a plain black knitted tie.' " Hemingway gives up, apparently convinced of Fitzgerald's unreliability. What his narrative carefully constructs, however, is his own unreliability. If the British were there with him and if they were indeed obnoxious, what may one believe about the tie (which has changed in draft anyway and then turns out to have been bought in Rome) or about any of Fitzgerald's behavior?

This carefully constructed destabilizing process opens the relationship in the text between Hemingway and Fitzgerald and underlies apparent certainty about the very smallest details. When they plan to go down to Lyon together and Hemingway fails to find Fitzgerald and goes down by himself, revisions in the draft versions demonstrate Hemingway's fine-tuning of the narrative so that it develops from righteous self-justification, an anxious intrusion of explanatory matter such as he cut from the preface, to a spare presentation of the two men interpreting their circumstances. Early drafts of this chapter work and rework the plans for this journey. They set a tentative date, meet twice more, set a final date, and then check that final date the night before departure. It is inconceivable, according to these early draft variations, that the two men could fail to turn up on the same railway platform at the same time. Fitzgerald's failure to appear with the tickets for the journey is therefore a major betrayal. Its seriousness is magnified by revisions in the draft versions that emphasize the Hemingways' financial straits and their attempts to save money for a trip together to Spain. These early reworkings are particularly remarkable because so much of the chapter appears in print virtually unchanged from the first draft. These, in other words, were very clearly the issues with which Hemingway was struggling. The drastic cutting, then, whereby plans for the journey are sketched only briefly and Hemingway's distress over money is stated but not elaborated, does not exonerate Fitzgerald: "I had never heard, then, of a grown man missing a train," he writes (157). But it does clear space for the same kind of reversal that we have already experienced with the tie. Fitzgerald is sorry there has been a mix-up; he had taken a train originally "right after" (revised to "not long after") Hemingway's, and adds: "'It was a very comfortable train and we might just as well have come down together'" (160). Hemingway's text expresses both his own frustration with this unreliable friend and the strong possibility that his, again, has been the unreliable perception.

Hemingway inculpates himself still further by assuming Fitzgerald needs a drink. "Scott," he says, "had obviously been drinking before I met him." His perception, conveyed in that use of "obviously," is most assertive, but nothing in the text so far has allowed for anything at all to be obvious. Fitzgerald denies that he is a morning drinker and asks if Hemingway is; his denial does not impinge on Hemingway's determination that they should have drinks. The paragraph ends with Hemingway's unsupported assertion that whisky and Perrier made them both feel much better. When they drink white Mâcon wine with lunch, and when Hemingway then buys four more bottles which he uncorks as they need them, one wonders whether he has not heeded his own story of Fitzgerald's inability to hold alcohol. When Fitzgerald becomes hysterical and ill, Hemingway orders a succession of double whiskies and then "a light, pleasant white wine of the neighborhood" with dinner. Fitzgerald passes out at the table so discreetly "it even looked as though he were careful not to spill nor break things" (174). Illness by now has far less to do with hysteria or hypochondria than with a failed or perverse communication between the two men that Hemingway's narrative seems deliberately to create.

Meanwhile, their discussion of books and illness and marriage has spun a tissue of lies. The scene in which Hemingway manipulates a bathtub thermometer to prove that Fitzgerald is not ill is both very funny and quite poignant; the large, inappropriate thermometer is lumpishly factual and remains impervious to the imagination of either man; it proves neither that Fitzgerald has a fever nor that he does not. It proves nothing at all, except, perhaps, the irrelevance of provable fact, an irrelevance that Hemingway's narrative both does and does not take into account in its treatment of Fitzgerald's story. Fitzgerald claims that he and Zelda have never spent a night apart before. Hemingway wonders about the preceding night. He is being literal, like the thermometer. But he then listens to the story of "something tragic" that had happened to them at St.-Raphael. It is the story of Zelda's affair with the French aviator, and Fitzgerald tells it several times. Notably, Hemingway does not provide the story itself but only his own unaskable question: if this story was true, how could Scott have slept in the same bed with Zelda each night? The story is sifted, in other words, through Hemingway's experience of hearing it in a particular context; he listens to the evolution of a fiction that originates in significant fact and that he hears through the medium of his own very literal-minded doubts. He is moved by the first version, which he believes is true. Later, he says, Fitzgerald tells him other versions "as though trying them for use in a novel, but none was as sad as this first one and I always believed the first one, although any of them might have been true. They were better told each time; but they never hurt you the same way the first one did" (172).

In the context of the construction of his own time with Fitzgerald, Hemingway enables Fitzgerald to construct his own time with Zelda. Both writers enact the process of translating lived experience into fiction in order to contain and control the affective meaning of that experience, but they respond to each other as to literal truth. Credibility is a central issue for them both, and they both doubt each other. "On this night," says Hemingway, "he wanted me to know and understand and appreciate what it was that had happened at St.-Raphael" (173). These verbs are urgent, and Fitzgerald is impelled by this urgency not to describe but to make the reality of what he wants known and understood and appreciated. "I could see the single seater seaplane buzzing the diving raft," says Hemingway, "and the color of the sea and the shape of the pontoons and the shadow that they cast and Zelda's tan and Scott's tan and the dark blonde and the light blonde of their hair and the darkly tanned face of the boy that was in love with Zelda" (173). All this exists in the power of Fitzgerald's narrative but is then read in the context of the narrator, who must be lying or forgetting when he says that he has never slept apart from his wife, and of the listener, who has already failed to hear or believe and who has imposed his own agenda of expectation and interpretation on what he hears. What sense, then, can one make of the story within the story when narrator and listener repeatedly doubt and distort and create separate meanings? Hemingway, furthermore, like the earliest readers of *A Moveable Feast*, would be familiar with Fitzgerald's (non-literal) rendering of this experience into fiction in *Tender Is the Night*, which was serialized in *Scribner's Magazine* from January to April 1934.

Writing some thirty years after the events that already exist as oral narrative in this 1925 conversation, Hemingway is once again highlighting transitions from experience to fiction and the epistemological insecurity of every stage of the process. His incredulity about Fitzgerald's failures of memory therefore reads as a culminating irony and echoes Fitzgerald's incredulity that Hemingway cannot remember whether he and Hadley had slept together before marriage. " 'Why did you want to make the mysteries?' " he asks. " 'It isn't the sort of thing I thought you would do' " (153).

Within *A Moveable Feast*, the story of Zelda, like *The Great Gatsby*, represents Fitzgerald's power as a writer, a power that is made clear by its impact on Hemingway. Unlike *The Great Gatsby*, Fitzgerald's attempts to tell the Zelda story continue and do not within this context become complete. Both writers, in fact, are tampering with life in this chapter in order to make stories. Only Fitzgerald, however, tampers with stories to make them commercially viable and so becomes the false practitioner who might ruin the writer's *métier*. Such is the textual symbiosis of these two writers, however, that Hemingway shares this guilt. Greed for success forms the hidden crevasses and the deadly avalanches of the final chapter. It is truly irrelevant that there were no avalanches that year. What matters and what is so urgently adumbrated in this Fitzgerald chapter is the consummate skill required to survive danger—in this case the precision of balance whereby the writer uses but is not betrayed into the literal.

In the penultimate chapter of *A Moveable Feast*, Hemingway has an extraordinary conversation after World War II with Georges, now the bar chief at the Ritz, who claims to remember everyone but does not remember Scott Fitzgerald. When Françoise Feret was working for her doctoral dissertation at the Sorbonne, in 1957, she interviewed Georges and he remembered Fitzgerald very well indeed.[9] So one must bypass the literal information, recognizing of course that it calls memory into question once again, and read only the text in which Georges seems to parody Hemingway's introduction to Fitzgerald. " 'It is strange that I have no memory of him,' " Georges says, picking up on Hemingway's word "strange" (192). Many strange things have happened with Fitzgerald, but this chapter of shared experience and fiction has been too strange for Hemingway to forget. When, furthermore, Hemingway promises Georges that he will write about Fitzgerald " 'exactly as I remember him the first time that I met him' " (193), his promise is qualified within his own text—not only because he has shown that memory of literal fact is irrelevant but also because this fiction has been explicitly about the process of fiction, which perpetually erodes foundations in fact.

None of this attention to Hemingway's process of crafting relationships and situations alters, to my mind, the nastiness of Hemingway's last words on former friends who could no longer speak for themselves. His treatment of Fitzgerald, in particular, is remarkable for its apparent lack of self-awareness; could Hemingway not see, one wonders, that such self-aggrandizement does not read as he might have wished? His "lies" are damned both because they implicate others in shocking and offensive ways and because they damn the writer who promulgates them. At issue here, however, is not an ingenuous, Houyhnhnm-like exposé of untruth but rather an appreciation of Hemingway's finely tuned and witty crafting of interacting fictions. In another unpublished manuscript entitled "Writing in First Person," Hemingway gets the last word: "What is, if not easy, almost always possible to do," he writes, "is for members of the private detective school of literary criticism to prove that the writer of fiction written in the first person could not possibly have done everything that the narrator did, or, perhaps, not even any of it. What importance this has or what it proves except that the writer is not devoid of imagination or the power of invention I have never understood."

What has engaged me in this exploration of the manuscripts has been Hemingway's transition from crude early scribblings, through strenuous revisions that draw attention to particular problems, to the tightly controlled writing of the final text in print. Where a happier man might have been more compassionate toward Fitzgerald, or exercised more discretion in his choice of materials, Hemingway demonstrates a pyrotechnic display, like that of his fire-eater in Lyon, which combines hunger and need and illusion and fact with dazzling skill. Numberless autobiographies, of course, originate in that hunger and need to own and explain the past and to create some permanent meaning that will endure beyond death. What Hemingway does that seems both valuable and new is to remind his readers of several things throughout the final text: that the self is constructed in relation to and in terms of other selves; that life writing and life reading are simultaneous and mutually corrective processes; that self-definition cannot be true in any objective or verifiable sense; indeed, that autobiography is a matter of wrestling with angels; that naming one's self involves strenuous conflict and maiming, and that one's story in the end is an explanatory myth, explanatory primarily of its own processes.

AN AUTOBIOGRAPHY BY MARY MEIGS[10]

Mary Meigs also has old scores to settle, but her text is more conventional in appearance than Hemingway's, so less liable to misreading. Moreover, she posits as her central concern not the destabilizing of the narrator's perspective but the construction and validation of her own perspective in opposition to that of others. For her, as for Hemingway, autobiography depends on mirror talk, but where he works to strip his own ego from the final text, Meigs's task is to assert hers as the final word on who she feels herself to be. Like Hemingway, she establishes the terms in which her work is to be read. In the course of unraveling a complex situation, Meigs provides, in *The Medusa Head*, an image that encapsulates her distinctive approach to autobiography. "I remember as a child," she writes, "seeing a carved ivory ball in some grand palace in Holland. Through the tracery of the outer shell I could see an inner ball, and inside it another, and inside that one still another. The outer shell was necessarily made first but when the tiny ball at the centre was completed, the outer shell came to seem like a final truth" (1983, 142). Similarly, for the first of four autobiographical works, Meigs has chosen in her title to create an outer shell, through the tracery of which one sees an inner ball, and through that another, and so on.

Meigs's autobiography is offered as a self-portrait by a painter (Lily Briscoe) who is a fictive creation of a novelist (Virginia Woolf) who is, to some extent, creating her own life story. This interconnectedness of life with art and of art with the lives of artists provides continuous mirror talk among people and among genres of art, a matter both of recognition and of cross-fertilization. More important, Meigs uses this elaborate trope in order to create reflections, alter egos, who become both tools with which to consider the act of self-representation and alternatives in relation to whom she constructs herself.[11] She provides the means, in other words, that enable the reader to participate in assembling the work of art. But she is doing a number of other things as well.

First, she is an artist, consciously making sense of her experience in terms of painting and writing; this is a natural course for her to take because she believes very strongly that all art is autobiographical. In her responses to painting and literature, as to the writers and painters she knows, she insists both that the text creates character and that an original character exists behind and beyond the text, the referent, who is, however, an artist and has made a new reality, not a simple reflection. (So Hemingway insists he is writing fiction, even as he frets about whether people will be hurt or will fail to understand.) Meigs's choice of her own text, then, is crucial to her own integrity. This point becomes particularly important when she moves from her self-chosen role as Lily Briscoe to the less acceptable role in which she is cast as Dolly Lamb by Mary McCarthy. (Although Hemingway creates responsive strategies for Fitzgerald, he would surely have been outraged had Fitzgerald himself written back.)[12] The artist as generating subject resists becoming anyone else's object. The perceiver chooses how to be perceived. She cannot sit still to be rendered by any artist other than herself. The theft of self and the violation of her central "I am" by such external definition become central issues.

Then, Meigs is a lesbian who has struggled for a lifetime to come to terms with the person she knows herself to be and with the appearance of herself that others will accept. Defining herself in love, therefore, as in art, Meigs resists being altered, diminished, or destroyed by societal pressures, cultural reflections, or the expectations of those closest to her. From her doubly marginal position as a woman and a lesbian, her most important tasks are to redefine herself so that both she as artist and her public may recognize the same appearance; to redefine the art, language, or medium in which her perception can name — and therefore control — the ways in which she wishes to be perceived; and possibly to redefine the society that marginalizes her. In this last task, again, Meigs is writing within the mainstream of North American feminist thinking, valuing the normative impact that art has on life. In this sense, too, her autobiographical agenda is largely political. Finally, in order to connect art with life and seeming with inner reality, she presents autobiography as a unique and necessary creation from inside the self, effective in determining what is true and, as art, what face or outer shell that truth shall wear.

What is true in varying degrees for all autobiography is of particular interest here because Meigs is articulate about the choices she is making; she invites the reader (from the outside peering in) to watch the artist at work in this creation of a mask or a persona that makes integral sense. Meigs aims for a more secure persona than Hemingway. Where he destabilizes human behavior, vindicating the artist only in terms of his art, she finds human behavior all too intractable and looks to art for interpretive survival skills. Where Hemingway creates crises of credibility that paradoxically provide a credible relationship, Meigs responds to the crisis she perceives in self- and other-perception of her sexuality in order to establish the realities that can be shared. Sexuality as crisis involves body and reflection in very particular ways (see discussions of Lorde, Joslin, and Butler and Rosenblum in Chapter 4 and Chapter 6) and identifies the personal as necessarily political. Grounded more comfortably in modernism than in the political activism of the 1960s and 1970s, Meigs exemplifies my suggestion that mirror talk may well originate in modernism's attempt to create solid presence out of contradictions.

Formed in the expectations established by her mother's public life, Meigs is courteous, reticent, gentle in style. Her autobiography develops through friendships, family, art, dreams, and her love of birds, wildflowers, and landscape. Beneath the even tenor of such discourse, however, inside this outer shape, lie the imperatives that alter the whole work. Just as Hemingway constructs himself in relation to a number of other writers, so Meigs constructs her autobiographical self (rather more kindly) as much in strenuous relation to her mother as to the fictional characters Lily Briscoe and Dolly Lamb; the mother-daughter relationship, indeed, provides one of her most fruitful uses of the Lily Briscoe trope. Mary Mason describes the "discovery of female identity" as commonly acknowledging "the real presence and recognition of another consciousness." She finds that "the disclosure of female self is linked to the identification of some 'other'" (210). For the lesbian, this "other" is commonly the heterosexual woman against whose norm the "woman-identified-woman" identifies herself. Charlotte Wolff has described the "emotional incest" that is "the very essence of lesbianism" (72), but it seems more fruitful in this context to recognize mother as also wife and housewife and, in particular, as part of the myth of fertility, posing quite specific problems for the lesbian artist who wants to identify what she is not. "I carried the baggage of that inheritance for a long time," Meigs writes, "though I gradually made decisions . . . not to marry, to be an artist, to listen to my own voices" (11).

Learning to accept her sexual nature, to acknowledge it as a part of her whole appearance, becomes accordingly an important part of her autobiography. It involves a continuous tension between the expectation imposed by others and the self that chooses expression. Similarly, learning to be an artist involves, as one might expect, tension between inner aspiration and external realization, but tension, too, between the dedication necessary for artistic achievement and either personal love or political action. How good does one have to be, Meigs asks, for dedication to be appropriate rather than selfish? ("Does every life deserve an autobiography?" she asks. "Does mine?" [11].)

What emerges through the external form is an evolution of choices and, through the tension, the courage to recognize and assert those choices as herself for all to see. Others' choices for one's self, even when made in love, are prisons or cages, damaging and inescapable. The artist, therefore, creates what Canadian painter and autobiographer Emily Carr has called her "yourself shell"; it protects and contains, yet, made from the inside out, it is true to the self inside. For Meigs, in other words, unlike Hemingway, the inner / outer dynamic of the traditional autobiographer figures significantly, which may account for her repeatedly turning to fictional characters for illumination as well as to their creators.

Narrative, of course, is one of the forms of art, and autobiographical narrative is a specific creation not to be seen as a transparency onto any given reality. One cannot, as Kermode puts it, clean the glass in order to reveal some undistorted truth. "How much more sensible," he suggests, "to study the mode of its partial opacity" (1972, 199). The mode of partial opacity also works, however, as a mode of illumination. Meigs introduces her mode at the outset in her title, indicating the role of Lily Briscoe, Virginia Woolf's artist in *To the Lighthouse*, in Meigs's creation of herself. The relationship extends well beyond the immediately apparent similarities between two women painters and is crucial to understanding Meigs's creation of autobiography.

For example, Lily Briscoe is one character among others in a work of fiction. The novel represents a world of which she is just a part. Similarly, Meigs creates an incremental context of which she herself is just a part; her world of family, friends, and fellow artists diminishes the egocentricity of the narrator. Like Lily Briscoe's, Meigs's role is that of interpreter and recreator of her world. Meigs's relationship with Lily Briscoe's role is further complicated, however, because Lily Briscoe is, in a sense, Woolf's autobiographer capturing Woolf's parents as she lovingly apprehends the presence and the memory of Mr. and Mrs. Ramsay. Toril Moi suggests that Woolf is developing here her crucial concept of androgyny:

> *To the Lighthouse* illustrates the destructive nature of a metaphysical belief in strong, immutably fixed gender identities — as represented by Mr and Mrs Ramsay — whereas Lily Briscoe (an artist) represents the subject who deconstructs this opposition, perceives its pernicious influence and tries as far as is possible in a still rigidly patriarchal order to live as her own woman, without regard for the crippling definitions of sexual identity to which society would have her conform. (13)

One value of the Lily Briscoe trope for Meigs, then, is the discretion of a representation (at three removes) of ancestral and heterosexual polarity mediated by the (fertile) daughter/artist. Woolf's sister Vanessa Bell was impressed by the likeness to their parents: "[A]s far as portrait painting goes," she wrote to Woolf, "you seem to me to be a supreme artist & it is shattering to find oneself face to face with those two again" (quoted in Bell, 2:128).

Shattering, in part, because the passing of time in *To the Lighthouse* is described as a downpouring of immense darkness. The rendition of such darkness, however, depends on moments of light, in terms of which, if only by contrast, the unspeakable and silent dark is representable. Mrs. Ramsay thinks in terms of such illuminated moments alternating with the darkness, like the beam from the lighthouse. She knows, for example, that her radiant dinner table has become, as she gives "one last look at it over her shoulder, already the past" (Woolf, 173). Like Lily Briscoe, who focuses primarily on Mrs. Ramsay, Meigs, focusing on herself, is conscious of her responsibility to hold that image, thus creating the permanence of the work of art from the flux of life and from changing impressions of it.

From her partial viewpoint, the artist also tries to understand the complex, multiple, mood-dependent viewpoints of those around her. Lily Briscoe, at the heart of Woolf's novel, sees what other characters also see. From the center and the periphery simultaneously, she sees a whole. Her perspective is partial and necessarily colored by her own character and experience, but objective reality, like the removal of the autobiographer from center stage, is stressed in both books. Meigs's use of documentation, for instance, is the *donnée* of her work. More important to the creation of her world is the attention she gives to the perceptions of others not simply in order to understand or to forgive but also so that her characters, like Woolf's, may vouch for the reality of what the painter sees.

The subject of Lily Briscoe's painting, moreover, is not just there for other characters to see; it is as central to their imagination as to hers. Mr. Ramsay, for example, looks up to see his wife and son framed in the window and is "fortified" (Woolf, 56). More important to the context of the whole novel and to the completed painting, Mr. Ramsay in distress actually seeks the figure of his wife reading to the little boy (Woolf, 73). Mr. Bankes looks at Lily's picture and sees Mrs. Ramsay, but he wonders what is meant by a purple shadow, whether this is truly an acceptable way in which to represent the time-honored image of a mother and child. In part, of course, Lily Briscoe is creating herself. Her thirty-three years are there and she must remain true to what she sees regardless of fashions in painting. (Meigs's cover contains a strongly delineated visual self-portrait with her mother's face outlined and faint but inescapable behind her—another unusual adumbration of mother and child.) What Lily is also achieving, however, is the elusiveness of meaning. When Mr. Bankes is annoyed at the dinner table, he feels that Mrs. Ramsay does not matter. Her beauty means nothing. Sitting at the window with her little boy means nothing. Lily's purple shadow, accordingly, is composed of the mattering and the not-mattering of Mrs. Ramsay and of "all this," which she and Mr. Bankes and Mr. and Mrs. Ramsay all love. It contains what Meigs, specifically identifying with Lily Briscoe, has called, like the rhythms of the beam of the lighthouse, "cycles of sight and blindness" (94).

Stasis and flux, the momentary truth or fact and its shifting meaning, can only be combined if the purple shadow represents an aspect of reality that every character in the text can recognize. The novelist provides explanatory context for what become cryptic images in paint. Word and image, for the artist and autobiographer, as for God in the beginning, are one and the same. "If only she could put them together, [Lily] felt, write them out in some sentence, then she would have got at the truth of things" (Woolf, 228). Meigs, who has created her mother's life in paint, voices dissatisfaction with her self-portraits and clearly shares Lily Briscoe's desire for the comparative unambiguity of the word. Yet Woolf deplored the railway track of the sentence and wanted to achieve "those splashes" of the painter (Bell, 2:106) and Lily also recognizes that "words fluttered sideways and struck the object inches too low" (Woolf, 274). For the Medusa-head of lesbianism, of course, face-to-face recognition is ugly and dangerous; Meigs's whole approach enacts Emily Dickinson's suggestion to "tell all the truth / but tell it slant." The generating crisis, which for the modern autobiographer remains unresolved even by the act of autobiography, makes sense here, as for Hemingway, of autobiography by reflection, bounced off the wall, or containing multiple perspectives, as for Cézanne, that preempt a singular vision.

For novelist, painter, or autobiographer, the object has less to do with some incontrovertible fact than with the mode of comprehension and expression. Lily Briscoe's purple shadow, for example, is part of her continuous process of understanding what she knows in terms of shape, color, and image. Similarly, thanks to Andrew's explanation of Mr. Ramsay's work, a scrubbed kitchen table, or even a scrubbed kitchen table lodged in a pear tree, comes to represent Lily's profound respect for Mr. Ramsay's mind. Sections of potatoes describe Mr. Bankes's dedication to science. The specific, even absurd particular provided by subjective comprehension extends, in visual expression, into form and balance; for Mrs. Ramsay, whom she cannot know in full but around whose secret knowledge and wisdom she hovers, Lily creates "the shape of a dome" (Woolf, 83). Disturbed by imbalance in her painting, she moves a salt cellar at the dinner table to remind herself to move a tree. Years later, at breakfast, she conjures up the salt cellar, the tree, and the painting which now, in defiance of the passing of time, despite the unlikelihood of success, she will finish.

The image becomes a code, a cryptic and intimate reduction of total experience to its meaning. The painter's effort, then, to recognize what is distinctive about another person or, in Meigs's case, about herself, involves expression of the inner secret in just such terms that are specific and visible and that fit so that others, too, can recognize who or what is meant. Lily Briscoe, for example, knows that Mrs. Ramsay is unreachable. She would understand Mrs. Ramsay's feeling that we are known only by childish "apparitions" when we rise to the surface (Woolf, 100). Novelist and painter combine in recognition of the wedge-shaped core of darkness into which Mrs. Ramsay shrinks, "something invisible to others," despite the fact that she continues to sit upright and knit. Repeatedly, Meigs explores her characters from new angles, in new relationships, sounding them to different depths and holding up images of them that serve to represent her recognition of internal life — Marie-Claire Blais as Astarte, for example, or Edmund Wilson's mind moving easily upon silence like Yeats's "long-legged fly upon the stream" (28).

Lily Briscoe imagines a glove shaped by the hand that wears it; the artist's image needs to belong beyond any doubt to its owner. She achieves this perfect match when she recognizes Mr. Ramsay in his boots, which are "his own indisputably" (Woolf, 237). Her recognition is so acute that he too accepts it gladly. "It had taken him the best part of his youth," he tells her, "to get boots made as they should be made. He would have her observe (he lifted his right foot and then his left) that she had never seen boots made quite that shape before" (Woolf, 238). The fit, of course, grows and evolves with the person, which is how it becomes — in Gerard Manley Hopkins's phrase — "counter, original, spare, strange," indisputably one's own. Woolf uses those empty shoes at the end of *Jacob's Room*; in their very ordinariness, they describe the absence of Jacob.

The artist looking for the glove or boot (or, indeed, the necktie) that fits another is particularly sensitive to any fit imposed upon her by another and asserts herself vigorously against it. Meigs learns who she is and produces her self-portrait in a constant battle against the limitations others create for her. Description of herself by another she sees as a shirt of Nessus: painful, destructive, impossible to take off. Lily Briscoe provides the idiom or mode here, too. By means of her ability to understand and ascribe meaning to people and to relationships — by virtue, in other words, of her creative role — Lily Briscoe resists as irrelevant the limiting perceptions that others have of her. Mrs. Ramsay, for example, sees "only Lily Briscoe . . . and that did not matter" (Woolf, 31). One could not take her painting seriously and she would never marry. Yet observing the Ramsays and their houseguests, Lily Briscoe retains years later the clear memory that she had saved herself exultantly from the pressure to marry by knowing what she needed to do in her painting (Woolf, 271). She bends like corn under a wind before Mr. Tansley, who says that women cannot write, women cannot paint, and erects herself again by hanging onto her painting (Woolf, 134–35). She can laugh and let Mr. Tansley talk all night because she is moving the tree in the morning. In the context of inherited wealth, Meigs identifies with the rich young man who could not give up all he had in order to follow Jesus, thus describing the continuous inadequacy she feels as an artist, her failures of dedication or attainment. Yet, in terms of her potential for translating her own experience into a new and public form, she too resists the pressures to behave as others think appropriate. Lily Briscoe's exultation, furthermore, is fully justified. Mr. Ramsay, who responds to Minta's glow on the evening of her engagement and has referred to "poor Lily Briscoe" as "skimpy" (Woolf, 154), is nonetheless known and created by her both in his person and in the completion of his journey to the lighthouse.

The process of this creation provides a continuous theme through Woolf's novel, connecting the activity of the novelist with that of the fictive painter. This, too, is important to Meigs, whose autobiography records the process of exploration, recognition, understanding, and creation in paint and in words. The self is part of the medium of perception and of creation, which is why Mr. Bankes sees Lily's thirty-three years on the canvas and why both Lily Briscoe and Mary Meigs are afraid to have people look at their painting. "It had been seen," thinks Lily Briscoe. "It had been taken from her" (Woolf, 86). She can only say what she means with a brush in her hand, the saying being not a finite accomplishment but a process. Yet the moment between seeing and putting brush to canvas is traumatic because the brush stroke makes shape out of chaos, stability out of eternal passing and flowing, something finite out of the essentially unfinished. Lily Briscoe's final brush stroke represents the ultimate possibility for the artist because it penetrates the obscurity of perception in which the painter struggles to integrate a total picture; it contains Lily's process of seeing and making, Mrs. Ramsay's identification of herself with the last, steady stroke of the lighthouse, the end of Mr. Ramsay's journey, and therefore the end of the book. It demonstrates the complete integration of life, perception, and art that is central to Meigs's process of autobiography. The activity or process in flux creates the presence with its illusions of stasis.

For Meigs, all art essentially expresses its artist. Lily Briscoe is present in her rendition of a mother and child because she refuses to compromise her perception of what she sees in order to suit the prevailing norms in art. Meigs's love for Marie-Claire Blais is so apparent in a portrait of her as to make Andrée, of the triangle of *The Medusa Head*, fiercely jealous. In the work of Mark Rothko, who wished, Joyce-like, to abstract himself from his painting, Meigs sees "abstractions of [his] inner torment" (38), a form of self-portrait. She believes, indeed, that

> the most resolute minimalist is *there* in his work . . . that even if one reproduces photographs of soup cans, those cans of soup proclaim not Campbell, but Warhol. The painter or sculptor enters into fluorescent lights, chunks of wood, electrical gadgets, steel girders, by the fact of his having given them new instructions and a new order. (38)

Certainly she would subscribe to the notion that all writing is a form of autobiography. She cites the *Alice* books as forms of subconscious self-analysis that kept Dodgson/Carroll relatively sane. Rilke, she recalls, objected to analysis on the grounds that it would "derange his poetic universe" (216). Inadvertently when not intentionally, the artist produces a form of self-portrait or autobiography.

For art is spun out of that wedge-shaped core of darkness that is so difficult to identify in another, so often unrecognizable in the self. Recognition of such secret places, furthermore, is potentially dangerous because it penetrates the public mask or apparent role. Giving a Wildean spin to the relations between life and death in autobiography, Meigs asks: "Isn't the threat finally, *death* to an essential image of ourselves, to the way we hold our egos together?" (39). In frequent anecdotes about family and friends, Meigs indicates the explosive possibilities inherent in truly recognizing oneself, or, in Meigs's own case, acknowledging that she is lesbian. So art, which specifically thrives on this uncensored inner life and translates it into acceptable form, becomes, like dreams, a medium for expression and recognition of the secret self.

It makes sense, then, that Meigs's efforts to come to terms with her
own homosexuality, especially within the context of liberation from all the foot-binding expectations with which she grew up, should lead her to identify with characters in fiction and, through them, with their creators. She identifies, for example, with Isabel Archer before her marriage to Osmond. Like Charlotte Brontë's Jane Eyre or Shirley, like Jane Austen's Elizabeth Bennett or Emma, indeed, like Lily Briscoe, Isabel Archer has "a sense of her own right" (20). Meigs speculates on Brontë's marrying and on Austen's remaining single. Unmasking heterosexist assumptions, developing and articulating her own unique perspective, Meigs argues anxiously with Edmund Wilson about James's homosexuality. She is distressed by Wilson's denial that Proust was homosexual. Proust, he says, wasn't anything. Such denial, she feels, makes "discussion impossible and conjecture indecent" (27). It forces the morally acceptable correlation of great art with heterosexuality. (Were Emily Dickinson or Virginia Woolf less great as artists because they loved women, she asks?) It serves to protect great reputations for the sensibilities of conventional opinion. It also blinds one to the autobiographical in art.

James's treatment of independent women becomes for Meigs part of his treatment of homosexuality. He mocks the feminist Miss Peabody in *The Bostonians*, for instance, and is ruthless to Olive Chancellor, whom he has "pinned on a board, a perfect specimen of a repressed Lesbian" (20). Wilson has written about the governess in *The Turn of the Screw* as a neurotic monster who frightens the boy Miles to death. Meigs, however, sees her own mother and governess in James's governess. She recognizes their moral rigidity and righteousness. Theirs is the moral outrage that the homosexual has to face, and Miles is one of three Jamesian characters whom Meigs identifies as "not strong enough to bear the image society has of their guilt. Each is suspected of being homosexual, and, in one way or another, James repeatedly killed the homosexual in himself" (58). The tension and anxiety inherent in Meigs's discussion with Edmund Wilson result, of course, less from her identification of James as evidently homosexual than from what such perception says about her. James was lucky, she feels, to die before his secret was run to earth. It is one thing to translate inner turmoil into art and quite another for it to be identified from the outside.

Where Lily Briscoe triumphs through her work over the limited and limiting perceptions that others have of her, Meigs describes how recognition and assertion on her part grow out of such an instinctive resistance to others' perceptions of her. The aunt who wonders why she has not married when she is just an ordinary American girl is like the young man at the party who hesitantly half-speaks his sense of her sexuality. They provide alarm signals according to which the young Meigs, in her bewilderment, must begin to define herself. Wilson, both courtly and sensitive friend and brutal male minotaur, later asks her whether she is not "really a sort of Lesbian" (14). His "sort of" identification deeply disturbs her "shadowy world of denial and pretense" (5). It stiffens her pride and opens the whole process of acceptance of herself.

The serious implications of external identification and the need to create oneself are developed in the second part of *Lily Briscoe*, titled "Dolly Lamb and Lily Briscoe." Quoting from *To the Lighthouse* as preface to this section, Meigs shows Lily Briscoe clasping "some miserable remnant of her vision to her breast, which a thousand forces did their best to pluck from her" (143). For Meigs, these forces take the particular form of Mary McCarthy and her characterization of Meigs as Dolly Lamb in *A Charmed Life*. McCarthy, as woman and artist, repeats the creative mother role that opposes Meigs's self-definition; Meigs finds herself misread, like James and Proust, and reacts with a reader response to her own life.[13] McCarthy's "acceptable" characterization of her as repressed (for which she is at the time partly grateful) becomes part of the resisting and defining process by which Meigs can assert a freed sexuality which she names for herself.

Before McCarthy's book was written, Meigs had "felt this terrible judgement without appeal settling over [her]" (151). She had felt, despite their kindness, as if McCarthy and her husband, Bowden Broadwater, had "slowly, very slowly . . . swallowed and reconstituted [her]" (148). Casual details of her life as their neighbor provide constant material for the portrait that she knows is in process. They identify her type, for example, in her choice of a "smoke-grey sleeveless dress of pleated chiffon" and fit their definition over her like a "ghostly skin" that she cannot shake off (150). "How to prove," she asks, "against the weight of evidence, that you are the person you feel yourself to be?" (151).[14]

Dolly Lamb is Martha Sinnott's friend and neighbor, a single woman with an independent income, and a painter. What Meigs winces at is the portrayal of the repressed virgin, "'industrious, even in her pleasures, like a sober little girl making mud pies'" (152). Her work, says one character, is sick and cramped with preciosity and mannerisms. If there was anyone else inside her, "'it was a creature still more daunted and mild and primly scrupulous than the one the world saw'" (150). Her collection of shells becomes a "hoarding" of her own "shit" assembled in neat, "constipated little packages" (152). She is controlled, in her meekness, by everyone with whom she comes in contact. Her money gives her a certain power in the novel but may prevent her from ever becoming a painter. McCarthy's picture of a person almost totally re-pressed, coming at a time in Meigs's life when she was "still resolutely hiding [her] head in the sand like an ostrich" (155), wields significant destructive power. It is "saturated with a kind of burning poison, like the shirt of Nessus," and sticks to the skin of the self, "for although there is an affirmative voice that cries, 'Can't you see that this is my real self?' another self-doubting voice is slyly whispering, 'Could it be true?'" (107). It is, in part, "a germ of truth" that makes external observation so dangerous, to be resisted "with the blind instinct of self-preservation" (121). It is also a matter of the power of definition which may turn semblance into reality, thereby altering the self from the outside in; it is no joke that Gertrude Stein could come to look like Picasso's portrait of her. "Mary seemed to want to quench my faith in myself," Meigs writes. "She activated the dormant seeds of doubt that made me so ready to hate myself and my work. . . . I dragged myself about in a state of doubt and self-loathing for a long time" (152–53).

In keeping with Meigs's thesis that all art is autobiographical, how-ever, McCarthy's sword is two-edged. She herself is Martha in relation to Dolly Lamb's "Mary" and is neglecting her higher calling amid the busy and complex results of her return with a new husband to an old home territory still housing her former husband, Miles Murphy as Edmund Wilson. Murphy's dominance in Martha's life is irrational and strong. Her pregnancy by him is disastrous. More interesting still, his purchase of her portrait at an exorbitant price that he refuses to pay is surely most precisely that theft of a soul that leaves Meigs feeling in-dignant and bruised. These multiple and explosive interrelationships between living artists and their creations of themselves and of each other suggest that for McCarthy, as for Meigs, Woolf, Hemingway, and Fitzgerald, autobiographical narration reflects both human rela-tionships and the forms of art in which others might pre-empt creation of one's self.

Words and paint steal from reality even as they define and create it. The citizens of Wellfleet, including Edmund Wilson, express fear of Marie-Claire Blais because she might put them in her book. Wilson, Meigs feels, had no right to complain for he too had the ruthless eyes of a writer and had "prepared his own friends for a ritual feast and served them up in recognizable form" (111). So Marie-Claire, treated like a witch, feared like a prophet, is slandered or ignored while she, with her "strange power" (111), sees and hears everything, recording and storing it away for future use. Meigs sees in her the "mighty writer's will that reconstructs the lives of others" (211). These two have recognized the "unchangeable 'me's'" in each other (107), but another writer friend provokes a quarrel "when she, with her writer's zeal, tried, so to speak, to write my life" (212). The curious dilemma for the creative artist, whether portraying another or the self, is to realize the full potential of the creative act without damage or distortion to the sitter. Meigs's portrait of Marie-Claire is an extension of her love, and illustrations for one of Marie-Claire's books integrate their imaginative lives. The issue is one of taking or giving, which is as subtle and as potentially dangerous in art as in love. "Indeed," says Meigs on the subject of a love that has passed, "it becomes dangerous, the possession of parts of one's self by someone else, and not only have all the pieces to be taken back, but also one has to be careful not to let any escape" (234). Rothko, the minimalist, preferred Tintoretto's portraits to Rembrandt's because "Tintoretto told the truth about human beings without trespassing on their integrity, and this was the duty of a great portrait painter" (37–38). While resisting Rothko's downscaling of Rembrandt, Meigs describes in numerous ways the importance of respecting the sitter's "I am," which is, after all, the sitter's own most significant creative act.

Meigs, I have suggested, is less concerned with interaction among people than with that between the individual and her artistic medium. Other people are important to this text essentially for their misreadings of her, which she is eager to correct. The most serious question becomes how to work with this crisis of misrepresentation to arrive at a representation that satisfies herself. Marie-Claire guards "the secret of her 'I am'" (109), but Meigs has to wrestle like Jacob with the angel to create a likeness because she has proved elusive even to herself; she must track herself down through memories that include joy, anxiety, and regret, through friendships, and through work, which is the context for her growth and change both as a person and as an artist. Meigs finds two beings in herself: "one, who has been free to make choices and shape [her] life; the other, bumbling along, trying this and that" (105). The first is a free spirit that she connects repeatedly with light and with flying. The other is caged in armor, impersonal and rigid. The first enables her to choose and to insist upon those forms of work and love that liberate her. The second, imposed by the sense of duty and the guilty conscience that are inseparable from her class, draws her into roles of social and political responsibility. "The suits of armour in my life," she writes, "served to teach me what I wasn't and what I couldn't do well" (106). Alternatively, Meigs's "pursuit of happiness," or — the same thing — of what is "natural" to her, enables her repeatedly "to wriggle out of all those suits of armour, just before the nuts and bolts had been tightened for all time. . . . I slithered repeatedly out of traps I had voluntarily entered when they began to threaten the indestructible sense I have always had of my 'self'" (106). Roles imposed by societal expectation are external perspectives on the self. "They make us what we are, even the bad roles, for every choice is both a kind of mask, to which we conform, and something inner, that alters us from the inside-out" (106). What artist and autobiographer are concerned about is this inside-out process, the life behind the face, the integrity that must stand clear of trespass, the invisible self that is impossible to know (238). A significant aspect of autobiography becomes the rendering visible of that secret identity.

For Meigs, the painful and lifelong issue has been the naming of her homosexuality. It needs to be said in words. The young man's hesitation, Wilson's "sort of," McCarthy's repressed virgin, all containing merely germs of truth, generate Meigs's own expression, which has less to do with sex than with love, less with difference than with wholeness, less with eccentricity than with artistic integrity. It is the whole person of whom the nameable parts are only parts that she needs to create from the inside out. And for her, as for Lily Briscoe, the mother becomes the absent referent, both desired and feared; in language as in life, the mother's presence contradicts such naming, such fertility in self-procreation.[15] Her sister, years after their mother's death, accepts Meigs's sexuality and says their mother would have, too. Even now, however, her "heart begins to thump with the old fear and sickness . . . at the very thought of talking" (67). She recognizes other women "consenting to hypocritical silence and coming to believe in the necessity, imposed by their mothers, of lying low and pretending to be invisible" (67). Fleeing hurt and humiliation in love, Meigs at one point seeks just this invisibility. "I spent the month with my mother in Washington," she writes. "I could not tell her the reasons for this surprising and welcome attention to her, but I felt strangely happy with her, as though her ignorance of my life made it invisible, as though a spell had been cast over me that made my New York self cease to exist" (223). This life, however, is what she calls earlier "a dishonest shadow-land" (69), and she cites Lewis Carroll's parable about the power of words to change love into fear. In *Through the Looking Glass*, Alice wanders through a wood "where things have no name," her arms lovingly clasped around the neck of a young fawn. Only when they leave the wood is the fawn startled to realize that she is a fawn and should rightly fear a human child. "Like Alice and the Fawn," Meigs writes of herself and her mother, "we could only be friends in a wood 'where things have no names'" (70).

Art, in whatever form, is precisely a matter of naming, however. If Rothko is present in his abstract paintings, if James is present in the homosexual characters whom he repeatedly destroys, if Woolf is present in Lily Briscoe, and, we might add, if Hemingway is present in Fitzgerald, how much more present is the artist in the deliberate self-portrait. For Meigs, her stubborn self as she and not as others perceive her remains elusive, like the garden in *Alice in Wonderland*, always just out of reach. She is suspended in a moment of what she has called, in a dream, "transparency." "I once heard this word on the edge of sleep," she writes, "and knew that it meant the relationship between trying to understand and the moment of understanding, the open eyes of real attention" (178). She has experienced this in the gap between seeming to understand Yeats in ways that convince others that she should teach and then truly discovering Yeats for herself. The point of recognition, understanding, or realization of vision is a freedom from effort, a moment of grace, which needs to be repeated again and again. It is easy, like Yeats's long-legged fly upon the stream that reduces Wilson to tears, like walking on water with the simplicity of Jesus. Similarly, Meigs describes as "intense attention" (192) that love that is not possessive, not characterized by sexuality, not restrictive of the other's self-definition. "A real flowing of attention into another being," she writes, "is like a transfusion of life" (193); it creates a new thing without damaging the old. Meigs articulates an ideal for intersubjective relations that art, like living, so commonly overrides.

Learning to fuse the inner life and its external manifestations, in art as in love, is a process of growth. Meigs describes the movement in her life from copying, as the genteel art of a young lady, to the discovery of color with all its implications for form and space. "Perceiving colour at last," she writes, "was . . . an awakening that simultaneously released dreams, like marvellous paintings unable to make the leap into conscious life" (163). Similarly, she has "dreamt marvellous paintings that fade to a confusion of dim colours when [she wakes]" (169). Use of color, for her as for Lily Briscoe, is dogged repeatedly by disappointment in the realization of the vision; but for her, as for Lily Briscoe, it becomes central to how she perceives. (She angers her father with her pleasure in Van Gogh and wears outrageous colors with a keen sense of abandon.)

For Meigs, conscious use of color involves repeated effort and repeated disappointment, like the self-portrait, precisely because it signifies, in its connection with the inner life of dreams and self-expression, a move away from the making of a copy to the making from the inside of a new reality entirely. The new face is not the original face but an expression of what that face means, to which other characters in her life-book respond and react. If she holds the portrait up to the mirror, she can see "everything one has done wrong" (255). If she concentrates, however, on "the elements of a portrait of a Lesbian; [her] life with its mixture of shame and pride must be visible in [her] face" (255). The life, in other words, translated from its manifestations onto canvas, as into print, becomes manifest less in seeming than in a new reality, an art form governed by its own laws. Adherence, indeed, to the original life form will dispel the illusion of profound relationship. Lily Briscoe creates a purple shadow that does not look like a mother and child but is a new and satisfactory definition of Mrs. Ramsay reading to James. And Mary Meigs, in reticent memoir, creates her lifelong struggle to be herself. In personal terms, the evolution takes her from hiding her head in the sand to allowing other people to see her portrait, the form of herself that she has made. As an artist, she has discovered the mode in which her outer appearance becomes a satisfactory rendition of her inner self.

Meigs envies the snake which repeatedly sheds its skin and continues to grow. Continuous growth and change in life are stunted by a shirt of Nessus or by any mask or armor that restricts such movement. Life, in a sense, resists and escapes art, refuses to stand still. The necessary movement of life conflicts with the necessary finality of art. So Woolf envied the painter "those splashes" that allow for impressionistic accuracy. Restricted to language herself, she created the character of a painter with a work in progress who could then create the Ramsays and their world. A fictive painter, whose work is invisible, provides the process or activity by which reality may be apprehended but at a remove from the text on the page which is most fixedly there. That is, engaging the imagination through the printed word about a fictive character engaged in an invisible process of recreation, Woolf asks each reader to make Mrs. Ramsay at the window with her child and to recreate the journey to the lighthouse. Lily Briscoe uses "those splashes" denied to Woolf but she, too, like the novelist, must call her work at some point "finished." It may contain, like a kaleidoscope, many alternatives, many variations, no single fixed picture. But it is also, unlike life, complete. The process may match the evolution of a life and define its character through change. Unlike life, however, the process does at some point become a product. The making of fiction becomes in its own right a fact. It stands still, enduring further change only from the outside in the eyes of its beholders.

Meigs clearly sees the language of art (like the language of dreams) as both a symbolic or created expression of her life and an original self about whom and for whom that "artifact" is true. This is why she describes not exposure but liberation as a result of autobiography. Her final images are not of vulnerability as she releases her portrait for public view but of freedom and flying. For, unlike the naive auto-biographer who hopes to say something about life, the artist knows that self-creation, like love and friendship, is "a long process of simulta-neous attention and letting-go" (260). The separation of the finite work of art from the continuously changing self leaves the autobiogra-pher to be assessed not at all in terms of life but in terms of the genres of autobiography. In this outer shell, Meigs demonstrates what has been for her a continuous process. Revealing tension, contradiction, and this momentary stasis between dynamic inner core and finite outer ap-pearance, Meigs creates the face that she has chosen for herself as an act of deliberate resistance to choices that others might make.

BREYTENBACH'S *MOUROIR*: THE NOVEL AS AUTOBIOGRAPHY[16]

Hemingway's anxiety about maintaining artistic integrity, by not allowing success or easy money to damage his *métier*, generates the continuous crisis informing *A Moveable Feast* and generates, too, the original genres of this autobiography. Fitzgerald provides the perfect foil because he faces the same dangers, and the two men reflect for each other the ways in which fiction improves the reality on which no two men can ever agree. Meigs, on the other hand, driven by her need to correct the perception others have of her sexuality, contradicts those perceptions with the multiple voices of other artists and their fictive creations; she establishes a single perception by means of others that are self-confirming and that work from the inner life rather than the external. For the Afrikaans poet Breyten Breytenbach the crisis is po-tentially life-threatening; imprisoned for anti-apartheid activism, he faces the problem of total disjuncture from the normal conditions and connections of his life and needs to recreate a self that has been effectively removed from recognizable realities into a situation of extreme danger. If genre responds to and represents crisis, the question for Breytenbach is what tools best serve the skilled and experienced writer who reconstitutes himself in darkness and in secret?[17]

In 1975, Breytenbach was sentenced to nine years in a South African prison for his anti-apartheid activities. He served two years in solitary confinement at Beverly Hills Maximum Security in Pretoria. In a television interview made after his release, he has described living among the death cells, saturated with the chanting of the condemned, able to see only the passing feet of his fellow prisoners. He smuggled out line drawings of a bed, bars, a folded blanket, bound wraiths of men. It was here that he wrote *Mouroir: Mirrornotes of a Novel*, thirty-eight semi-connected prose studies of life in death. After a second trial in 1977, Breytenbach was transferred from isolation in Pretoria to Pollsmoor, a criminal prison at the Cape. He has said that he did not expect to leave prison, death being frequently an accidental result of prison's explosive violence, and the courts being clearly able and determined to order the course of justice to meet political needs. His early release in 1982 was, therefore, unexpected. Breytenbach returned to Paris, where he dictated *The True Confessions of an Albino Terrorist*, which appeared in 1983. ("Now I must get rid of the unreality. I must vomit. I must eject this darkness. . . . You must allow me to regurgitate all the words, like the arabesques of a blind mind" [27].)

Both *Mouroir*, written piecemeal during Breytenbach's time in prison, and *The True Confessions*, produced after his release, grow out of the same experience. Both accounts employ a variety of tones ranging from the cynical to the passionate, a variety that affects style and treatment and the processes of narrative. And, as if finger-printed beyond verbal patterns, both describe an integrity apparently undamaged by that damaging time. Breytenbach has spoken of writing in prison as a conduit, as a means of pouring out of himself that which could not be sullied, as a means of maintaining inner purity despite constant pawing, physical and mental, despite constant desecration. His prose makes both the need and the achievement very clear. He describes groveling self-abasement in pursuit of small luxuries like conversation, along with lies, subterfuges, desperate remedies, but all with the pellucid objective of keeping himself intact. The achievement common to both books, accordingly, is a clear voice, trustworthy in part because of its variety and range, urgent, personal, intimate yet witty, restrained and self-mocking.

The two books, however, are by no means parallel texts. *The True Confessions*, telling the story from hindsight, beginning from the certainty of a known end, tells the story of Breytenbach's experience in prison, giving background information about his family, his political activities, his arrest, both trials, and describing relationships with warders and prisoners, the processes of work and visits, the material of his prison life. It is a clear, comparatively straightforward "and then" account of what happened to the central character, Breyten Breytenbach. It has all the usual advantages of traditional autobiography, the authority, the perspective, the ability to make sense for others of what is already intelligible to the narrating self. *Mouroir*, on the other hand, does not work at this public level of sense-making. It is a more problematic book, harder apparently in the writing, certainly harder to read. In particular, as an autobiographical work, it raises a number of questions about the uses of fiction for the rendition of lived experience. Reading *True Confessions* as descriptive and explanatory material, the best factual authority available on the subject of *Mouroir*, one can see in the disturbing series of prose poems that constitute *Mouroir* deviously coded and interconnected genres of autobiography in crisis. In particular, their treatment of a mysterious and elusive narrator and of repeatedly destabilized narrative create a peculiar tension for the reader; we are permeated by the anxiety of the man in hiding, for whom death seems inevitable, and we are simultaneously, by virtue of our efforts to decode his narration, the sleuths who will identify and destroy him. Breytenbach's disturbing episodes accordingly suggest a shifting or multiple target and a hide-and-seek rendition of subjective experience.

True Confessions on the Subject of *Mouroir*

In a chapter entitled "The Writer Destroys Time," Breytenbach describes the conditions under which he wrote *Mouroir* in prison. He received permission to write so long as he did not show his work to anyone or attempt to smuggle it out of prison. He was to hand in everything he wrote as soon as he had written it and to keep no notes. In return, he was assured that his writing would be kept safe. Unable to trust such assurances, Breytenbach nonetheless wrote, knowing, as he puts it, that the enemy was reading over his shoulder. He wrote to an audience outside prison knowing that he could not reach it and knowing too that he was "laying bare the most intimate and the most personal nerves and pulsebeats in [himself] to the barbarians, to the cynical ones who [would] gloat over this" (1983, 159). Referring to the censored, Afrikaans edition of his *Season in Paradise*, Breytenbach says the prison authorities, the "Greyshits," knew about it long before it was published. Such keen connoisseurs are they of literature, they will inter-

cept a manuscript between author and publisher. Indeed, he suggests, "They may even read a book before it is written!" (1983, 157). This writer's first level of encounter, therefore, is with hostile readers who have the power to censor his work and, indeed, his life.

Privacy and personal integrity become, then, a matter of writing in the dark:

> In the dark I can just perceive the faintly pale outline of a sheet of paper. And I would start writing. Like launching a black ship on a dark sea. I write: I am the writer. I am doing my black writing with my no-colour gloves and my dark glasses on, stopping every once in a while, passing my sheathed hand over the page to feel the outlines and imprints of letters which have no profile. It makes for a very specific kind of wording perhaps akin to the experiments that the surrealists used to make in earlier years. There is the splashing of darkness, the twirled sense. (1983, 154–55)

Mouroir takes place essentially in the dark, moments of pellucid illumination being necessarily only moments or serving only to define how lost one is or how limited is one's vision. Many characters are myopic or wear dark glasses and some pretend that they can see. "Writing," he says of the origins of *Mouroir*,

> becomes for me a means, a way of survival. I have to cut up my environment in digestible chunks. Writing is an extension of my senses. It is itself a sense which permits me to grasp, to understand, and to some extent to integrate that which is happening to me. I need it the same way the blind man behind his black glasses needs to see. (1983, 55)

This extension of senses, this discovery through words of what is comprehensible, becomes in the dark and without external checks or references, a labyrinth, "the exteriorization of my imprisonment. My writing bounces off the walls [a literalized version of *jai alai*]. The maze of words which become alleys, like sentences, the loops which are closed circuits and present no exit, these themselves constitute the walls of my confinement" (1983, 155). Breytenbach's situation is extreme, but he describes the processes whereby words and the activity of writing (as for Hemingway, or paint and painting for Meigs) provide the genres and the meanings that the particular life requires.

Just as he needs to write as deeply down inside himself as he can in order to evade the enemy over his shoulder, creating comprehension in isolation, externalizing an inner experience with no assurance of its meaning for others, the maze comes also to represent the mind in the process of such creation. Working without notes or certain memory,

> you do not know whether you are writing in circles, raking over cleaned soil, coming back to sniff again and again at the same old sour vomit. . . . [A]nd since you write your dreams and dream that you are writing, you do not know what you have actually written and what you have only imagined. You write your mind. (1983, 160)

The episodes and fragments that constitute *Mouroir* can be read, indeed, as so many possible directions or possibilities leading repeatedly to further confusion or to yet another dead end. The only constant is that of search or inquiry or puzzlement. "That which links us all," he writes in *Mouroir*, "is exactly the unknown" (192). The mind creates its own reflection, the words become the mirror that holds the otherwise shifting image. Or so one imagines, until the mirror also becomes water washing the stones of experience, leaving no trace of an origin to reflect. "[I]t is unbalancing something very deeply embedded in yourself," Breytenbach writes in *The True Confessions*, "when you in reality construct, through your scribblings, your own mirror. Because in this mirror you write hair by hair and pore by pore your own face, and you don't like what you see" (155).

The problem, in the heart of this very private labyrinth, is the collapse of time and of the usual distinctions between the necessary and the arbitrary, between past and present and future, and the absence therefore of logical sequence. Not liking what you see consists also of not recognizing it. But the mirror "won't let you out again. . . . Who am I? Where and who was I before this time?" (1983, 156). So images recur that make sense only afterward or in the context of later events. Watches tick, unpeel like onions, open like coffins or bodies, tell a time that is irrelevant, or break down altogether because time has run out. Many episodes in *Mouroir* specify a distant past or future or a reflection that precedes the image, or a sequence of events in which conclusion precedes origin. The mirror image, of course, is not a replication but an opposite. In a mirrored labyrinth all hope of escape must be desperate.

Breytenbach played chess in prison, from which he creates a metaphor of hopeless encounter: "a schizophrenic experience, playing white against black, I facing I, me against Mr. Investigator. I cannot lose. I cannot win. I am free" (1983, 154). *Mouroir* provides one chess table that describes the nature of time and space and the player's inability to control any aspect of either, though the chess game, the contest, the illusion of a possible win, of having some control, is a recurring image. This chess table is clear glass with no legs, a transparent block:

> When a piece — pawn, bishop, knight, or rook — is eliminated, it sinks through the board into the glassy depths of the table. Then it shrinks, slowly at first and gradually ever faster, but it remains part of a game with the other pieces. The two players also are moves in the ritual. Invisible threads of correlation entangle everything. All go down in the game. There are different layers of volatilization amplifying and tied into each other, and all dimensionless. The two contestants are manoeuvred. Arrive at a position of tension or aggression or defence in relation to the pieces on the board and those again to the pieces moving in the glass depths. From the result of each move hang life and death. A game endlessly renewed. . . . Smaller and smaller. In this way and at this distance there is no difference between life and death. (1984, 97–98)

Placing these two accounts side by side demonstrates the transition from angry imagination in a series of deadlocks to the surreal quality in which life encounters death in the mirror of *Mouroir*.

Mouroir is permeated by death and dying, by rot and decay, by the expectation and the smell of death. In a powerful section called "The Double Dying of an Ordinary Criminal," Breytenbach describes the death-song of the condemned blacks which he heard constantly during his isolation at Beverly Hills:

> When the Unwhite are informed (when the countdown starts) they directly open up in song, they break and let the words erupt. There is a pulsating urgency about the singing, as if one can hear how scorchingly alive their voices are. All the other prisoners — in any event only awaiting their turn — help them from that instant on: the basses, the tenors, the harmonizers, the choir. Every flight of the prospective voyagers' voices is supported and sustained by those of the others. . . . The sound of the voices is like that of cattle at the abattoir, the lowing of beasts smelling the blood and knowing that nothing can save them now. . . . In this fashion, during the final week, that which is fear and pain and anguish and life is gradually pushed out of the mouth. (1984, 52)

The bruises of such experience remain with the witness until he is compelled to become part of the ritual: "The pen twists the rope. From the pen he is hanged. . . . He hangs in the mirror" (1984, 62). The danger inherent in isolating such images is that Breytenbach might seem too clever by far. In cumulative, dense, and persistent metaphor, however, he shares the death-song of the blacks. "Uncoloureds," he says, do not sing easily. But from him, as from the condemned, expression of life in the labyrinth of death rises frequently "to a shriek of limpid knowing" (1984, 53).

Mouroir as Fiction

Breytenbach's *True Confessions* situates *Mouroir* in a specific time and place. It also specifies the sources of what in *Mouroir* becomes a surreal presentation of violence, helplessness, fear, decay, and death. Nowhere in *True Confessions*, however, does Breytenbach describe *Mouroir* as autobiographical. Indeed, in its own presentation, he seems explicitly to disqualify it as autobiography, calling it *Mouroir: Mirrornotes of a Novel*. This novel is by Breyten Breytenbach, the author well known for *True Confessions* and for volumes of poetry, but he appears within this text as one of the many passing characters in several fragments as Braytenbach, Breathenbach, Brethenbach, Turd Breytenbach. The narrator is similarly unstable, unfixed, on occasion first person, at other times third, and yet again impersonal, paring his nails. If instability here becomes hide-and-seek, the connections to be avoided between writer and narrator are the connections to be avoided between silencing and death. (The desperate circumstances of Breytenbach's writing should not blind us to the complex parallels between his construction of the subject and that of Hemingway or Meigs.)

The difficulty of this work for the reader originates precisely in the writer's practical difficulty. Just as he had no certainty of a book accumulating in some official file as a finite body of meaning, so he restricts the reader to one page at a time. Even in the completeness of a bound volume, *Mouroir* provides only fragments telling no definable story, involving no single discernible character nor, even, a central narrator, and no clear references to any known world. It engages many disparate and usually nebulous situations, none of which is resolved — except, presumably, the overall reflection of the processes of death clearly suggested by the title.

Furthermore, *Mouroir* tells no story. Though all the names recur in many variations and interrelate among the episodes in ways that suggest meanings, continuity is never even suggested. In the final piece entitled "Index," Juan T. Bird takes responsibility "to finish off these accompanying documents; not to complete them — that, you'll agree, would be unethical — but to *book* them." He claims "this dubious honour" because he has "collected the diverse fragments over several years" and because he did know, or had met, "some of the memoirists and their companions" (1984, 252). Narrator here shifts from (plural) memoirist to recipient and reader of fragments ("I facing I"), a mediator between the hiding place and the public world.

Because of the shifting grounds of these multiple encounters, all explicit signals place this work as fiction. To all appearances, Breytenbach removes himself as a point of reference or departure just as he repeatedly shifts place and time and context. So fictive is this work that nothing remains certain within one episode or from one episode to the next. It may, indeed, seem positively perverse to explore *Mouroir* as autobiography. Yet I suggest both that Breytenbach himself presents, within the text, many reasons why one should do so, and that the self that avoids direct encounter creates a new idiom for extreme and continuous crisis.

Mouroir as Autobiography: Naming of Parts

The verbal wit that characterizes all of Breytenbach's writing inevitably includes his use of names. Juan T. Bird alerts the reader to his own absurdity by his wish to "book" his confusing documents. The name, in fact, is claimed by Breytenbach in *The True Confessions*: "*Mister* Bird, if you don't mind, which means the jail bait" (1983, 178). Within *Mouroir* alone, however, the name connects with caged birds, seagulls that evoke the blinding of Gloucester and the cliffs of Dover in *King Lear*,[18] birds that out-Hitchcock Hitchcock, and frequent Icarian images of useless flight. In this way, virtually every name connects with thematic images or with momentary sense-making, thus reverberating beyond its own statement of a character who maybe does thus and so to a personification of some possibility. Lamourt Lasarus is an obvious example. The name needs no explaining. But its meaning, like all else in *Mouroir*, shifts and modulates. Lamortcek, or LL, for example, tells a story in prison about another prison, possibly in Czechoslovakia, and the story there of a pistol that is possessed by the treacherous uses to which it has been put. But LL, it turns out, has hijacked the identity of the original LL in whose disappearance he possibly played a part. Which LL, one may then wonder, is actually the friend of Gregor Samsa, who appears in this and other stories and is referred to on other occasions by variants of this name? LL, furthermore, is given the disturbing pistol of this story by Keuner, also known as K., a companion of several narrators. Breytenbach's choice of literary allusions adds resonance to each given context and may help to describe the ways in which he builds meaning out of suggestion.

K. and Greg Somesome are also part of another group in which Lamourt appears with his wife Mooityd. When Juan T. Bird "books" these characters in his "Index," however, Braytenbach turns up "in Paname out of the blue and . . . he there one day approached a lady (on a public thoroughfare) insisting that he was her husband returned from nowhere in Niemansland, claiming that he's been looking for her and persistently addressing her as 'Mooityd'" (1984, 254–55). So complex are the labyrinths through which the reader seeks understanding that identifying Braytenbach, husband of Mooityd, with Lamourt probably happens first at a subconscious level. Braytenbach, apparently, was so distressed by her failure to recognize him, "recalling incident upon incident, creating pell-mell a rickety structure of supposedly shared memories and impossible imaginings, that the strange lady was ultimately moved to play along" (1984, 255). (Much of the text reads like commentary on itself.) On his death, she writes off to the authorities in Niemansland in order to fill the gaps in her own supposed past, and receives confirmation of records on "a certain Brethenbach, who, so he claimed, had been united in the state of matrimony to one Mayted" (1984, 255).

The names shift and slide, both undermining the certainty of knowledge and creating, cumulatively, an amalgam in which these names belong, in many different circumstances, to companions either in distress or in the world of art and letters, or in that of politics. The contexts, too, are varied. Quite apart from the likelihood that Breytenbach is encoding character or narrative in ways that only a few readers might understand, the cumulative effect within *Mouroir* is that of a merging of Lamourt and Don Espejuelo in particular with Breytenbach himself. Don Espejuelo appears in one episode as a dead uncle in the back of the car, endangering their passage, despite the presence of a warder, because of his tendency to cough dust and speak in riddles. But D.E., like Juan T. Bird, has papers that he needs to deal with. Like LL, he is responsible, too, for some of the quotations that head the different episodes. The papers that he has inherited and leaves, notably, to his executors, present a proposal for a grave in Rotterdam to the Unknown Poet. Such a grave would celebrate Homer and Pushkin, Villon and Brecht, as well as Lamourt Lasarus and, indeed, Don Espejuelo. These names belong, then, both to the husband of the same wife and to writers within the text, even, it would seem, of the text.

In a remarkable section called "Book, a Mirror," the writer Angelo, in company with his disturbed friend, Gregor Samsa, who is director of a prison, is taken to an underground traveling library. Not only does Angelo find one of Breytenbach's titles by D. Espejuelo, but he also reads about the Pope and the space travel already encountered in *Mouroir*, and then finds himself reading the story of which he is now a part. Like Aureliano Babilonia at the end of *One Hundred Years of Solitude*, he reads ahead, ostensibly to discover what happens next, in fact to discover his own dissolution: "the visitor truly loses all sense and knowledge of his own suchness (*quiditas*), decomposes, becomes absorbed in—" *Mouroir* (180). The *quiditas* that decomposes is the story, which fails to continue. It is also the writer, who is only a character and must read ahead in search of a conclusion. And it is the character who has no writer to provide a denouement.

Despite the fact, then, that Breytenbach provides none of the usual overt signals that he himself is faithfully recording his own experience, and despite the fragmented, apparently disconnected nature of the various episodes, he does provide, through the text as a whole, a relationship among several names and thematic images, an identification of several names with one husband and one writer, and indeed a booking of documents into one text that reflects that writer. The text effectively creates him but can tell him no more than he himself can understand.

In Search of the Autobiographer

If an autobiographer's central concern is to make sense of his life for others to understand, Breytenbach's apparent disappearance from this text is problematic, to say the least. One can say that he is writing in code or that he has incorporated himself in several different characters for the attentive reader to hunt down. It is, of course, important that several characters coalesce into the possibilities of one character, that he emerges from this fragmentation as a South African writer who is in prison, that he has a wife and home and friends outside Nomansland, and that he has brought his wife on occasion back to South Africa. He is also concerned about his parents' suffering; the recurring image of a helpless old man destroyed by tears is particularly distressing. To say so much, however, is to identify specific elements whose affective power derives not from such facts as can be stated but, rather, from their fragmentation. One can take the work apart to show that it is in so many details about Breytenbach himself, but these details work, in a straight reading, at a subliminal level. The reader grasps them momentarily only to lose them in confusion. One sees a recognizable pattern only insofar as it enables recognition of the disruption of the pattern and order. Repeatedly, one glimpses the autobiographer only to lose him again, losing the thread in the labyrinth. The disappearance of the autobiographical narrator/protagonist is central to the emotional impact of this work.

What Breytenbach reveals of himself, in other words, is his own absence from any familiar context that could make sense to others. The mirror reflects alternately absence and death. On a ship of death, Lamourt Lasarus, identified here with another recurring character, Fagotin Fremdkörper, discovers that he must be dead. He is not welcome at a formal table where his two brothers sit like scarred cadavers, because "he is absent already" (1984, 46). He searches the ship because "he wants to situate himself again; he, Fagotin Fremdkörper, needed a clarification of his own condition, a focal point, an I, a departure" (1984, 45). All he finds, however, is the duplication "not much further than a scream away" of his own ship of death (1984, 46). Trapped in his own death, as in the game of chess, the narrator duplicates his own helplessness in the form and content of the work, creating a nightmare world in which he himself does not exist, from which he cannot escape, and over which he has no control, apparently even in words.

As a writer, Breytenbach is faced with a twofold problem. First, in order to be accurate, a mirror image is necessarily impermanent. Consciousness, in a continuous state of Heraclitean flux, does not stand still to be reflected in any way that makes lasting sense. Therefore, second, the words that create any image are either untrue to the next reality, or they are permanently true, in which case they dissolve or erode the reality that they began by reflecting. This twofold concern with the reflection and with the disappearance of what is reflected constitutes a recurring theme through many episodes.

Because the original reality is uncertain, fleeting, and above all, incomprehensible, narrators and protagonists alike are constantly looking for traces and clues both of facts and of their meaning. Lamourt Lasarus in "The Other Ship" knows that he will understand if he can see what flag he is sailing under. The possibility of past human habitation in "Wiederholen" is unverifiable: "All dust now. Passed and extinct. Or had it always been thus? Nothing, no indication or track could ever prove the hypothesis or its refutation" (1984, 29). The extremes of permanent desert and one-time life are reconcilable, however: "aren't we all, and everything around us, finally the wind-blurred drawings of the structure of decay?" (1984, 29).

Decay and dissolution may be all that is to be understood or may be all that these myopic characters can understand from what they see. Tracks, traces, and excreta indicate life, the wherewithal of interpretation. But they are bewildering and, whether the investigation involves roads in the making, as in "No, Baba," or tunnels through a mountainside, as in "Hanging on to Life," the movement is that of maggots in rotting intestines, the mirror reflecting the process of decay and, accordingly, the hopelessness of finding life or of finding a way out.

This helplessness, elaborated in many a search or attempt at escape, is a central feature of an episode like "Forefinger," "a veritable book of darkness," in which through dense and varied images, a hand hovers trembling, fumbling, shivering, fluttering over the chess board: "But it was too late: the queen had already been removed and now he was mated. . . . There was no way out" (1984, 161). This chess game takes place in prison, but all threads of memory and association, all fragments of narrative through the process of the game, are about an impotence and frustration that are then articulated in the necessary loss at chess.

This is not, however, the helplessness of an ineffectual or spineless character. One effect, indeed, of fragmenting the author/protagonist into many characters is the proliferation of attempts at escape and efforts to understand. But the situation is always, it would seem, under someone else's control. For the most part, as in the defeat at chess, the antagonist is anonymous. Sometimes warders are named, never as characters in their own right or as sources of power, but essentially as role-bearers. In one specific and repeated situation, however, two characters emerge who seem to be friends but are not to be trusted and prove to be dangerous.

Tuchverderber and Galgenvogel, in their twinned combination of the comic and the sinister, suggest Rosencrantz and Guildenstern not simply at center stage, as Stoppard places them, but actually wielding effective power. They request a simple story of adultery and betrayal which they themselves are already in the process of enacting. They produce the "blade a steely-white flash-tongue of all clarity and knowingness and simplicity" by freezing the narrator's comprehension and so ending the story that they had requested (1984, 126). That conclusion, which the writer Angelo has had to read ahead to discover, is here manipulated by the very pair that had also initiated the action. In truth, there is no way out. The crucial feature, however, of power in the hands of such a pair is precisely the absence of Hamlet. When the friendship and the betrayal are thus enacted for narration by the central character whom they destroy, Hamlet is revealed as murdered prematurely, deprived of revenge, which is, in any case, no more than a reassertion of power after defeat. Like Angelo, this narrator anticipates his own conclusion, explicitly naming prolepsis as prolapsus.

This absent hero, the central character with whom the reader could identify, whose narrative one could follow with interest and comprehension, is "a man whom I didn't know," whose identity could not be established then or since, whose death by his own hand or otherwise took place at a time when he no longer knew who he was, "and in a weird place I may tell you." In place, as it were, of his presence, this missing character has left an uncompleted document addressed "To Galgenvogel and Tuchverderber; make no bones about it," that proposes a tomb to the Unknown Poet. The anonymous editor/narrator of this episode wonders whether these are "two gentlemen — or ladies? a couple perhaps? a publishing firm? tailors? —" (1984, 189), but has never succeeded in identifying them, either.

Within the fiction that moves within the fiction, this pair remains, then, as minor characters, unimportant in their own right but traitors to personal loyalty, tools of a hostile power, as when they come at Claudius's bidding. What they achieve here is not a new importance but an association that defines the black hole into which the central character has disappeared.[19] As if to underline this role and purpose, Brother Galgenvogel turns up in a story called "And Then" as "a sort of mechanic or technician of religion" (1984, 150) to help Nefesj, yet another central character, interpret the god that he has created. Like the autobiographer, Nefesj is creating his world by means of fiction, finding it necessary "to create that which you don't understand" (1984, 149). Brother Galgenvogel, charlatan and traitor, devalues, undermines, and eventually appropriates this god, leaving Nefesj in a vacuum. It is possible, Nefesj discovers, that he, who must have been conceptualized by his god if his god was indeed godlike, has, with his god, ceased to exist. Like Angelo the writer, Nefesj also stands in for the autobiographer who is both discovering and creating his own nonexistence.

The Failure of Narrative

Just as the autobiographer creates a self as narrator/protagonist, so it is also customary to create a narrative out of what are otherwise merely events in his life. By selection and omission, by sequence and emphasis, narrative gives meaning to events. For autobiography, of course, it gives, furthermore, the author's own understanding of the meaning of his own life. Even where the autobiography covers only a small part of a life or a particular crisis, its object is understanding and its medium is narrative.[20] Clearly Breytenbach is flouting these norms. His forty-eight fragments do not create a story line. Despite the interweaving of increasingly familiar names, these episodes do not build on or support each other as narrative. For one thing, the familiar names do not retain familiar roles or relationships. For another, the setting is constantly shifting, from beach to desert to ruined city or labyrinthine complex, to shipboard, prison, airplane, or mysterious countries called Paname or C.

Time shifts, too. It is long, long ago "when we were young," or "when it was still the modern epoch." Or time is strangely vague: "it must have been after the war." Or it functions as if part of an ongoing narrative: "in those days." Frequently time is present: "when it is dark . . ." Or it is measured as part of the present-tense problems of narration, as in: "At last, I've found the solution." And it can be future, as in "Departure," a reconstruction of Breytenbach's mission to South Africa which plunges him into the labyrinth and discovers his own body, bloated and bleached, teeming with uncountable ants. Such play with time evolves its own narrative idiom, creating as explicit fiction that which cannot be true because time future in a world of logical sequence has not yet happened. Giovanni XXXV, the "intransparent" Pope of a future time in which "nothing is now invisible or our own" (1984, 68), is also covered by ants, almost before he is dead. As with "The Self-Death," in which the second section turns out at the very end to precede the first, time has broken loose from conventional sequences that create conventional causes and effects. Of time, as of character and place, this work provides only fragments. Nomansland, like Hades, is a land of shadows; comprehension of it is tentative and confused. More important, if this is autobiographical narrative, this world is unverifiable.

The corollary of Breytenbach's rejection of all the usual constituents of autobiography is the creation of a mind, a mode of perception, and a voice that create consistent meaning out of facts that are in themselves bizarre and meaningless. In this slip between the substantial and the elusive, Breytenbach achieves quite dramatically that self-presence with which Hemingway and Meigs also override the controls of language. *Mouroir* presents a small world in all its variety and complexity, continuously amalgamating the possible with the actual or the momentary truth with many of its branching alternatives. This world keeps shifting and is incapable of substantiation. No aspect of it is verifiable. It is, furthermore, a world in which the narrator himself can trust nothing that he knows and, as he makes clear in *The True Confessions*, no person, either. Writing in the dark, then, and without any of the checks and balances upon which an autobiographer can normally rely, the narrative voice that emerges despite the absence of a central narrator, telling of places that refuse to provide a clear context, in times that spin and change, can only claim authenticity to itself and be convincing if that authenticity is, in itself, sound and reliable. Breytenbach uses three distinct but interconnected narrative techniques to establish authority for the telling and significance for what is told.

Narrator as Narrative

First, a recurring and troubled theme is that of the story that is difficult if not impossible to tell. It is delayed, postponed to allow attention to immediate detail. It is begun and fades out because it is inexplicable, or painful, or both. The labyrinth implies both a central secret and danger as well as no evident way out. The chess game involves strategy and danger. Endless clues provide evidence only of loss and death. Frequently the attempted narrative responds to some request and its failure then becomes a failure in communication. Repeated and subtle implication of a listener who is anxious to understand creates a tension within the text that is twofold: on the one hand, the listener is an intimate with access to the narrator, and on the other the failure of each attempt to satisfy or to conclude disturbs that relationship because each attempt aims at explanation or shared understanding. And while this tension can be created by means of fiction, it serves effectively to reflect efforts in reality, as distinct from in fiction, to explain private experience. Where the novel creates a whole, Breytenbach is at the very least mimicking the disjointedness of experience. His chosen techniques take his narrative close to the problematic beginning from which external reality or private experience are to be described before any order has been imposed on them.

From time to time the narrator is too troubled to continue or must weep in the dark or in secret. On other occasions, the listener is part of the story, walking hand in hand, ordering breakfast, but the narrator is isolated with the untellable, confronting fears that are the more alarming for not being told despite the presence of one who is eager to hear. By means of this implied audience or companion, with whom the reader strains to listen, Breytenbach's cryptic, encoded, and essentially private language acquires public sense. Not a little of its emotional power derives precisely from this narrative device which indicates that the text is private, urgent, and impossible to produce. Undoubtedly fictive as such devices are, their effect, once again, is to recreate the difficulties of telling one's private story, of making one's private life comprehensible to someone else.

Then, also recurring through the text, one finds the public voice, the direct narrative in which South Africa and prison provide entirely explicit context and meaning. Even here, however, where the story is unambiguous, Breytenbach crams every rift with ore, developing emotional meaning through imagery and metaphor. "The Double Dying of an Ordinary Criminal" is dense and complex in its treatment of institutionalized death and its effects on all who are involved in it. It treats also of hope and of despair, both in the specific ("his mother arrives with her grey hair and her black back" [1984, 59]) and in the detail that extends into metaphor: "When she prays, her hands, the knuckles and the joints, are so tightly clasped that it must be a tiny god indeed who would find asylum in such hand-space, a god like an idea worn away over the years, rubbed small, like a seed" (1984, 59). From this suffering mother and her praying hands grows "the forbidden place where fruit will be hung on the trees of knowledge of good and evil." When she prays beside the still empty coffin, "There is no more room between the hands. From her body something like bleeding bubbles up, the reminiscence of a foetus, and breaks in her throat like the dark cooing of a dove" (1984, 60). Sharp focus on one mother and one son is thus extended to embrace all such suffering. Indeed, by virtue of such images that stretch into metaphor, Breytenbach involves the reader not only in someone else's reality but also in the reader's own possibility. Such language becomes a shared meaning, creates a common experience so that, as with the private code, readers participate in what is not originally theirs to know or to understand. Reading as Breytenbach writes, deep inside oneself, where such meanings as these are clear, one is trusting not the fact but the metaphor with which this mind and voice make sense of fact.

Similarly, "The Break," which clearly develops two fantasies of escape, the second a correction of the first, extends the specific and the local into the metaphoric and the abstract. Prisoner 3926/75 recognizes a friend unexpectedly among the PODs, or "prisoners of death," and realizes that "the selection of executees is arbitrary. South African roulette" (1984, 113). The character of his own desperate break grows out of his internal response to this shock. The prison becomes a human abattoir. The charred carcasses, scorched flesh, stacked bones, the cacophony of terror in raw crescendo or fading rattle, and the pervasive mess of blood connect this apparently straight narrative with the more abstract nightmares of other episodes — ashes in the eyes, severed horse heads in the lap soaking pants with blood, the reek of rotten eggs, foamy mucus at eyes and lips, clusters of meat flies, the salty sweat of phlegm and grime and tears.

Prisoner 3926/75 identifies with the hare escaping from the hunters, "the long ears down in the neck like blinkers which have slipped down" (1984, 117). In his final haven, however, among vague, friendly people, he is offered "a few peaches" (one is taken back to the fruit of the tree of knowledge) but finds only "[t]he stone of a fruit without any flesh" (1984, 119). The stone, of course, is a seed, like the hope held earlier in praying hands, but it becomes here the hard center of irreducible experience.

Such uses of imagery and metaphor, affecting one's reading of the least ambiguous episodes, direct our response away from matters like verifiable character or fact to an emotional plane on which the specifics, whether familiar or odd, serve essentially as purveyors of meaning and not as facts important in themselves. By cross-referencing, as it were, the language that is direct with that which is secret and suggestive, Breytenbach provides a continuity of narration that transcends the variety of separate narrators in their separate situations. The bizarre situations developed in the isolated imagination work in league with others that one understands are part of the world of fact, relying on the same language to establish their necessary combination into a whole, a communicable and consistent meaning. Similarly, precise, small details that create a sense of immediacy, and therefore of reality, serve as hooks for comprehension of the indefinable, or what Breytenbach has called "the grey outcrops of your indistinct condition" (1984, 182). The result is an impressionistic turning of fact into feeling, a creation from the surreal, so specifically attached to factual detail, of an emotional reality. Like the Ancient Mariner, this narrating voice is so urgent and compelling that one cannot choose but hear. Overriding dislocation, fragmentation, and upheaval of the norms of autobiographical narrative, these modes of narration, like the overlapping names and the relentless sense of helplessness and death, provide the sense, the meaning, that narrative imposes on facts. The apparent lack of order that replicates immediate experience directs the reader to listen to the teller rather than the tale.

In the long run, no one except Breytenbach can say for certain whether or not this work is autobiographical, and his title page suggests that it is not. The crucial difference, however, between autobiography and novel is not the public pronouncement of an intention, which can be tilted either way by sleight of hand and must simply be taken at face value, but the nature of the reference within the text to the author, the quality of the reflection/creation that forms the idiom of the work. Breytenbach uses techniques that are reminiscent at times of Kafka or of Marquez, but his world is also clearly related to Auschwitz as recreated by Primo Levi or Elie Wiesel.

When Marquez creates a bizarre situation dependent on no commonly shared logic, he invites readers to hear a private language — to suspend disbelief and accept his elaborate and coded histories as fiction. Because Kafka's works lack enchantment, one is more likely to assume that the bizarre, in his case, describes psychological distress or desperate prophecy. What Breytenbach achieves may be described, rather simplistically, as an amalgamation of such fictive techniques and effects but with a grounding in external reality that anchors the bizarre or surreal and ensures that it is not simply fiction, however effective, but a reasonable response to a bizarre reality. It is, furthermore, distinguished from aberration or insanity, about which the informed analyst could say much the same thing, because of its conscious, articulate, mirror-purpose.

In *Mouroir*, the situations and episodes that seem most disconnected from the logical forms of any familiar world are painful because they are crafted beyond the level of idiosyncratic response to a situation; they represent or reflect a condition that most of us otherwise cannot know, in terms that we can learn, through the process of the text, to feel and believe. Breytenbach is dealing with experience in ways that are common in experimental fiction but is also drawing on a power that springs from an authentic claim to empirical truth. Given that such a claim is a *sine qua non* of more conventional autobiography, autobiography theorists may need to take it less for granted, to reconsider the nature of the ballast it provides to autobiography. One could spend time on distinctions raised by the observer observing the self, what one might call the distortions between the artist, the face in the mirror, and the resulting self-portrait with the earnest regard. My concern with *Mouroir* is not such distinctions, which Breytenbach has kindly provided, maybe precisely to deter naive readings, but rather the significance to the text of the glimpses that he does allow of himself, of his prison, and of his very personal distress. "The least we can do for him," as he writes of the Unknown Poet, "is to give him the face he struggled for" (1984, 191).

But if one does so — if one, so to speak, recognizes him — then *Mouroir* ceases to be a novel and makes claims on its readers' responses — not that we suspend disbelief but that we look, like the artist, with concentration at a world we might rather not see.

HEMINGWAY, MEIGS, AND BREYTENBACH: "BOOKING" THE LIFE

Literary strategies for Juan T. Bird's project of "booking" a life prove to be numerous and as subtle as the serpent of old. They pretend and deceive, play games of hide-and-seek, create illusions of reality and then open trapdoors or shift trajectory, as if determined to undermine credibility and to prove that sleight of hand was all that was intended. They focus, precisely, on the role of art in rendering life even while suggesting that art, too, is ephemeral or, at best, untrustworthy. Cézanne's apples do not tumble, but they always look as if they might. The writer's preeminence, or sexuality, or very life does not cease to be in question; the crises that these texts engage are now forever crises, regardless of changes in the lives from which they sprang. This "booking" is of crisis. In each case, it replays crisis. And its methods for doing so resonate throughout contemporary autobiography.

These three variations on autobiographical writing take on objective reality but their repeated foregrounding of the processes of fiction complicate reference to any world of fact. Repeatedly, and in different modes, these writers use but are not seduced into the literal (which involves, after all, in varying degrees, their concern with their own non-existence, erasure, or death). Their devices for reflecting themselves and their realities, furthermore, suggest the value of many modes of mirror talk to the modern and postmodern enterprise of autobiography. All three writers examined here depend on mirror images not even to reveal their "selves," as in self-portrait, but to posit the existence of an original self as reflected from various angles, responsive, that is, to literal truth, and therefore likely to be real. No Cartesian self emerges, and yet ephemera do become solid, the unlikely does become familiar, and narrative positions do become persuasively associated with a conjunction among author, narrator, and protagonist. To focus, for example, only on the distinctions between uses of the "I" in Hemingway and in Meigs is to recognize a determined presence among all the slippages of literary devices. Similarly, Breytenbach's absence, creating tension and anxiety throughout the text, is forceful in its ability to convey a presence that has been disappeared. Carrying forward the reading experience of detecting living characters behind the literary artifacts, I propose to look now at some of the strategies that can be found in drama and in film for creating the autobiographer through mirror talk.

3

Speculation in the Auditorium
Film and Drama as Genres of Autobiography

Literary autobiography is a shape-shifter, a chameleon, blending and distorting genres in response to the pressures of life circumstances. It raises questions about the role of life in the rendering of art. Certainly the three writers considered in the last chapter cannot be described as writing from the margins; privileged by race, education, social standing, and comparative wealth, their distortion or resistance to master narratives arises not from their being otherwise silenced but from their need to fit the glove, the skin (Mr. Ramsay's boot), to particular circumstances for which no traditional genres exist. Just as such writing implicates the reader in pursuit of the subject through its camouflage and hiding places, so too it implicates the reader in its generic permutations. Disrupting the contractual obligations of genre disrupts both expectations and satisfactions, enforcing an intense level of interpretive participation in the autobiographical act. Furthermore, as writers reflect the conditions of their relatively uncharted experience, they foreground their processes of artistic construction, as if to guide their readers through the quicksands of interpretation. Writer and reader in sequence create the narrator and subject of such autobiography, and this sequence, furthermore, can become an ongoing dance as the reader rereads or as the writer produces more autobiographical work. Given the complexities of these transactions, the subject emerges as the result of generic negotiations, responding to particular difficulties, permeable, unstable, essentially in distress. Hemingway's deployment of Fitzgerald as subject exposes his own most fatal flaws; having wrested control of her own subjectivity, Meigs must also let go;

physically confined, politically silenced, Breytenbach builds a perpetually disintegrating world from his own isolated subjectivity. Finally, one feature of these literary autobiographies (and it may be an inevitable feature of interactive autobiography altogether) is the concern, propelling the text and built into its structure, that some other or others have or will take control of the self, that the subject risks expropriation, a subtle and dangerous form of erasure.

Because film and drama involve so many people in their making, and because their traditional genres deploy both technological interventions and competing subjectivities, the autobiographical subject in these genres lacks even that degree of control that the writer enjoys and may well fear an unfriendly merger. The issues remain the same, in other words, but generic implications alter the rules of the game. The reader becomes a viewer and a listener. (Even the reader cannot ignore the shift in role because the printed page now includes speakers' names and stage directions, which may range from factual information to interpretive suggestions for the director.) The *mise-en-scène* and sound effects contribute to meaning and effect. The screen or the lighted proscenium replaces the printed page. The camera eye, the editor, and the director all intervene between author and subject, whose representation can also depend upon a performer. How, then, can the autobiographer claim a narrative point of view or control over the production in film or theater? Given the possibility that the writer and performer are one, as in the case of Guillermo Verdecchia's *Fronteras Americanas*, how can the autobiographer negotiate the specular control of the audience? Even when participant in the text, writing or directing, or interacting with life partners, how can the autobiographer in film or drama avoid appropriation of the subject by any or all of these others who are, after all, implicated in the production of autobiography?

To explore these issues, I propose to look, first, at some varieties of autobiography in film, considering along the way some of the generic traps and advantages that film provides, and then to concentrate on one play in particular that focuses on subjective representation among layers of appropriation. This play, furthermore, is embedded (or booked) as *The Book of Jessica*, in which the drama of the making of the play replays, so to speak, the life issues that are transformed into theater. My discussion of theater will therefore involve attention to the printed text in which the two main participants negotiate the making of the play. Both the play and its context of struggle and negotiation threaten to blur distinctions between interacting subjects, with the serious risk that one will absorb the other, that encounter may simply become obliterating appropriation. In all these cases, the discussion will focus on the discovery and the claiming of authentic selves (invariably present tense and in a state of conscious transition). These selves, furthermore, resist (with varying degrees of success) the appropriative tendencies of the genres in which they are working, altering in the process the generic tropes that threaten autobiographical integrity, and implicating the audience, so that film and theater become rich resources for mirror talk.

ENCOUNTERS IN CAMERA

Just as autobiographers increasingly identify themselves in relationship, and work self-consciously with their chosen medium, drawing attention to the effects of any given medium upon their self-representation, so neither they nor their viewers can assume a stable or solipsistic "self" or even affect naïveté about the manner of its presentation. Films seem to raise these problems quite explicitly. Involving both technology and significant collaboration of people with each other, film calls deliberate attention to varieties of interaction and to issues of medium. With the camera lens as a literal and necessarily figurative means of access to experience, I need to examine some of the problems that arise in thinking about film as autobiography.

My discussion of this creative interaction, personal and technical, begins with Michael Apted's British film, *35 Up*, and Janis Lundman and Adrienne Mitchell's more recent Canadian project, *Talk 16*, followed by *Talk 19*. These films depend on formal interviews in which the filmmakers invite participants to talk openly about themselves. Apted's *35 Up* suggests a grounding in lived experience with avowedly historical and sociological purposes; Apted works from the Jesuit hypothesis that the child at seven reveals the "man" [*sic*], and its concomitant — in this case, that he can reveal the face of England in the year 2000. Lundman and Mitchell, following the lives of five young women for the year after their sixteenth birthdays, seem more concerned with the personal issues that evolve over a limited period of time. Their revelations, however, are also of sociological import, as research grounded in human experience is likely to be, so that they can comment on the gender biases and double standards, for example, that still operate for these young women in areas such as sexual experimentation. Originating in specific contexts, fulfilling many of the possibilities of historical documentary, these films invite discussion of editorial control, of the interaction of subject with interviewer, and of the effects of replaying past experience for present consideration. Each subject's opportunities for and limitations in scripting a past and a future feed into the narrative tensions between the lived moment and its celluloid "proof," or the fiction that it seems to become.

In an interesting development from these techniques of formal interview and documentary, American filmmakers Jim Lane and Tom Joslin have experimented with more self-consciously interactive autobiography on film. With deliberate foregrounding of the camera and of the relationships that help them to define their personal experience, they control the camera eye, the strategies of interview, and (with one significant exception) the editing. As Peter Friedman describes Tom Joslin at work, these approaches foreground the contingency of lived experience; they do not suggest opportunities for scripting a future so much as they result from ways of seeing: "seeing life from 'above' while simultaneously participating in it." As a "performer," Friedman writes,

> Tom [Joslin] was certainly aware of audience, but he was more concerned with that place (something like the "upper room" of Christianity, he said, although it plays a role in Buddhist thought also) from which we can watch everything, including ourselves, as detached observers. It is a place to retreat to when in danger, since nothing can touch us there, and it is the place from which we can find the ability to watch our unfolding experience as though it were a film — in sympathy with the characters but never in total identification, even with ourselves. Life to . . . Tom was a series of stories, unfolding dramas and adventures. Even the worst experience could and should be viewed/experienced that way. And it was the source of vision. I think what Tom cared about most was vision. That is, ordinary daily life, made vivid, significant and even entertaining (an important but dangerous word) from this other level of awareness.[1]

"Entertaining" is clearly a problematic word to describe *Blackstar*, about a gay relationship, or *Silverlake Life*, in which that same gay couple is living with/dying of AIDS, but these films demonstrate both the capacity of this genre to move close to subjective expression of experience in film and the ways in which the medium may affect original perception of lived experience. Lane (with *Long Time No See* [1981], and *East Meets West* [1986])[2] and Joslin (with *Blackstar* [1976] and *Silverlake Life* [1993]) demonstrate, in other words, the potential for living life "like a story."[3]

And finally, extending these fictive elements of pre-scribing or overseeing, I would like to consider a Canadian film, Cynthia Scott's *The*

Company of Strangers (1990), which places eight women in a fictive frame and surprises them into revelations that are profoundly auto-biographical. Where the formal interview tends to fictionalize "subjects" into a controlling narrative, the "make believe" of this film, in which the women play themselves but in a fictional situation that they share, serves to release the subjective in unexpected ways, most specifically as they encounter one another in dialogue. The fictive frame provides the vision, the over-seeing, because it provides context and purpose for the filming. This fictive frame, imposed from outside, prevents them from seeing their lives as film, as Joslin does; they do not look at their situation as from an upper room but respond to the pressures of the moment, with a few notable and scripted exceptions, "in character." As seven of them are also elderly women, they do not in conversation tend to prescribe an arc of experience for themselves, as the younger subjects of interview do. They rely on the past less to indicate a future than to position the present as a time of poignant loss. Their dialogues are quintessentially autobiographical as they remember and re-present themselves to each other, coming to terms simultaneously with the person that each situation discovers and with the imminence of death, overdetermined in this case both by their age and by the fictive crisis in which they find themselves.

Different as they are, what all of these films have in common is an assumption that film offers both a convincing idiom for grounding representation in some prior reality and an opportunity for intimate expression of subjective experience. One essential interaction that this discussion will need to take for granted is that between the image, with its apparently indexical relation to the natural world, and the use of language with its ranges of signification. The combination of these two provides rich opportunities for simultaneous objectivity and subjective "swallow-flights of song."

Surely no art form is better equipped to dramatize the intersubjective qualities of experience than film. For a start, it involves encounters among several people in its simplest making. Technically, it involves the crude objectivity of the camera eye with the editorial skills that cut and paste to create narrative images. Documentaries, writes Bill Nichols, "do not differ from fictions in their constructedness as texts, but in the representations they make" (111). Not unlike written text, film implicates the viewer here and now in the auditorium in interpretation of the then and there of the filmmaking. Like conventional autobiography, furthermore, documentary film interacts with other genres in its medium. "[A]s a concept or practice," to quote Nichols again, documentary "occupies no fixed territory. It mobilizes no finite inventory of techniques, addresses no set number of issues, and adopts no completely known taxonomy of forms, styles, or modes. [It] . . . must itself be constructed in much the same manner as the world we know and share" (12). Like autobiography, too, documentary resists the easy pleasures of the imaginary and derives its prestige from the referential illusion it produces. As Moholy-Nagy expressed it in the early days of cinema: "Everyone will be compelled to see that which is optically true, is explicable in its own terms, is objective, before he can arrive at any possible subjective position" (quoted in Sontag 1973, 203).

Partly at issue is the coexistence of image and language. Robert Scholes points out that cinema resolves Lessing's dichotomy between the mimetic possibilities of verbal narration and of pictorial representation. Although he sees language as crucial to the interpretation of image, Roland Barthes has described the image as the "perfect analogon" of reality (1977, 17). Central to the viewer's reception of the photograph, as he puts it, is knowledge of the *"having-been-there"* of the person or thing itself (44), the "zero level" of objective reality. Film is peculiarly able to present this quiddity, this presence, because, as semiologists of cinema tend to agree, cinema is a language that differs from verbal language in seeming to have no code. ("Seeming," of course, needs to be stressed.) Cinema mimics the natural and real, effacing its hidden structures by reference to the visually empirical world out there. Barthes's pupil Christian Metz describes photographic images as natural rather than arbitrary signs. André Bazin stresses the existential bond between this sign and its object. In a curious conflation of this indexical relationship with the transformative powers of his medium, he describes the photographic image as comparable to a death mask, a Veronica, the Shroud of Turin, an imprint; it takes its impression by a manipulation of light. Following Barthes and Metz, Bazin's aesthetics of realism assert the primacy of object over image and of the natural world over the world of signs (Wollen, 125–26).

The implications of this aesthetics of film are clear for autobiography, which also depends quite crucially on the "having-been-there" of its subject. Further problems arise, however, because power of reference is a feature of all film, so that further distinctions are necessary between fiction and autobiography. With film as with the written word, one question crucial to autobiography is the subject's means of self-representation. In her 1980 discussion of film as autobiography, Elizabeth Bruss begins with the apparent disjunction of subjectivities involved in film: "The unity of subjectivity and subject matter—the implied identity of author, narrator, and protagonist on which classical autobiography depends — seems to be shattered by film; the autobiographical self decomposes, schisms, into almost mutually exclusive elements of the person filmed (entirely visible; recorded and projected) and the person filming (entirely hidden; behind the camera eye)" (297). Her identification of the classic autobiographer depends, of course, on Philippe Lejeune's pellucid and minimal definition. Her term "mutually exclusive elements" echoes the familiar deconstructionist reading of autobiographers writing themselves out of (and therefore into) existence — an element of crisis that cannot be underestimated for the postmodern autobiographer.

The interaction of at least two people involved in filmmaking clarifies perception of these fundamental problems. Assuming that just one autobiographer at a time is requiring attention, this medium in particular seems to challenge and block that would-be autobiographer. As Catherine Portugues has put it: "It is perhaps undeniable that in view of the divergent specificities of the two forms, no exact equivalent of autobiography is possible on film" (340). Bruss and Portugues identify the impulses and themes common to autobiography and to autobiographical film, but they come adrift on the apparent disjunction of subjectivity and subject matter which they understand as central to definitions of autobiography.

Once again, I suggest that traditional reading of this genre is problematically exclusive and obstructs interpretation. Writing on reflexivity in cinema, Jay Ruby suggests that personal art films rather than documentary should be the medium for autobiography. They derive from the documentary tradition but their subject matter tends to be exotic to the genre because it downplays the "natural" and "true." (He cites as examples Jerome Hill's *Portrait* and Miriam Weinstein's *Living with Peter*.) Nichols seems to pick up on this point when he discusses the problems of combining documentary with overt declarations of subjectivity. One fundamental expectation with the documentary, as he points out, is that sounds and images bear an indexical relation to the historical world. Subjectivity seems to jeopardize such grounding; expecting an indexical relation, the viewer devalues the subjective and reads it as fictional. Nichols raises the failure of the American Academy of Motion Pictures Arts and Sciences to nominate *The Thin Blue Line* or *Roger and Me* for Academy Awards, each film being reckoned "too subjective" or "too personal" to fit their generic categories. If significant elements of the subjective blur the genre boundaries of the documentary, the autobiographically creative fiction fares no better. Insisting on "one and only one authorizing source who is responsible for what is said and done," disturbed by apparent alternatives in film between the "all-perceived" and the "all-perceiving" (309), Bruss admires the subtlety with which the actor, Mastroianni, plays Guido, representing the subject, Fellini, but she concludes that "the gap between the person filming and the person filmed remains" (315).

Here, again, with film as autobiography, recognition of what this genre can do seems to have been limited by what it has done. What Fellini, Bergman, Truffaut, Godard, and Allen achieve in film is autobiographical fiction that plays wittily and self-consciously with its medium and with the halo effect these "characters" enjoy as public figures whom viewers recognize. They may work from profound autobiographical impulses but they do not ground their work in what Louis Lumière called catching life "sur le vif" (Barnouw, 6). For all their reflexive devices, their narratives are contained: they do not break out of the proscenium into the real world. They limit the excess that might remind viewers of life beyond what they can see, of film's status as merely synecdochic representation of a larger and more complex "reality." They provide subtle forms of closure that depend on reader response for distinctions of genre. For example, when a character in verbal fiction translates into an actor on film, readers-become-viewers experience a sense of closure to imaginative possibilities (Laurence Olivier, for example, forever "fixes" that most elusive of verbal fictions, Brontë's Heathcliff). Autobiographical performance by the original subject also provides closure but in a referential grounding that creates confidence. Nichols distinguishes the talented actor capable of representing a wide range of characters from social actors who "perform" themselves, who create "virtual performances" and need to provide character continuity and coherence (122). In each example in the discussion that follows, both interview subjects and the autobiographers who take more independent control of their text are performing themselves; in each case, furthermore, the medium of film is friendly to their varying opportunities for subjective expression.

FILMED INTERVIEW AS INTERACTION

When Michael Apted selected thirteen seven-year-olds in 1964, he articulated sociological concerns that grounded these children in their own beyond-the-film reality (a children's home, the Yorkshire dales, private preparatory school) and in the wider concern of British viewers to explore, on an individual basis, the face of England in the year 2000. The authority of his hypothesis (that he could indeed show this, that the child at seven would reveal "the man") pervades his assumptions about class and gender, opportunities and limitations, and what constitutes failure or success, in ways that his subjects only gradually learn to challenge as he returns every seven years for a follow-up interview. The latest film as of this writing, *35 Up*, contains scenes from the earlier films and provides its own editorial confirmation of Apted's original assumptions. These are more clearly about the individual children than about the face of Britain, and they are challenged by the people these children have become. Sociology, in other words, becomes a form of (auto)biography in which the subject speaks back.

Apted's assumptions are confirmed, for example, by Paul (whom he follows from the deprivation of a children's home to the fulfillment of family life in Australia), but they are refuted when he cannot persuade the working-class women Jackie, Lynn, and Sue that they resent others for their privileges and opportunities; as one of them puts it, and as they all agree, they don't think about these things at all until he comes around with his regular interviews. They have limited choices and, at the end of the day, they are going to do what they can. Other subjects resent Apted's assumptions about women's roles or cut off the interviews because they resent his perceived bias against their upper-class status; they find comparisons invidious and object to being typecast. It is one thing, they say, to show small children describing the conveyer belt that would take them through a sequence of expensive schools to Oxbridge and then into the professions, and quite another to leave out the sweat and toil that ensured that they maintained those privileges.

But one wonders, too, about Symon, who begins in the same children's home as Paul, who grows up without a father, feels responsible for his fragile mother, and wants to be a film star or an electrical engineer. He begins work in the freezer room of Walls's sausage factory fully expecting to move on to more challenging possibilities but, when he refuses to interview after *28 Up*, he has been freeze-framed as content to remain in the same job and to give his five children what he never had — a father. Has he withdrawn from the camera and the interviewer because they intrude on a private life over which he now enjoys some control? Or has Apted's attitude to his limited opportunities belittled a man who has not enjoyed control of the sociological storying of his life? Another man, the East Ender Tony, tries to control his own story. He wants to be a jockey, and he rides with Lester Piggott. He wants to be in films and works as an extra with Steven Spielberg. He enjoys being a London cabby and tries a stint with his own pub. He says there is nothing he has set out to do that he has not done on his own terms, but when Apted insists he is a failure, that he has not pulled anything off successfully, Tony is closed down on the line that we all live on dreams.

The invisible interviewer, in other words, with his pattern of brief questions, controls to a large degree the possibility of what can be said. As editor, he juxtaposes filmed scenes that reveal inconsistency and contradictions in his subjects' lives. Just as the would-be film star is shown working at Walls's, so the woman who does not want children is shown enjoying playtime with her infant. At the end of *35 Up*, Apted returns to the opening shots of the children playing, and he claims to see the characters that have unfolded over the years in these children for whom, at this conclusion, he reinscribes the future. Fascinating as these interviews are, they are limited by the authority of such inscription; indeed, what proves most engaging in the end is the occasional escape of a subjective element from this objectifying control. Apart from explicit resistance (repeatedly, every seven years, Nick refuses to answer questions about girls), subjects also respond spontaneously to the pain of their lived experience; a business may fail, parents do sicken and die, ill health does threaten equilibrium, a brother's profound deafness may reduce a man to tears. The contingent erupts into the pattern and the subject struggles with emotion. But the most obviously disruptive element, and accordingly one of the most poignant, is Neil, who confounds Apted's hypothesis; the seven-year-old is a beautiful, happy, and articulate child who wants to be an astronaut or a coach driver. For Neil, however, the teens bring "personality disorders" that take him from homelessness at twenty-eight to a desperate harbor in the Shetlands at thirty-five. Apted asks if all his original hopeful vision is lost to him, and Neil says it does seem to be. "Do you think you have failed?" Apted asks. Neil cannot judge; his life is not over. But he brings the whole biographical experiment up against the contingency of lived experience and the difficulty, as he puts it, of accepting the reality of the particular and personal situation. Neil's inability to "fit" the interviewer's story engages Apted, and drew a warm response from viewers of *28 Up*. Of necessity rather than desire, he disrupts hypotheses, resists editorial control, and delivers within the interview format powerful expression of subjective presence.

Lundman and Mitchell's questions for the sixteen-year-olds of *Talk 16* seem more flexible than Apted's, more prepared to follow the particular and personal situations in which the subjects find themselves.

Their pursuit of the Apted model, however, in the 1993 follow-up, *Talk 19*, clarifies their concerns with gender and power. Erin, who pulls out a drawer of childhood treasures in the first film and talks about her rubber Santa and her pacifier, becomes one of the "wild girls" at Bishop's University and talks about wielding "pussy power"; she will get anything she wants, and her husband will do what she wants or he will not be her husband. Beautiful at nineteen, she is absolutely certain that she will have cosmetic surgery later in life if her beauty fades. One might assume that her anxieties are the price she pays for beauty, but she is echoed by Lina, who distorts her face in front of the mirror, pushing her nose and pulling her eyelids to show what has to happen to her face before her life can really begin. The future belongs to the beautiful and she is "stuck in nerd hell" until she can be transformed. Rhonda, too, knows that men like certain kinds of bodies, doubts that she is attractive, and stays home a lot, unable to push her desire to act, fearing defeat. Helen, both beautiful and gifted, speaks with anger in her first year as a pre-med student about feeling like a toy to men, feeling objectified, and wanting romance, which she equates with respect; she wants a man to enjoy talking to her on the phone, to like her voice and to listen to what she says, to treat her like a person, not like lips or hair or body.

These young women look back on their earlier film to discuss both their subsequent maturity and their freedom from real worry in an earlier, happier time. Like Apted's subjects, they tend not to like what they see of their earlier selves. Like Apted as interviewer, Lundman and Mitchell assume a progression, asking "Who are you now?" or "Where are you now?" Like *35 Up*, *Talk 16* and *Talk 19* demonstrate the contradictions and inconsistencies within personal and particular situations; Astra's boyfriend, for instance, who would never hit a woman, is convicted of assault on a former girlfriend. And, just as Apted assumes that class barriers must cause resentment or that success consists of describing and then clearly achieving remarkable purposes, so Lundman and Mitchell assume that adolescent women face a disempowerment specifically related to gender. They may well be responding to what they hear; Astra matures into the recognition that she needs to preserve her own integrity in a relationship, whereas her new boyfriend has never felt his personal integrity threatened or subsumed. But the limitations of the interview technique for autobiographical expression originate in the emphatic control of the interviewer/editor which determines what can be said or heard, seen or filmed. That the subjects of *Talk 16* and *Talk 19* do not subvert their interviewers' program, do not resist like the subjects of *35 Up*, who create small explosions of subjective expression by means of that resistance, may be due to their age, to that engagement so common in adolescence with exploration of themselves and their lives, and to their relationships with their interviewers. The three-year as opposed to seven-year gap between filmings also emphasizes the therapeutic value of self-review; Lina condemns her earlier self as a complete idiot and the more reflective Helen thinks of her earlier self as judgmental. Film clips demonstrate aspects of that earlier person whom the later person assesses with a combination of detachment and embarrassment, objectivity and a subjective sense of responsibility. Although such reflection and analysis are significant features of an auto-biographical experience, the very notion of chronological progression or linear narrative has become counterintuitive for the reflective auto-biographer who actually controls the content and technology of the autobiographical narrative.

INTERSUBJECTIVITIES

If Apted and Lundman and Mitchell work as ethnographers inviting but controlling subjective response, Jim Lane and Tom Joslin foreground the camera, situating themselves both behind and in front of it. Both use long shots of the man behind the camera filming himself reflected in a mirror, the source and the object of the camera eye. Both also resist linear narrative, using unexplained off-camera voices, including apparently random, decontextualized people and activities, defying all but the loosest possibilities of narrative. Lane's *Long Time No See* and Joslin's *Blackstar* both suggest a focus for exploration but arrive at no clear conclusions; each film, indeed, identifies a problem in the process of living for which the autobiographer finds no solution. Emotional intensity, therefore, derives from the apparently pre-filmic living moment, the shifting angles of vision that select and frame that moment, and from the foregrounded effort to articulate in the combination of sound and vision a spatial rather than a linear concept of subjective experience.[4] Both filmmakers use the camera, furthermore, to dramatize specifically the wider range of the original material and the random nature of the specular; for both of them, furniture, rooms, scenery, and people burst out of the frame as constant reminders of that original experience to which the filmed experience refers.

As soon as the filmmaker foregrounds himself and his activity of filmmaking, the grounds shift for film as autobiography. Whereas the interviewer provides controlling vision and reception in the Apted and the Lundman and Mitchell films, developing interaction as in a game that can progress toward recognizable goals, Lane and Joslin create visual spaces and develop film idiom in ways that enable them to defy the expectations of Bruss or Portugues and to offer film as subjective representation. They, too, conduct interviews but in terms of plural subjectivities; they explore their own relationships, passing the camera back and forth as they respond in filmmaking as in life to the needs of other protagonists. They work, furthermore, within an idiom that is filmic rather than sociological or narrative. They use, for example, cartoons, old photographs, and family videos both as components of their autobiographical library and to contextualize their present work with camera and sound. Both Lane and Joslin, furthermore, with handheld cameras, or with the camera attached to the interior of a moving car and swinging through seemingly random shots, suggest a contingency in the very filming that dissociates even the autobiographer himself from any controlling vision.

Stressing, then, the contingency of lived experience in the most minute particulars that the camera picks up, both autobiographers also develop through these films that which is not visible to the naked eye. For Lane, the issue is relationships. He is wrestling with guilt, a guilt that goes back to an occasion when, as a boy, he broke his father's glasses. On the phone in voice-over, and into the camera, he talks about his father and about Debbie and Ellen, whose apparent coldness he finds hurtful. His attempts at resolution include journeying between the city that has alienated and frightened him and his childhood haunt of New Found Lake, the scene of his original sin. In this film he also talks to Ed, whom he has known since they were both small; in *East Meets West*, Ed takes his turn to talk about struggle, disappointment, and anxiety in his life. For Joslin, the issue is his homosexuality; *Blackstar* explicitly brings him and his lover, Mark Massi, out of the closet, making visible on film and in dialogue not only that which has been hidden or private but specifically that which is subjectively experienced and determined.

Subjectivity explored in these ways expresses itself in voice and gesture, space, movement, and response. It also resists narrative explanation and closure. Working "in the middest" of their experience, Lane and Joslin do not provide originating impetus or concluding satisfactions. Lane opens *Long Time No See* with a long-distance call to Ellen against the background hype of television programming for the new year. For *Talk 16*, such programming opens the narrative frame for the "year-in-the-lives-of" these young women, but Lane provides no such framing and seems to offer this opening device to accentuate his isolation and need rather than to measure time; his use of this convention of time plays with such filmic conventions in order, paradoxically, to suggest "speculation" of interior space. Wrestling with the ways in which film can or cannot meet their needs, Joslin and Massi conclude not in terms of their lived experience but in terms of what their medium can offer, and ask whether they are satisfied with that. Lane's film wraps back on itself, returning to photographs from childhood, his voice wishing he could feel less alienated from family and friends, wishing that the people he has been searching for could acknowledge him, wishing he could stop feeling guilty.

Friends accuse both filmmakers of living their lives in movies, of hiding behind movies. Both try to abnegate authority and control, or, as Joslin puts it, to throw everything away, but for both of them the camera seems to function as an extension of the body, as a source of experience rather than design. Subverting autobiographical conventions, they explore subjective expression by means of the technology that has come closest to suggesting objective realities. By virtue of their particular autobiographical needs or of new conventions that are even now in formation, or in order both to use and overcome the objectifying features of film, Lane and Joslin explore, define, and develop their subjective expression in close relationship with their medium and with other people; they cannot be separated from their relationships with camera or friends and therefore work very clearly in an interactive mode. True to the contingent nature of lived experience, furthermore, both autobiographers offer in their films mere nuggets of experience that lack final explanation. It seems most appropriate, then, to this experiential autobiography that Joslin's later film, *Silverlake Life*, should provide an absolute conclusion only in the sense that its narrators carry the camera up to the experiential finish line of death from AIDS.

Silverlake Life, which I discuss more fully when considering the genres of death in Chapter 6, opens with Massi apologizing to Joslin that life is not like the movies; he has tried to close Joslin's eye in death, but it refused to stay closed and popped open again. This ironic but deliberate discovery of the disjunction between lived experience and the conventions of genre is important for *Silverlake Life*. Not a creative art film, and not a depersonalized documentary, *Silverlake Life* posits pre-textual life as the controller of the text and uses the film medium quite explicitly in order to record the surprises of contingency. Because of the nature of their relationship, furthermore, and of the crisis they are dealing with, Joslin and Massi take their viewers beyond what is public domain in any person's life, beyond, indeed, what many may be able to watch. As Sobchack puts it: "[D]eath . . . in documentary films . . . is experienced as confounding representation, as exceeding visibility" (287). Joslin and Massi's constant, collaborative interaction, however, controls audience response; viewers participate by invitation, their "view" moving back and forth between the two men with the camera eye. Like Joslin on the phone to his mother, their film asks "Do you understand?" Like *Blackstar*, this movie involves family and friends. They analyze the reactions they receive, defining themselves in response and resistance. Joslin's mother learns to understand; she moves from a benignly liberal position that marginalizes their relationship to a fuller recognition through her son's death of Massi's love for him. Joslin's father, on the other hand, refuses to pay attention. He spits off camera and talks about "normal" people; he does not "understand." The first film had grown out of their inner secretiveness about being gay; they reject both the lies and the transformations of personality that they feel lies engender. In *Silverlake Life*, too, the issue for Joslin and Massi is unabashed expression of the relationship that is central to their lives and, beyond that, of the further intimacy, the personal and secret territory of dying and death. Teresa de Lauretis has written that "[c]inematic representation can . . . be understood . . . as a kind of mapping of social vision into subjectivity. . . . In this manner cinema powerfully participates in the production of forms of subjectivity that are individually shaped yet unequivocally social" (8). Joslin and Massi seem to reverse de Lauretis's suggested order. Their combination of the very private and even the inexpressible with the deliberately public forum of television film, defined and controlled by the decorum of their interaction with each other, with their inescapable experience, with their medium, and therefore with their audience, transforms their subjectivity into a social vision and their most personal experience into a manifesto.

Conscious anticipation of death creates that intensity of living that characterizes contemporary autobiographical expression. If film facilitates development away from linear narrative and singular and authoritative selfhood, and if resolutions or conclusions have ceased to describe experience effectively, then autobiographers need to identify those relationships or confrontations (as with imminent death) that surprise them into intense expression manifesting the quality of particular moments. Joslin's relationship with Massi enables him to explore both homosexuality and imminent death not insignificantly because

Massi shares the same concerns most intimately. Their experience precedes the vision with which they can represent it. The last film I would like to consider, however, suggests some ways in which the controlling editorial vision that is more common in film and that causes problems for Bruss and Portuges, for example, can be used to release autobiographical expression with an intensity equivalent to that achieved by Joslin and Massi.

In a remarkable "revision" of the documentary based on interview, *The Company of Strangers* (retitled *Strangers in Good Company* for U.S. release) originates loosely in script that was then revised as the eight participants performed themselves within the scripted situation. Mary Meigs is one of the participants, and she has described the activity of discovering, through trial scenarios, where participants were true to their own characters and where false. Like actors, in other words, they adjusted the nature of their participation, revising the film in keeping with their own sense of what was "true to life." The original scenario, which had suggested "a story," was, accordingly, "taken by the wayward movements of the cast away from and beyond the 'story' to an unanticipated place where it wanted to live" (Meigs 1991, 29).

The original vision of elderly women marooned at a remote lake in the Quebec countryside invites these women to think about survival, to recognize the possibility of death, and to connect with each other through their memories and their desires. When this elderly cast hobbles out of the mist (which "symbolizes the absence of explanation" [Meigs 1991, 10]), anything is possible: in their scripted survival, they share the bits of food they have with them, then eat frogs and fish and berries and build fires for smoke signals. They sleep on packed grass, play cards, talk, watch birds, and move into harmony with the landscape. Catherine fails to fix the bus but rubs her arthritic feet with castor oil and hikes out to get help. When she returns in a small seaplane, the "story" merely confirms the emotion of the film that the women themselves have created; it confirms the livingness of this time that is foreshortened by the expectation of death, and the richness of the women's capacity for survival. What the filmmaking has done is effect a transformation that blends "the dancer with the dance"; as Meigs puts it, each woman was transformed by her experience of the film and by her relationships with all the other women. The film works from many individual expressions of experience with which the women surprise each other, or confirm each others' experience, or adjust their understanding in relation to each other.

Building on trust, each woman takes opportunities to "discover" herself to another. Could you fall in love again now? Alice asks, and they chuckle over this real possibility, ponder the bitterness of past failures, and anguish over lost youth. Beth, elegant and coiffed, a city person who does not care for country, talks about the light going out of her life with the death of her only son; bouncing off Michelle in conversation, she also unbuttons her collar and whips off her wig. Although Meigs has described their resistance to certain scenes as "out" of character (Constance would not throw away her pills, Mary would not try to fish by hurling rocks), such scenes function almost as cameo possibilities within the long meditation on age and its confrontation with death. Cissy looks at the stars and says her husband is up there looking down on her, but Alice does not believe in heaven or hell: when we are buried, then it's all over. Death is around us everywhere, says Constance, looking at Mary's painting of a dead bird. Her inability to hear the white-throated sparrow, repeatedly audible on the sound track, and her longing to hear it again, most poignantly define the losses of age that precede death. Cissy, who has recovered from a debilitating stroke, struggles with emotion as she talks about her fear of losing everything, of being destitute, and nobody wanting her. What are you going to do? she asks herself. What are you going to do? But there is nothing she can do. This anguish, shared by Alice and hushed in her embrace, is not in essence scriptable but arises from the opportunity that the script provides. Constance is afraid of dying, says Mary, and so is she. Ironically, the only young woman in the film, the driver of the bus that breaks down marooning the entire cast, sprains her foot badly at the outset and cannot exercise her youth and strength in the tasks of survival. Ironically, too, Gloria Demers, with whom the vision originates, and who had considered scripting the death of Constance, herself dies before the film is completed. "Gloria is invisibly there," says Meigs, "and her scenario still remains as the invisible scaffolding of the film" (1991, 12).

Death and disability are no respecter of persons. The vision that invited elderly women to contemplate dying, however, could not afford for any of them to die — in fact or in fiction. At issue was not that inevitability but rather their confrontation with it and with mutual fears. Like all other forms of art, autobiography is transformative, providing not so much records of the past as tropes for discovery, for processes of recognition and letting go, for the construction of emotional meanings that depend not on literal accuracy but on the free play of psychic possibility. Even as film suggests, then, the referential grounding of its fiction, it also demonstrates fictive possibilities that serve profoundly subjective purposes.

Clearly grounded in a world that precedes and extends beyond any given fictive construction, filmed autobiography offers one convincing mode of referentiality. Unlike traditional autobiography, film constructs interaction — certainly between the subject and the camera but also, for various reasons, among subjects. Technical and personal collaboration interfere with and become part of the living moment, altering perception and creating, therefore, new "realities." What engages me is the brinksmanship that film seems to invite, the intensity of interaction that these examples demonstrate: among subjects, between subjects and their medium, between subjects and their most intimate concerns, and ultimately between living and dying. When the women walk off screen, retreating into the mist from which they have emerged, they have been changed from strangers into company because of the intensity of what they have shared. "Goodbye house," Winnie says to the ramshackle shelter that represents St. Augustine's house of memory, Henry James's house of fiction and, in terms of the autobiographies it now contains, a retreat from ordinary time into a rarified space for meditation. Each of these films makes clear that "what happens next" happens outside the scope of the film in the world of contingent realities. What happens in autobiographical film, however, which refuses the story that could explain the past or describe the future, happens as transformative intensification of lived experience in process. Elusive and mercurial, autobiographical presences erupt on screen, as in life, in relation to other presences and to the idioms that film uniquely provides.

THE BOOK OF JESSICA: THEATER AND A HEALING CIRCLE FOR AUTOBIOGRAPHY[5]

Healing — and for me that's theatre, writing — is that you try to find . . . you find what's beautiful, the essence, and that's what you give back.
— *The Book of Jessica*

Theater raises many of the same questions for autobiography as film; the absence of the camera is, of course, significant, as is the presence of live actors and the formal constructions of scenery. For both genres, nonetheless, the audience responds to various levels of "performance," and the actors depend on the necessary involvement of others in their scenario. In both instances, furthermore, the autobiographer works against the risks of appropriation — a live form, perhaps, of upstaging. Unlike film, however, theater has ancient associations with religion and with healing; *The Book of Jessica* interests me as an example of autobiographical drama because it "acts out" both its own agenda and these elements that distinguish theater as a genre, suggesting a perfect match between autobiographical and generic issues even while the autobiographical pushes at generic boundaries.

The Book of Jessica crosses a number of significant boundaries: between life and art, between context and text in autobiographical genres, between ceremonies of religion and of theater, between oral and written narratives, and between two women, one Métis and one white. Absorbed at a very personal level by the ways in which we make sense of ourselves, I have been reading and listening here to a multi-storied "poetics of differences" (Neuman 1992), and I wonder whether it is not what I understand as a Native aesthetic (which certainly inspires and guides this text despite the final editorial control of the white co-author) that challenges all these boundaries, transforming the conflictual binaries of the original situation into a continuous and, I will suggest, a healing circle.

Because this text depends on elements of Canadian history, including colonial appropriation of land and power and the possibility of an imperialist feminist appropriation, in this case of the Métis voice, it is ironic that I, as a white academic with an appropriately British (read imperialist) education, should pronounce on it in any fashion. I am reminded of Lenore Keeshig-Tobias's scathing point that university professors have stepped into the shoes of the missionaries and the Indian agents. So I enter the dialogue, attentively, from this limited and specific position because the complexities of the text raise important questions: first, for women's writing and its efforts to identify women's experience. In the book that precedes the play, the Métis woman, Maria Campbell, mothers the actor, Linda Griffiths, into discovering her own subjective identity even as the two of them battle through clichés of mother-daughter relationships — of love and anger, of need and withdrawal. She does this, furthermore, as the two of them explore other stereotypes of female sexuality and weakness with which the play, *Jessica*, challenges its audience. Then this work raises questions about cross-cultural reading and its problems for interpretation; Griffiths's misreadings of Campbell and of their interaction in preparation for the play clarify her own needs and assumptions and Campbell's justifiable wariness about appropriation. And the play with its preparatory context adds significant material to discussion of transitions between life and art, oral and written expression, and the dynamics of autobiographical interaction between people and between the texts and contexts of their separate beginnings.

Jessica is a play. It grew out of a collaborative process that began in the Theatre Passe Muraille in the fall of 1976. This mobile "guerrilla theatre" without walls made docudrama its trademark during the early seventies, focusing on local communities and alternative histories (see Wasserman, 16). Brian Arnott stresses the "conscientious effort" of the Passe Muraille "to give theatrical validity to sounds, rhythms and myths that were distinctively Canadian" (107). Maria Campbell, who had already published *Halfbreed* in 1973, approached Paul Thompson of Theatre Passe Muraille because she had been convinced, by Clarke Rogers's production of *Almighty Voice* and then by Thompson's production of *The West Show*, that this kind of theater could empower the Métis community. "My weird world appeared normal to him," she says in *The Book of Jessica*, "so I talked and talked" (16).

At this point, in 1976, they agreed to an exchange; Campbell would learn from taking part in "the process," and in return she would "give [her] bag of goodness knows what." (This "exchange" between Maria Campbell of the Métis community and the Theatre Passe Muraille provides a cross-cultural subtext to my discussion of "appropriative autobiography"; notably, in this instance, Paul Thompson is careless of Campbell's interests in the contract he draws up [55].[6] It also foregrounds the parallels in this play and in the book between theater and religious ceremony.) "The play," Campbell explains, "would be about being a woman and the struggle of trying to understand what that meant." Campbell's life story, or "goodness knows what," was drawn from *Halfbreed*, but the idea took on a life of its own when Thompson called in Linda Griffiths, the white actor/improvisor, to "study" Campbell and to play the role of a young Métis woman from her experience of Campbell's life. Their extended sharing of life and of art reenacts the control and the resistance so evident in documentary interviews, but it also evolves into a complex interaction that creates autobiography for each woman as subject. Between them, painfully the two women evolved a third; Jessica's name comes from a Waylon Jennings song they heard on the car radio as they traveled through the interior of Saskatchewan together.

Jessica

In narrative outline, the play *Jessica* covers the ground that Maria Campbell had already laid out in *Halfbreed*. Like Breytenbach's, her autobiography takes two forms, the sequential narrative serving as an informational matrix for the play. The play, however, is less concerned with such information — the loss of her mother, her rape as a young girl by a Mountie (which had been edited out of *Halfbreed*), her time as a heroin addict and prostitute, her focusing of her life on leadership in Métis issues. Even while using these ingredients, the play, described in the book title as "a theatrical transformation," combines the ceremonies of theater and religion to reassemble all the elements of Jessica until she can take control of her own life and identify and name herself. A relatively recent development in the genres of theater, theatrical transformation ensures, for *Jessica*, that this autobiographical assertion of presence is neither monologic nor conclusive.

Helene Keyssar distinguishes transformational drama from the enclosed world of traditional theater to which Bakhtin was hostile, suggesting that the continuous recreation of meaning or heteroglossia of communication is "the basic condition and phenomenon of theatre" (1991, 89). Whereas most Western dramas pivot on a recognition scene and arrive at a stable "truth," Keyssar suggests that drama can present and urge transformation of persons and of images people have of each other; transformational drama, in other words, affects the ways in which people see and respond to each other, pushing them toward mutual transformations in the processes of their interaction: "[I]t is becoming *other*, not finding oneself, that is the crux of the drama; the performance of transformation of persons, not the revelation of core identity, focuses the drama" (1991, 93). Often, Keyssar suggests, "and perhaps inevitably, transformation strategies go hand in hand with the dialogic imagination" (1991, 93), which develops the structural elements of drama that avoid enclosure in a singular point of view.

Closely connected with Joseph Chaikin's Open Theatre of the 1960s and with the drama of Megan Terry, whom Keyssar calls the mother of American feminist drama (1985, 53), transformational drama shifts characters among roles, times, and situations in such a way as to destabilize any sense of unity and to fragment the materials from which understanding is constructed. Such drama, according to June Schlueter, is "designed to play with the epistemological question of how the self takes form, without identifying a self that is morally accountable, psychologically consistent, or socially defined" (61). Schlueter also suggests that the audience tends not to relinquish its recognition of one role for another as rapidly or as thoroughly as the actor, with the result that sequential shifts in performance become layered in the mind of the viewer. "Transformational drama," she writes, "demands that the audience not only be aware of the multiplicity of selves generated by a multiplicity of roles but that it become an active participant in the process of definition and redefinition that never ends" (65). Furthermore, and central to the creation of *Jessica*, transformational drama tends to be collaborative drama. *Jessica* crowds the stage of autobiography; it relies upon the circle — of bodies, of spirits, of times and situations, and of ritual — re-presenting in metaphor the processes through which Maria Campbell finds her voice and develops the strength to resist appropriation.

The play's preceding text of *The Book of Jessica* returns repeatedly to a blending of theatrical and Native ceremonies, the acrimony and the anxiety involved in this collaboration, and the tightropes between need and appropriation that both women tread. Theatrical transformation, however, involves walking through the walls of traditional expectations — with changes to backdrop, to dramatic role, to the permeable barriers between make-believe and reality. The play responds, in other words, to the crises of its engendering. In the play, the Elder, Vitaline, creates the spiritual circle that contains spirits manifest as animals, and animals that transform into human characters in Jessica's life. Vitaline herself transforms on occasion into Coyote, the trickster. Disturbingly, as Jennifer Andrews points out, "Jessica is transformed into Wolverine, a haunting metamorphosis, because it is Wolverine who enacts the role of Jessica's childhood violator" (303). Yet spirits, animals, and humans also remain condensed as single characters, simply manifesting different qualities at different times and taking appropriately different positions on the stage.

Liam Lacey's review of the Passe Muraille premiere of *Jessica* draws attention to the three-tiered set, on which spirits take the highest level. Transformed by bursts of music, darkness, and lights, the characters wear masks that indicate who they are at any given moment but that also foreground the visual nature of performance and the shifting layers of identity that any one character may "wear." When Larry Lewis directed *Jessica* at the Northern Light Theatre in Edmonton, however, the dream visions took place in a roughly circular ceremonial space downstage. "This space took the shape of an earthpit surrounded by a ramp usually inhabited by the animal spirits and giving a more immediate sense of their hovering presence at all times" (Bessai, 239). In part, this play, necessarily dependent on spatial architecture and on actors' bodies and voices, is about those elements of a life that are not visible or audible, that are experienced rather than seen or heard. Transformation in both ceremonies, religious and theatrical, is about the shapes of experience, about shape-shifting, and about choosing the shapes that explain and enable one's life. Jessica's evolution into a strong survivor involves her acknowledging and accepting all of these shapes in her own life, the dangerous qualities of Wolverine as well as the warmth of Bear and the white and Western elements of the Unicorn.

Not only are traditional theatrical genres undergoing transformation as they blend with the religious ceremonies of Campbell's Métis community, but the ceremony itself is mixed, as is found to be most suitable in the recreation of a woman of mixed blood. Jessica fluctuates between white and Native communities, not at home with herself in either until she absorbs the elements of both. So the Unicorn is a new and troubling addition to the animal group; they are not sure whether she has come from as far back in time as the grandmothers or whether she belongs on a candy-cane rainbow at the Hudson's Bay Department Store. But she is the element that has been missing and that adds, both in religious ceremony and in theatrical representation of Jessica's life, the quality that needs to be recognized. Representation of life is also mixed, including life experience, dream, and trance, as well as analysis of Jessica's development and chances of survival. And the language, too, blends incantation with dialogue and both with the irruptions of the unexpected into the "scripted" situations of ceremony.

The "Book" of Jessica

It is ironic that Maria Campbell should have sought out the "process" of improvisational theater for her own story and that the product now available is a printed book, but this mingling of the oral with the written is one more element of *métissage* in this performance of autobiography. In part, language and translation perform the negotiation of boundaries that Campbell shares with so many other articulate leaders. Original languages, of course, connect with ancient cultures. Campbell includes Cree words in her texts for children to ensure that the Métis adults of the future acknowledge and take pride in their past. But the issue is never simple. One positive feature of English (in this case) as a dominant language is that, as Beth Cuthand puts it, "we could communicate with each other. I fully believe that we can use English words to Indian advantage and that as Indian writers it's our responsibility to do so" (53).

And the concern is not simply one of language. Added to the alien language is the problem of authoritative voice, an issue that becomes particularly complex in the extended discussion that is *The Book of Jessica*. Jeannette Armstrong describes the Native struggle for authority. "I started writing by accident," she says. "[A]ctually, I started answering back. I would start by saying 'That's not true! Indian people don't see things that way; we see it this way'" (1985, 55). But at university she learned "that there is a certain elite way of writing that is acceptable, and if you write within that framework you can be heard by the public at large." Nowhere has this distinction between how Native people see things and how they are heard in the colonizer's idiom been more dramatically made than in Chief Justice Allan McEachern's decision on March 8, 1991, on the Gitksan and Wet'suwet'en land claims. Campbell may urge Griffiths to reconnect with her own history, saying magic and power and history are inextricably related, but McEachern dismisses Gitksan history because it is all oral. The *Vancouver Sun* of March 9, 1991, quotes him as saying: "I am unable to accept . . . oral histories as reliable bases for detailed history, but they could confirm findings based on other admissible evidence" (B2). If oral histories are neither reliable bases for Western understanding of "detailed history" nor admissible evidence in a non-Native court of law, one may well wonder just how the First Nations can translate from one form of authority to another and how one Métis woman can reinterpret and renegotiate the painful relations of Native and white.[7]

Cross-Cultural Negotiation

Explaining oral values, Beth Cuthand could almost be explaining the power of theater and ceremony in forming cultural identity as well as the present transition from spoken word to text:

> We come from an oral tradition where our values, our world views, and our system of beliefs are transmitted orally. In this process, there is something more than information being transmitted: there's energy, there's strength being transmitted from the storyteller to the listener and that is what's important in teaching young people about their identity. What we're doing as Indian writers is taking that tradition and putting it physically onto paper and getting a broader distribution of those stories, because it's really important for us, in terms of our continuing existence, that we transmit our identity and strength from one generation to another. (54)

This consciousness of loaded cultural value, this foregrounding of addressivity, and this responsibility of the individual storyteller to the community and to the future, all seem to derive from Native traditions and to include Campbell's "bag of goodness knows what," the ingredients that she herself brings to the play. Certainly *The Book of Jessica* challenges the hierarchies of discourse that block exchange or reciprocity. First-person dialogue, as Janet Silman noted in her *Globe and Mail* review of November 4, 1989, "was absolutely right for this book, because the spoken word has an immediacy and dynamism which, even when recorded on paper, still can connect as third-person prose seldom does" (C22). Immediacy perhaps equates with Walter Ong's sense of urgency at the heart of oral cultures, and dynamism with the effect of language on listener/s both within and without the text.

Bakhtin suggests that the addressee assumed in each speech genre defines the genre (95). In *The Book of Jessica*, these genre boundaries become permeable or mobile as Griffiths and Campbell address each other, address live audiences (very specifically the Native Elders and white critics) through performance, and address us as readers and even theorists, through the printed text. Printed text, however, poses the danger of a potentially final idiom that privileges one audience over another. "[I]t does work better when we talk," Campbell tells Griffiths. "Because when it's written, it just sounds too . . . it sounds written" (67). Print represents one conclusion of negotiated meaning and connects in this text with the written contract by which Campbell feels so hideously betrayed, and, quite explicitly, with land claims and with the continuous displacement of the Métis by white settlers. (In *Halfbreed*, Campbell positions her own life in the context of Métis beginnings, the history of white settlements, the Riel Rebellion, the Battle of Batoche, and the migrant destitution of the Road Allowance people.) The theater contract is like so many other white/Native treaties; the white authority draws it up and asks for friendly approval, but the different peoples mean different things. Such agreements are too rarely double-voiced and tend, rather, to be appropriative. Griffiths wonders whether *Jessica* is a treaty. "To me, it was a sacred thing," she says. "A treaty is a sacred thing," Campbell agrees, "but a treaty has to be two equals, two people sitting down and respecting what the other one has to offer, and two people doing it together, negotiating. Otherwise, it's not a treaty" (82). She is describing, of course, the ideal and the sacred, not the historical. The printed forms threaten, however, to fossilize both relationships and texts that are still volatile and in process of negotiation. Such forms represent ownership to the white, and ownership does not seem to translate into Native languages or to belong in the cultures that those languages express.

Interestingly, these two women focus their talk about contract and treaty on their feelings of joint ownership of *Jessica*, the land that they have both worked so painfully and hard. (This spatial metaphor for the text is possible only for print, not for oral narrative. Campbell's independent use of print, like her work toward the contextualizing of an improvised play in print, demonstrates once again that her traditions are hybrid and that "Métis" means "mixed.") Interestingly, too, Batoche, and the centenary celebrations of the Battle of Batoche figure largely in Campbell's ability to rethink and renegotiate their relative positions. As with her work with women in prison, Campbell seems to gain strength from positions perceivable as weakness: "[V]ulnerability is strength," she says in her interview with Doris Hillis. "That goes back to my grandmother, because she said that's what the circle is: give everything away and it will all come back" (50). She struggles in these dialogues not for ownership versus appropriation but for a listener who really hears her and whose response is appropriate to what she has heard.

For all Griffiths's serious attention and her remarkable intuitions (and Campbell acknowledges these — as in the dance of liberation, for instance, that Griffiths introduces after the rape scene), Griffiths has a lot to learn. As with her fear that their project would die unless she completed it, Griffiths expresses her passion for the treasures of Native spirituality in an extended explanation and appeal: "I'm just like all the other white people," she says. "I'm a gold digger. . . . I saw your culture, and it was like a treasure chest opening up. . . . I am a gold digger. I went for that treasure chest with everything in me, my fists were full of your gold, my fingers closed in on your jewels. . . . So I'm a gold digger. I was then and I am now. And it hurt so much then, and it hurts so much now, to see magic come alive and then have your wrists slapped because that magic can never be yours" (84–86). In terms of negotiated meaning, of the processes of interactive readings, and of the limited value of the printed word, Maria's answer is particularly challenging:

Nobody ever said the magic wasn't yours, that the power wasn't yours, nobody ever slapped your wrists, that was your interpretation of what you were being told. You just said that you were tired of interpreting all the interpretations of the Cross, all the witches, all the things that theatre and poetry had done to those images. All I was trying to tell you was that if you were tired of it, then why are you trying to do the same thing to us? Then one day the same thing will happen to our stuff, the same thing that happened to European culture. . . . Maybe I get overly uptight when I tell you, "Don't do that," but it's only because, if we exploit it and don't even fully understand it ourselves, then we're giving something away to be abused. (86)

Exploitation here may describe claims and "treaties" that fail to acknowledge the varieties and dynamic continuities of lived experience,
or the ways in which lived experience can spill into its own representation. Campbell seems to be privileging the living that generates life-
story and fearing the story that may prematurely "conscript" the living.

The Book of Jessica dramatizes their "struggle of trying to understand."
The struggle, of course, is not simply that of understanding what "a
woman" means but also of understanding how women across barriers
of "race," culture, privilege, and age interpret "a woman" for themselves and for each other. "Eighteen years separated us," Griffiths says,
"as well as race, class, culture, social work, political work, and, in its
own category, what Maria called 'the street'—almost every boundary I
knew, and lots I didn't know" (21). Griffiths persisted with revisions to
the play despite Campbell's anger and withdrawal, and the final text
carries her name as first author. (Introductory notes to the play text
indicate that the first version of *Jessica* in 1981 was written by Maria
Campbell, Linda Griffiths, and Paul Thompson; the second in February 1986, and the third in the fall of 1986, were written by Linda
Griffiths in collaboration with Maria Campbell.) It was Campbell,
however, who suggested both that they talk through their difficulties
with each other and that the edited transcripts from these talks contextualize the published form of the play. Interestingly, Campbell withdrew from the final editing of the transcripts in order to run for political office—a move that Helen Hoy suggests "resonates with earlier
repudiations, [and] pushes against the reconciliatory drift of the narrative" (26). Griffiths took final responsibility for the editing and for the
narrative thread that ties the transcripts together.

Appropriation in this context probably begins with Clarke Rogers's
production of *Almighty Voice*, which had the Native community, as
Campbell puts it, "in an uproar. It was a play about Native people done
by whites; it also delved into a spiritual world that we felt should be
interpreted by Natives themselves. I went to denounce it, and ended up
defending it" (16). Campbell became complicit through her acceptance of Linda Griffiths for the performance and through her introduction of Griffiths into the Native community and their spiritual practices. Most immediately, she met opposition from Hannah, her friend
and teacher, who was "absolutely against it" (25). She exposed herself
both to Griffiths's possible desecration of these experiences and to the
possible outrage of the Native Elders when the play opened in Saska-
toon in 1982.

Griffiths's appropriation is obvious and has come under fire. Hoy

is categorical: "However well-intentioned, *The Book of Jessica* rede-
ploys the strategies of intellectual colonialism" (26). Hoy also wonders
whether Campbell would have focused this work so narrowly on the
two of them if she were editor (28). Griffiths herself cringes with complex embarrassments: "I was white," she writes, "really white" (15). Yet
she first read, then enacted, and then wrote the life of a Métis woman
who was old enough to be her mother, and did so, furthermore, in
terms of Native spirituality. Without downplaying the questionable
nature of all these decisions, I would like to focus here on the possibility that the text that now exists actually reasserts a Native voice in a
situation that seems to be one of white appropriation. At the simplest
level, for instance, Campbell stops Griffiths in her description of the
sacred ceremonies at the farmhouse. "[Y]ou were invited into that
circle," she says, "to help you understand, not to write a book about
it" (27). Repeatedly, through this brief argument, Campbell corrects
Griffiths's assumptions about her role and challenges her to use experience, not interpretation, as her artistic medium. She bullies and
coaches Griffiths into autobiographical work that is reciprocal, interactive, responsive, a matter for two subjectivities rather than the creation by the white actress of the Métis subject-as-object. I think the
empire speaks back throughout this text in unexpected and insistent
ways that inform the final product beyond anything Griffiths could
have controlled if she had wanted to.

In "Mimesis: The Dramatic Lineage of Auto/Biography," Evelyn
Hinz has argued thoroughly and convincingly, on historical and theoretical grounds, for the close relationship of drama and autobiography
in the Western literary tradition. In this case, Campbell's choice and use
of drama develop out of ancient and ongoing Métis and First Nations
traditions. Clearly, the methods of the Theatre Passe Muraille, which
were of specifically European origin, are relevant to this discussion, not
least because they were reacting to the perceived elitism of traditional
theater. The extended dialogue between Griffiths and Campbell that
constitutes the main body of the book repeatedly demonstrates the
ways in which Campbell controls the production of her life story as
process. Her recognition of drama as a powerful tool for community
work, her guidance of Griffiths through experiences that were foreign
to her and that activated all the white woman's anxieties, and the building of both play and contextualizing text out of oral exchanges — this
sequence describes a distinct aesthetic that depends on oral traditions,
recognizes the spiritual as central to daily life, the individual as centered
in the community, and art as closely related to political value.

Campbell also assumes the need consciously to negotiate thresholds between experience and the representation of experience. Just as she breaks into Griffiths's "description" of the native ceremony and insists she play back her own experience of it, so the rape scene and the creation of Wolverine become powerful as Griffiths reacts to Campbell's experience from within the previously unidentified sources of her own. The rape, for example, in which Griffiths becomes the twelve-year-old Jessica first "down on the ground . . . screaming and biting" and then sobbing, and finally singing herself a lullaby, reduces Campbell to tears. Dialogue between the two women is prefaced in the text as it would be in a play's text by the first name of the speaker. "Afraid to face [Maria]," Linda says, "I don't know if I sang the song you maybe sang, or if you sang anything, but . . ."

> MARIA: You really did sing the song.
> LINDA: My mother sang that song.
> MARIA: My mother too.

"As we held each other," Griffiths concludes, "it was as if I'd unleashed my own memories. Not a story, or even acting, but something else" (46). Such negotiation between experience and its artistic re-presentation is continuous through *The Book of Jessica*. The formal construction of such drama grows out of/spills into the whole process of exploratory dialogue that is both dangerous and explosive but that contains its own tropes for recovery. This repetition and replay, furthermore, deconstructs conventional binaries that privilege one and disadvantage the other. The relationship between the two women in the text refuses the oppositional and works instead toward a mutual recognition.

Finally, the circular drama of text and context, of life and art, and of cross-cultural reading is self-reflexive, so it resists both final appropriation and closure. Barbara Godard has described the Trickster workshops that understand the word (as in the oral context that enables progressive and emergent meaning) as "a process of knowing, provisional and partial, rather than as revealed knowledge itself, and [as aiming] to produce texts in performance that would create truth as interpretation rather than those in the Western mimetic tradition that reveal truth as pre-established knowledge" (184). Godard's Western, mimetic tradition, of course, is the literate tradition that privileges vision over the other senses and allows one to assume that meaning and truth become available instantly and can be firmly established. When Jessica recognizes and names herself at the end of the play, she has accepted the Old Way of the spirit world of her grandmothers and has been granted her "power song," but her reintegration is only the beginning of the healing process that Campbell wants for the Métis people. Her self-naming power is also part of an ongoing process in which such healing may be inter-personal and cross-cultural like the long dialogue between these two women that leads up to it.

Arnold Krupat has described aboriginal autobiography as a post-contact phenomenon largely dependent on the interventive ethnographer (much as the interviewer can control expression in an interviewee, who becomes, accordingly, not a subject but a creation). Narratives by and about Native people have changed in style and structure from academic analysis of the reified "primitive" to unreflective romanticism about the indigene, to the current self-consciousness that acknowledges not only that the ethnographer is inevitably biased but also, as Robin Ridington puts it in his introduction to *The Trail to Heaven*, that the modern ethnographer is involved in mutual, interactive interpretation, that the object of study is also a subject ethnographer. (Involvement and response of the subject, whether this Métis woman or the local farming community in southern Ontario, among others, seem to be central to the work of the Theatre Passe Muraille.)

The Book of Jessica posits Griffiths, as it were, in the role of the white ethnographer and replays variations of white/Native relations. Campbell takes Griffiths home to study the Native community but reverses the situation that Penny van Toorn describes as typical, in which the autobiographer is demoted to "native informant" under the aegis of the "patron discourse"; "the dominant culture," as she puts it, "issues minority writers with their licences to speak (which is also, of course, the site where mechanisms of exclusion and suppression operate)" (103).[8] At the personal level, Griffiths experiences the desires and anxieties that are commonplace in white Canadian interpretation of the Native. She does not encounter what Spivak has called "the Imperialist's self-consolidating Other" (quoted in Fee, 176). She, and not Campbell, is Other. She needs to "brown up," so Campbell applies makeup; this is both enabling ("like wearing an invisible cloak" [45]) and frightening when it turns streaky, refuses to work. She is ashamed and walks, as she had read in *Halfbreed* of the Métis walking when among white people, "with [her] head down around Native people. I felt ashamed," she says. "I felt them watching my skin" (50).[9]

Griffiths tells how Tantoo Cardinal taught her to chant on the banks of the South Saskatchewan River. "She never made me feel stupid, no matter what kind of sounds came out. Still, I had an image of myself on stage in brown greasepaint and borrowed feathers, singing a power song, with the elders going, 'You've got to be kidding'" (52). At the farmhouse ceremony, Griffiths had felt the need to chant: "If I had been able to chant, if I hadn't been afraid of my uncertain voice mixed in with the strange nasal call of the people around me, then it might have been easier. But I felt myself to be still a watcher, as if the comforts of the ceremony were not for me" (29). (Her sense of exclusion and her rendering of Jessica's power song are both important for this discussion.)

Although Griffiths attempts to efface herself, believing her role is that of medium, she is no better able than the ethnographer to be a truly blank receptor. For Campbell, this "blank receptor" is not blank at all but comes culturally endowed with abject guilt, with loss of history, and with the limitations of a rational straitjacket. At this continuously negotiated threshold between life and art, Griffiths's "professional" silence obstructs the transformative process. "Why is it okay to lay my guts all over the table," Campbell asks, "but you can only take some of yours, and by the way, madam, let's make sure they're the pretty ones. I've had a hard time with this the last few years, you being so virginal. Don't ask me to do something that you're not prepared to do, and if you're not prepared to do it, then understand why I'm nervous about working with you" (88). Only as Griffiths learns to stop smiling like the Virgin Mary and acknowledge her own self-hatred, shame, and emptiness can "exchange" reanimate the process. It's a late development in which Campbell says:

> [Y]ou're letting me see you, you're talking to me. You're letting me see you as an equal with things inside. When I say I saw the Virgin Mary, pure and empty, that's all I could see because you didn't give me anything else. . . . I'd come home after talking to you for hours and not feel you at all. . . . Do you have any idea what you did for me when you told me you'd been a booster? I just about fell off my chair. You're freaking out now because someone might read this. Hey, she's real, she's been in conflict, she farts in the toilet too. Talk about not being able to feel me, because I was "dignified," well, you sure had me fooled. (87)

Because this Métis woman, furthermore, is very much alive in the present tense, and very much in the process of working within and for her own culture, conventional Eurocentric responses of nostalgia, romance, or guilt are all appropriative/inappropriate responses to her which Campbell energetically corrects. Griffiths, for example, contrasts "the awkwardly modern people who had eaten lunch" with the (surprisingly) same people during the farmhouse ceremony who "were now what I imagined 'Native' to be" (27). Her imagination, of course, is based in Western literary traditions and assumptions. In dialogue, Linda has been "inspired and touched" by photographs of another ceremony. "Those guys that snuck in and painted pictures and tape-recorded and begged people to tell them things, were recording something that was dying." But Maria challenges her angrily: "[W]ho told you it was dead or dying? Those men who snuck in? Do you want to learn by sneaking around? That attitude of 'dead or dying' is what's killing us" (28). Griffiths's conventional responses create hierarchical binarisms that enable only limited, one-way, and linear movement from white to Native. Campbell rejects such binaries, associating the Church, for example, in *Halfbreed*, with cast-off clothes. Native communities do not provide handouts but redistribute wealth from their store of what is most valuable so that exchange is generous and social and bonding.

Campbell deflects Griffiths's liberal guilt about Native people by sending her back to her own history and culture and to her own sense of oppression. She sends her to books not about the Native but about the Celt and about the goddess traditions. "Passe Muraille was known to be a political theatre," she says. "[H]ow could you be political without knowing your own stories? And they were no different from the stories of Halfbreed or Indian people" (36). Driven back again on herself, Linda acknowledges her firsthand experience of being "semiotically controlled": "How could I speak about my own pain?" she asks. "All my life I'd been told I had it good—white, two parents, a nice home, only two kids in the family, two cars, . . . a decent education, no trouble about food, no beatings, no overt violence. . . . Everything repressed under the dining room table. . . . I grew up desperate for the stories that would fit my nightmares" (75–76). "I know I'm from the underneath," she acknowledges, "because of the way I feel, because of the anger I feel. I feel like I'm shaking my fist at someone on top of me, and I look. . . . I'm from the Canadian middle classes, who the hell am I shaking my fist at? . . . You say that if we understood our history, everything would be stronger. But it doesn't feel like that to me" (97). Historically, or from sense-memory in the Stanislavski tradition, Griffiths needs to learn the traditional Native principle of circularity that Tomson Highway has described as "the way the Cree look at life. A continuous cycle. A self-rejuvenating force. By comparison," he says, "Christian theology is a straight line. Birth, suffering, and then apocalypse" (quoted in Johnston, 255). Guilt, says Daniel David Moses in "Preface: Two Voices," sounds like the opposite thing to healing. " 'It seems that you don't want to heal, you want to keep the wound' " (xvii). (This preface in dialogue form shares several topics with the Griffiths-Campbell dialogue.) Campbell's responsibility for the healing circle includes Griffiths in its protective embrace.

As the ethnographer is transformed into two interactive subjects, so is the autobiographer. Her subject is not unified or autonomous but plural and contested. Hinz has already challenged the received distinction between the European as individual and the Native North American as a member-of-community in her brief analysis of the role of autobiography in self-interpretations: "Perhaps . . . the reason auto/ biographical documents are rare in primitive societies has to do with the fact that ritual performs a self-exorcising role for their members; and perhaps the reason auto/biographical documents are so abundant in the Western tradition has to do with the extent to which they provide a sense of the communal that we lack" (208).[10] In her introduction to *Life Lived Like a Story*, Julie Cruikshank contrasts the assumptions about autobiography in Native and European traditions and shows how these affect narrative technique. Whereas she wanted to know about the impact of change and development on the lives of three Yukon Elders, they understood their lives in terms of kinship and landscape and shaped their narratives to include mythological tales, songs, and long lists of personal and place names. Ong has suggested that the self is only visible in an oral culture through the eyes of others, that human beings depend on the technology of writing and print to split the subject for self-reflection (152). Cruikshank's questions, in other words, and the answers she receives demonstrate very distinct modes of understanding and vividly reflect their re-contextualized cultures of origin.

The years of dialogue that make up *The Book of Jessica* replay uninformed assumptions, renegotiate misunderstandings, play back to each other what each has heard. The ostensible purpose of those earlier, unrecorded conversations during which Griffiths was learning to be Campbell was to enable Griffiths to "sybil" Campbell—a strange verb that suggests the mystery of interpretation and the power of the actress to body forth another's life. Her sybiling powers must have been extraordinary because Campbell recognizes herself again and again with anger and pain. But this interpretive role is not one-sided. As with the circularity of exchange, while Griffiths sybils Campbell, so Campbell works as Griffiths's mother/shaman to induct and protect her in this shared and dangerous enterprise within the Native spiritual traditions. The Métis, she points out, have always been guides and interpreters (as, in another reversal, Griffiths is, too). They have linked the Native and the white in cultural/textual *métissage*, emphasizing a transcultural rethinking of identity, or what Lionnet describes as "relational patterns over autonomous ones, interconnectedness over independence . . . opacity over transparency" (1989, 245).[11]

Just as the ethnographer's reading of the Native translated, historically, into autobiography for white consumption and needs now to be regrounded in the Native experience and in appropriate media for expression of that experience, so, too, written literature affects what originates in an oral tradition. For Native people the danger is at least twofold. First, art is sometimes more privileged and therefore more powerful than ethnography, since it reaches a wider audience, and it may involve more significant damages of appropriation. Second, written literature fixes in permanent form precisely that which needs to be mobile, altering in the process what is said, how it is said, and how it is read and understood. "That's why I hate working with the English language," Campbell says at one point, "and why I have a hard time working with white people, because everything means something else" (17).

Theater was a natural choice for the author of *Halfbreed* precisely because it works as live performance and blurs the boundaries between contingent reality and its narrative interpretation. "Theatre . . . gives the oral tradition a three-dimensional context," Tomson Highway explains, "telling stories by using actors and the visual aspects of the stage" (quoted in Petrone, 173). It provided one more way in which Campbell could extend the story she needed to tell beyond the limitations of the printed word and ensure its return to the community. This particular theatrical drama, furthermore, enacts the drama with which this discussion began—about who may speak and who may listen and what the listener may do with what she hears. Drama can work as process—back into the past and forward into political effect. It contains revolutionary potential. In *The Book of Jessica*, such exchanges involve rage and silence and magnificent instances of hard-won empathy. The dialogue/drama continues and diminishes its own possibility of closure.

For this Métis woman, furthermore, the performance of relationship, the intersubjectivity with a white woman, becomes performatively significant for the autobiographical act. For her, as Jessica and as Maria-and-Linda, the woman-self is not singular but interactive, mediating and mediated. And this mediation, which is performed agonistically by two women with and for each other, sets up a cyclical motion. "This mind goes in circles," says the grandmother figure of Vitaline in the play. "[A]nd don't you forget it" (167). Her circles are those of the grandmothers, of the spirit world, of prayers for protection, of relationships in process, of recognition that all life forms are connected and responsible to each other, of performance that contains but does not confine evolution of character and of life story. Both the play and its dramatic context connect the inner life with its outer appearance in repeated transformations so that these women are both mother and daughter, both hurting and healing, both present and absent, as befits the best of autobiographers — readers, writers, and performers for each other.

It is possible that Campbell withdrew from the final editing of *The Book of Jessica* because she foresaw no possibility of an appropriate representation of her life experience. I wonder, however, whether her "bag of goodness knows what" does not include this crossing of generic boundaries between ethnography, autobiography, and drama, whether she does not overrule the traditional genre boundaries of Western literatures in order to connect her life with its spiritual roots and its dramatic presentation with sacred ceremony. She creates a safe place in which, as she puts it, she can move forward by looking at what she is afraid of and gain strength from recognition. The courage of her enterprise becomes vivid in a brief story she tells of turning to face the devil from whom she has been running by the river in Saskatchewan. The interactive value of her enterprise includes Griffiths and *her* worst fears — extending even to the creation of Wolverine and the danger that two women begin the work and only one may survive. Because Campbell understands the magical ability of language to create reality, she performs the ultimate transformations, through healing, of past times that have been intolerable to them both into a new and integrated order from which Jessica is born.

Writing from a non-Native perspective must, as Jeannette Armstrong insists, have much "to do with listening first of all, listening and understanding and waiting till that understanding has reached a point at which you can say, do you mean this and that person says yes, I mean this" (1990, 51). "People at large," says Louise Profeit-LeBlanc, "can have a glimpse of understanding." But, she adds parenthetically, "(You can never fully understand)" (115). My discussion, therefore, is interrogative and my questions remain questions. Whatever happens in *The Book of Jessica*, however, is important to my own search for the voices and genres of autobiography. Not only do two women struggle to collaborate on an elusive autobiographical project, but they also transform each other into versions of a self that each, at times, acknowledges or rejects. Their shape-changing, in other words, is interactive, fluid, and inconclusive. For their restless and unhappy venture, transformational theater pushes the traditional forms of drama so that generic mutability itself suggests the permeable nature of the boundaries between them.

Dialogues of Diaspora

But if I don't have roots, why have my roots made
me suffer so? — Trinh T. Minh-ha, "The Exiled," in
Surname Viet Given Name Nam

The immigrant must invent the earth beneath his feet.
— Salman Rushdie, *Imaginary Homelands*

I am a turtle, wherever I go I carry "home" on my back.
— Gloria Anzaldúa, *Borderlands*

STRATEGIC SPACES OF DIASPORA

Hearing aboriginal voices, Shirley Neuman points
out, does not mean that they are speaking in their own narrative conventions (1990, 351). As with other voices translated from their cultures of origin, they become original and hybrid. Maria Campbell's
work has been controlled by white publishers, editors, dramaturgists,
and actors, produced not in Cree but in English, and then read and
written about, within the academy and, in the present instance, by a
white and English-speaking academic. Specific qualities of this collaborative project clearly express its aboriginal subject — for example,
its orature and its valuing of art and drama as forms of politics. With
the important qualification that aboriginal politics are necessarily distinct from those of people who have left their places of origin, *The Book
of Jessica*'s treatment of deracination and the difficulty it manifests
with speaking and with being heard enable us to move easily from
aboriginal work to autobiographies of diaspora, which share these
same concerns.[1]

The subject of physical displacement claims what Avtar Brah calls
"diasporic space," because diaspora calls into question not only the
migration from land to land or culture to culture but also the interactions of center and margin, dominance and subordination, all con-
flicted ethnicity (16).[2] Space, then, describes place and boundary and
activities of transition in literal and in metaphorical terms. It names

the site of creative tension as more significant than the timeline of history. For autobiography, it privileges situation, struggle, and presence above exploration of identity, which would depend on narrative (see Eakin 1999). Referring specifically to a diaspora of color, and to the indigene as the dominant white, Brah suggests that diasporic space also belongs to "those who are constructed and represented as 'indigenous.'" Dominant whites may even doubt their possession of an ethnicity, but white ethnicity figures large in the critiques posed by writings of diaspora (209).[3] "Diaspora identities," says Stuart Hall, "are those which are constantly producing and reproducing themselves anew, through transformation and difference" (235). Building a third, or hybrid, space from two or more places of origin, the autobiographer of diaspora discriminates among a plurality of possible positions, all incomplete and in continuous process, in order to recognize who speaks, who is spoken, and just who might be listening.

Listeners, readers, or viewers, therefore, are closely implicated in the interactions that constitute even temporary meaning, and are accordingly required to be conscious of their own positions in relation to the autobiographer. The particular position of each participant constitutes a primary definition of place in autobiographies of diaspora. Many texts invite this self-consciousness, explicitly constructing an ideal or desired reader. On occasion, an original reading is built into the text, as with the joint project of Clark Blaise and Bharati Mukherjee, *Days and Nights in Calcutta*; here, a white Canadian husband and a Bengali Canadian wife visit India together, responding to each other as they respond in distinctive ways to their shared but very different experience. Similarly, gross misreadings by English-speaking Americans and by the Chinese community force Maxine Hong Kingston to identify her ideal readers as people like herself who speak from both cultures, Chinese Americans.[4] Trinh T. Minh-ha includes in her film, *Surname Viet Given Name Nam*, a discussion of the making of the film by Vietnamese women in America, a reflexive process that mingles performance with its own criticism and response. Salman Rushdie points his finger at a white "You," repeating Gandhi's magnificent retort that English civilization would be a good idea (138). Michael Ondaatje, who claims his family as his first readers, counting on him to "get it right," also addresses his Canadian friends, in particular at the party that opens *Running in the Family* with a dizzily drunken flow that blends the Canadian writer with his grandmother in the former Ceylon. When Shirley Geok-lin Lim publishes *Among the White Moon Faces* in the cross-cultural memoir series of the Feminist Press, she is selecting the theorists of such meaning production that form her present community, she herself contributing theoretical and critical work to the reading of Asian American literatures.[5] That Richard Rodriguez works with a wider, more popular culture, his text so frequently accompanied by his photograph, and excerpts of text so frequently included in anthologies, highlights the significant fact that choice of audience is political. Although these writers may all hope to become rich and famous by virtue of being widely read, their primary target describes their own primary positioning as autobiographers. Both likeness and unlikeness between writer and reader contribute to the dialectics of sense-making, corresponding to the processes of cross-cultural, diasporic identities.

Constantly producing and reproducing themselves anew, explorers of diasporic identity are surely the quintessential autobiographers of the late twentieth century — in their numbers and in their resistance to classification marking their effects on traditional Western understanding of the autobiographer as the universal subject. No longer migrants with a homing instinct for assimilation, they position themselves in transition, on borders, and in process, Janus-faced critics and analysts resistant to "pure culture." They move among genres with an imaginative ease that suggests all borders are permeable. Personal information and narrative as well as cultural history are embedded in the ironies of speculation and theory. Theory becomes autobiographical, as do political and cultural commentary, criticism, fiction, poetry, film. While rejecting the notion that they represent their people, these autobiographers define and represent themselves as members of communities whose stories require refashioning to make sense in changing situations. So, for example, Kingston speculates on the experience of No Name Aunt, whose secrets are important for the niece growing up in California, and she speculates, too, on the mysteries that made her father an American: "In 1903 my father was born in San Francisco, where my grandmother had come disguised as a man. Or, Chinese women once magical, she gave birth at a distance, she in China, my grandfather and father in San Francisco. She was good at sending. Or the men of those days had the power to have babies. If my grandparents did no such wonders, my father nevertheless turned up in San Francisco an American citizen" (1977, 237). Negotiating in a few sentences the information of her father's birth in the United States, the illegality of his mother's presence,[6] the stories that have encoded wily Chinese practices for fooling immigration officers, and the various alternatives available for their comprehension, Kingston, as ironic interpreter for both cultures, claims her own position as both American and Chinese.

Despite the date (1903), and her histories of Chinese grandfathers at work on the nineteenth-century railways of North America, Kingston's narrative enacts one distinguishing feature of diasporic autobiography in its creation of strategic spaces for a network of people rather than linear time or a singular story.

Brah favors the concept of space for diaspora. Linear time suggests that one thing succeeds another and enables the imaginative possibility of fulfillment or return to some place of origin. Similarly, Anne Mc-Clintock has criticized the term "post-colonial" for suggesting what she calls "prepositional time" (293), replacing the binaries of Western historicism with new binaries of before and after.[7] And autobiographers seem to support her sense of overlapping synchronicities. Certainly, the concept of space is significant to autobiographers for whom diaspora is a distinguishing experience. Crucial elements of their past inform their present just as their present, involving physical, cultural, and linguistic translations, affects interpretation of their past. All the writers to be considered here are simultaneously colonial and postcolonial; they write in the formal English of their education, which they permeate with their other languages and with the attitudes and vocabularies required by their other cultures.[8] These writers have also been sufficiently privileged by class, education, or generational position for choice to have played a larger part than enforced displacement in their own experience of diaspora. Notably, they are free to travel between their original and their adopted homelands. Their works nonetheless contain that critical analysis of imperial hegemony that transforms the colonial object into the "post"colonial subject[9] — a subject conscious of being formed by the processes of imperialism and simultaneously interested in shifting or blurring distinctions between centers and margins, presenting the processes of *métissage* as present space.

Frequently riding ideological shifts, personal experience also creates geographies of the mind that use space as a more pliable imaginative structure than time. Recalling a childhood moment of identification of herself as a writer, Lim establishes "Malaya [as] the middle of the earth": "Malacca was at the center of that crooked hunchbacked peninsula that filled an entire page, just as Australia or North America each filled a page" (75). Geographical centers are parallel rather than sequential. These writers destabilize boundaries fixed between places that are home, holding presence and absence in continuous and creative tension. For the autobiographer, several worlds coexist in this dialogic relationship dependent only on focus for full recognition. So Michael Ondaatje, working in his Toronto kitchen, plays back on his tape recorder the night sounds of Ceylon, noticing now not just the raucous peacocks but also "all the noises of the night behind them — inaudible then because they were always there like breath. In this silent room (with its own unheard hum of fridge, fluorescent light) there are these frogs loud as river, gruntings, the whistle of other birds brash and sleepy, but in that night so modest behind the peacocks" (136). Chronology can become almost irrelevant when the processes of perception and recognition focus on the present as a space in which worlds of difference are contained — contained but not complete, and fraught with contradictions.

Writing about "Diaspora Culture and the Dialogic Imagination," Kobena Mercer rejects the possibility of expressing "some lost origin or some uncontaminated essence," but looks for "the adoption of a critical 'voice' that promotes consciousness of the collision of cultures and histories that constitute our very conditions of existence" (56). Resisting appropriation by the language in which they have been constructed as other, critiquing their own complicity with colonization, representing affiliations in terms of "race," ethnicity, and the histories of particular peoples, autobiographers are necessarily committed to dialogic discourses. Indeed, by way of exemplary contrast, when Richard Rodriguez turns his Mexican world into a memory of lost childhood and wholeheartedly accepts the "education" that privileges him as an honorary (and therefore glamorous) white man, he resists his places of origin but not his places of arrival. He rejects or does not recognize his opportunity for critique and illumination of both cultures. Certainly he rejects the "[p]rocesses of diasporic identity formation," that Brah describes as "exemplars *par excellence* of the claim that identity is always plural and in process" (197). For Rodriguez, autobiography confirms a migrant identity of assimilation, suggestive of an arrival or homecoming that is not an option in postcolonial diasporas, with the result that he becomes, quite lyrically, monologic. bell hooks, less complacent than Rodriguez about her time at Stanford, writes of black students: "[O]ur sense of self, and by definition our voice, was not unilateral, monologist, or static but rather multidimensional" (12). hooks would likely agree with Anzaldúa about being sure to speak all the languages that one can speak, working against speaking as other to the white supremacist imagination.[10] Whereas Rodriguez defines anxious resolution, they deliberately perpetuate the very collisions of cultures and histories that constitute their present existence. "The postcolonial subject," Lionnet writes, "thus becomes quite adept at braiding all the traditions at its disposal, using the fragments that constitute it in order to participate fully in a dynamic process of transformation" (1995, 5). Lim describes the simultaneous existence in the mind of separated past and future as "the dialogics of identity for the immigrant American writer" (1992a, 28).

The concept of diaspora, Brah suggests, holds discourses of "home" and "dispersion" in creative tension, so that the diasporic subject exists in suspended or permanent transition, resisting stereotype. Campbell's struggle to incorporate both strands of her heritage and experience into the present tense contrasts, for example, with Griffiths's initial assumptions about what "real Indians" are like. Rey Chow, in a chapter titled "Where Have All the Natives Gone?" suggests that "[t]he production of the native is in part the production of our postcolonial modernity" (30), pointing out that natives are no longer staying in their frames — no longer positioned to "center" the colonizer (28). Negotiating complex terrains of historical circumstances and personal positions in which past and present transform each other, the autobiographer repeatedly reinterprets what it means to be Mexican in the United States, to be Indian but not in India, or to experience several stages of dispersion, as with Chow from Hong Kong or Brah from Uganda. Such critical reworking of possible positions and possible meanings ensures the aspects of dialogism so common to diasporic writing.

Because Rodriguez regrets his loss of familial (Spanish-speaking) intimacy in the same elegiac tones as he regrets his loss of the Latin Mass, his adopted English positions him in time, not space, and with loss more pronouncedly than conflict.[11] His explicit use of pastoral makes clear the impossibility of return; the rupture in his life is past-tense and present politics align him with the majority he would once have referred to as *gringo*. In fact, Rodriguez resists being considered, as Hall considers Caribbean identities, "in terms of the dialogic relationship between [the] two axes" of similarity and continuity and difference and rupture (226).[12] For all his sense of loss, Rodriguez's paradoxical move away from the private and communal life of his Mexican culture to the public and solitary life of mainstream America refuses to negotiate cultural identity. Gayatri Spivak warns against simple notions of identity that overlap neatly with language and location (1990, 28), and cross-cultural lives certainly allow for complex balancing of opportunities and choice. In Rodriguez's assimilation into mainstream America, however, he forfeits precisely those subversive responses that his time and place invite. The poignant tensions of his text are individual, even solipsistic, finding safety in monologic certainties rather than risking the unfinishable business of dialogic discourses.[13]

Describing diaspora as opportunity, Rey Chow uses Hong Kong as an example: "Their diaspora is a living emblem of the cryptic Chinese term *wieiji*, which is made up of the characters for 'danger' and 'opportunity,' and which means 'crisis'" (25). Hong Kong, Chow points out, is diasporic not by choice but by history. As an American from Hong Kong, she herself is doubly diasporic, "a kind of diasporic person in diaspora" (23). To affirm such a state of "crisis" is not to refuse assimilation, for example into the academy, but to embrace all the affiliations that contribute to personal identity, and to negotiate their particular meanings in time, place, and the specifics of the personal situation. Negotiation begins precisely here. As with class, gender, and sexuality, the meanings of "race," language, and ethnicity are predetermined in distinct relations; they are always already constructed. Negotiation, accordingly, involves a black woman in England identifying herself as Jamaican, or an Indian in Canada becoming more specifically Bengali on the subcontinent. Indeed, when Clark Blaise, in *Days and Nights in Calcutta*, makes the mistake of assuming that Bimal Chattopadhaya is thoroughly Westernized and must feel alienated in Calcutta, the Bengali resists being seen as less than his "pure culture" counterparts or less fortunate than his colleagues in the West, reminding Blaise that he in India, and Mukherjee in Canada, are also displaced persons (104–5). As Barbara Johnson writes, commenting on Zora Neale Hurston, "the insider becomes an outsider the minute she steps out of the inside" (318). Whereas the American school system seems to have determined one powerful identification for Rodriguez because he is an able student, the dialogics of diaspora engage in continuous resistance to such determination from outside, insisting that the inside, the center of the map, the place within all the times and languages the mind contains, is where autobiographical balancing acts begin.

Most autobiographers in diaspora describe separation, sometimes final, from their original families. However, family, for the postcolonial autobiographer, is not, as for David Copperfield, a matter of beginnings for a narrative that comes to conclusions; it provides, rather, a continuous web of identification. Lim, for example, outlines a childhood of desperate poverty, abuse, and neglect, but places her written self in that community for its richly identifying power. She writes of her grandfather's funeral procession: "The town through whose streets I mourned publicly, dressed in black, sack, and straw, weeping with kinfolk, united under one common portrait, is what my nerves understand as home" (1996, 20). Similarly, even in hunger, the ritual feeding of hungry ancestors "bonded [them] as one Lim family, springing from a common root and tied together in ways that could not be unknotted" (46). Despite her sustained efforts to free herself by education and then by leaving Malaya for the States, Lim is describing family not as a summary but as a *com*position for herself. In a more whimsical rendition of the family relations that "compose" *Running in the Family,* Ondaatje sees himself as "part of a human pyramid. Below me are other bodies that I am standing on and above me are several more, though I am quite near the top . . . chattering away like the crows and cranes. . . . [W]e are approaching the door which being twenty feet high we will be able to pass through only if the pyramid turns sideways. Without discussing it the whole family ignores the opening and walks slowly through the pale pink rose-coloured walls into the next room" (27). Remembered or imagined, painfully silent or chattering like crows and cranes, these families recur in the mapping of diaspora. Participating in a large Hindu wedding, ten years after his quick, registry-office marriage with Mukherjee, Blaise finds himself "beginning to understand why every Indian is so densely populated" (162). Mukherjee's autobiographical journey incorporates her Calcutta community of middle-class Bengali women, friends from her school days, whose lives enact what had been her own most likely continuities. Despite her own education away from family expectations, bell hooks understands southern blacks as existing in relationship and depending for their very beings on the lives and experiences of each other. "The self," she sees "not as signifier of one 'I' but the coming together of many 'I's, the self as embodying collective reality past and present, family and community" (31).

FILMING DIASPORA

Trinh T. Minh-ha's film, *Surname Viet Given Name Nam,* makes this point elaborately by means of a range of editorial decisions and camera techniques. In no conventional sense autobiographical, this film consists of a series of interviews in which the interviewer herself is absent. Fragmentary answers to unspoken questions build incomplete stories of five Vietnamese women during and after the war. The interviews, conducted in Vietnam, have been excerpted and translated from Mai Thu Van's book, *Vietnam, un peuple, des voix,* and then "played" by Vietnamese women in the States, who also play themselves. This layering and repetition of performance in two languages and two media and by two groups of women who merge into the one group made audible

and visible in film, foreground and, indeed, analyze the fragile, sometimes evanescent possibilities of diasporic identity.[14]

Visually, too, this film refuses singular impression, far less comprehension. The camera eye moves from artistic composition of a complete human figure or face to lopsided and partial images, intense but
passing attention to hands, a mouth, an angle or part of a face, fragments constantly stressing the partial nature of perception while also
serving metonymically for more or other than this one person. Faces
are overlaid with print. Halting English narrative merges with commentary, quotation, and songs in Vietnamese. Simultaneous voices
speak of different matters, or print and voice overlap but do not, as
when clear comprehension is required, coincide. Documentary footage
punctuates images and sounds of the women speaking, the familiar
"news" footage and the individual experience commenting reflexively
on each other. Even the text of the film printed in Trinh's *Framer
Framed*, which includes the director's elaborate line-drawing notes,
reenacts on the page the multipositionality of every aspect of this composition. An opening note explains: "In this film, women speak from
five places" ("place," in this context, is clearly not only geographical but
also positional); "these are represented here by different typestyles.
There are two voices-over reading in English (italic & plain); a third
voice singing sayings, proverbs and poetry in Vietnamese (bold), with
translations in smaller typeface; interviews in Vietnamese subtitled in
English; and interviews in English synchronized with the image (in-
dented plain and italic texts)" (49). The irony of these visual collages
plays off against the unseen but assumed recognition in Western culture of American-made films on the Vietnam War. "Each government,"
Trinh suggests in a different context, and one could say each positioning, "has its peculiar way of using and appropriating women's images"
(91). Foregrounding the varieties of appropriation in the same footage
in which the women speak for themselves (and for each other) provides disturbing commentary on the autobiographical activity of insert-
ing the self into turbulent discourses.

Affectively, too, *Surname Viet Given Name Nam* combines the terrible sadness of women exhausted beyond hope with the buoyancy of
survivors making new lives for themselves in the States. One result is
a tension and paradox of simultaneous realities — distinct experience
contributing to the communal experience, which is also individual.
Like Kingston, and like Mukherjee, Trinh incorporates the stories of
legendary heroic women, who were both warriors and poets, associating them with the courageous endurance of contemporary Vietnamese

women and with desperate gestures of self-immolation. So *The Tale of Kieu*, "written in the early 19th century in the people's language *Nom*" is so widely loved that "[i]lliterate people knew long passages of it by heart and recited it during evening gatherings" (60). Similarly, in the streets of Los Angeles, American Vietnamese celebrate the Trung sisters for their resistance to the Chinese. Their suicides, preempting submission, are then mirrored in the self-immolation of Nhat Chi Mai pouring gasoline over herself and lighting a match. "I wish to use my body as a torch to dissipate the darkness" is her "caption" (60). "In certain cases, the only way to enlighten one's surrounding was to burn oneself to death" is the commentary, many pages later, incorporated into memories of the refugee camp at Guam. There, the stories spread of refugees, especially mountain people, simply dying in their sleep. "'The reporters described this as one of those mysterious. inscrutable oriental phenomena, but I think they die of acute sadness,'" says one voice, yet another reminder of the experience of being stereotyped in the reading. "*Buon thoi ruot,*" the commentator continues, "sad to the extent that one's bowels rot, *as we commonly say*" (83, my italics). But appalling distress does not constitute a single or even a sustained element of the film, the stories of refugees, for instance, slipping between a conversation about adapting to the West and wearing spandex pants, and the Miss Vietnam 1988 Pageant in which contenders are asked (in Vietnamese but here in translation) "*what characteristics of Vietnamese culture we should preserve in American society*" (83). And the answers list the ideal virtues of submissive and virtuous women.

The dynamics of juxtaposing fragments provides continuous reflexive critique on the various materials of these women's lives and on the complex means of their representation; each shift in topic or perspective implicitly comments on the before and after of the linear experience of watching or reading even while suggesting that all of these fragments are moments in simultaneous realities. In the same way, individual histories from the south or the north, evoking French or Chinese domination, communist reeducation camps, American brutality, or the dominance of men in every area of these women's lives, suggest their continuously vigilant resistance to any singular representation, to being spoken for. Every observation comes weighted with several areas of application. "Dominated and marginalized people," Trinh tells Judith Mayne in "From a Hybrid Place," "have been socialized to see always more than their own point of view. In the complex reality of postcoloniality it is therefore vital to assume one's radical 'impurity' and to recognize the necessity of speaking from a hybrid place, hence of saying at least two, three things at a time" (140). So, when Thu Van says she is "caught between two worlds" (73), she is commenting on her own displacement which involves being truly "at home" nowhere, but she is commenting also on the powerless working world of women, on the Vietnamese experience of continuous conflict, on the suspension of her own image and words translated into film and into English in another woman's voice, and therefore also on the other Vietnamese women participating in multifaceted "translation," which they mediate by virtue of their own literal emigration, which suspends them, too, between two worlds.

One must then question the position of the viewer or reader to whom this film and this text are addressed predominantly in English.[15] We witness a literal carrying over of places, times, personal stories, and situations, the language and its stores of wisdom, all foreign elements to the English speaker, mediated by the women who have made all these translations in their own lives. These performers of diaspora speak the words of women in Vietnam as well as their own words, and they comment on speaking the words of others, on being mouthpieces for the shifting cultures of war and colonization as well as being, in their own persons, personal and cultural imports to the States and to Europe. Mai Thu Van ("author" of *Vietnam, un peuple, des voix*) writes from France: "Dear Minh-ha, 'Since the publication of the book, I felt like having lost a part of myself. It is very difficult for a Vietnamese woman to write about Vietnamese women'" (82). Maternalism being as important as it is in France, she feels she should have accepted a preface by Simone de Beauvoir, as her publisher had wished. Thu Van herself, Trinh tells Judith Mayne, is multiply displaced. She took five years to collect these interviews because of her own difficulties with assumptions about Vietnam that she had formulated in France (144). The "reader" multiplies both in the text and beyond, each speaker and each respondent interacting both with what she herself knows and with elements within the film and within the processes of making the film that are necessarily beyond her purview.

In the States, the recent immigrants combine their traditional responsibilities to family and community with jobs in which they are aware of their mediating role and of the value of their own voices. They recognize reverberations, for instance, to their own arrival. They know that "*[t]he Americans have always looked down on Vietnam as a second-class country*" (87), and must now learn to accept an influx of Vietnamese with Ph.D.'s competing with them in the professions. For themselves, adjusting to their new lives, they are "*mastering elevators and escalators, learning wristwatch-type punctuality, taming vending machines, distinguishing dog's canned foods from human canned foods, and understanding that it was not permissible to wander the streets, the hotels or anywhere outside in pyjamas"* (86). Irony and anxiety inform these observations, an intimate experience of distancing created by that which is foreign but needs to be understood.

These shifting grounds of multifaceted interaction make for a troubling film that offers no resting place. Its title plays with the notion of marriage to the nation, "surname Viet given name Nam," and underscores the inequities these women have suffered and the commitment they bring to recognizing themselves as nation even when displaced.[16] However, not only has their lifetime experience of this nation been one of trauma, upheaval, and transition, but they — "A million of Vietnamese dispersed around the globe" (83) — now also represent both nation and transition. Trinh's own role is central, as director, writer, editor, and unidentified narrator. As her book title, *Framer Framed*, suggests, the woman who makes the pictures is here included in the picture, with the additional risk that what is framed becomes canonical. Her presentation of self, nonetheless, is not personal but communal. Neither single character nor single story provides center or singularity. Vignettes of experience, like look and voice, provide spaces rather than linear sequences for communication. Communication itself, urgent because fraught with so much suffering, works as a continuous trial, acknowledging its shifting grounds and requiring of its recipients an equivalent fluidity of positions for comprehension.

CELEBRATING DIFFERENCE: AUDRE LORDE'S *ZAMI*

These shifting grounds preempt any possible search for roots, a process of which Spivak speaks with contempt (1990, 93). Hybridity of culture, like creolization of language, which makes no significant distinctions in tense, emphasizes processes of transition rather than places of origin. In *Zami*, however, Audre Lorde provides a strange twist in the familiar pattern of diasporic autobiography, suggesting some of the rich possibilities of diaspora as myth, including the myth of return. Like Kingston, she is an American responding to the systemic racism that devalues her; both writers mythologize the distinctive cultures of their ancestry to account for and appreciate the *métissage* of plural cultures in their own lives. Lorde, for example, works across the distinct cultures of her mother's childhood and her own to encapsulate the diaspora of her own experience — as a black woman, as a woman poet, and as a lesbian — for which specifically political work is her more usual agenda. Julia Watson reads Lorde's present as "uninhabitable because of its fractured political structure," and defines this myth of "nostalgic futurity" as Lorde's strategy for autobiography (154).

Writing what she calls "biomythography," Lorde describes her parents, trapped in Harlem by the Depression, unable to return even to the last place of enforced migration in the windward islands of the Lesser Antilles, which for them was home. "Little sparks of it were kept alive for years by my mother's search for tropical fruits 'under the bridge,' and her burning of kerosene lamps, by her treadle machine and her fried bananas and her love of fish and the sea" (1982, 10). Whereas Lorde's father is reluctant "to talk about home because it made him sad, and weakened his resolve to make a kingdom for himself in this new world" (12), her mother "would tell us wonderful stories about Noel's Hill in Grenville, Grenada, which overlooked the Caribbean. She told us stories about Carriacou, where she had been born, amid the heavy smell of limes" (13). The child, who has never seen this home, creates an "imaginary homeland," which she is literally unable to find on a map, but which begins with her mother's sensuous recall and feeds the child's imagination.[17] "She breathed exuded hummed the fruit smell of Noel's Hill morning fresh and noon hot, and I spun visions of sapadilla and mango as a net over my Harlem tenement cot in the snoring darkness rank with nightmare sweat. Made bearable because it was not all. This now, here, was a space, some temporary abode, never to be considered forever nor totally binding nor defining, no matter how much it commanded in energy and attention" (13). Where Trinh assembles variations on a Vietnamese woman through the persistent odds against her being heard, Lorde constructs her own diaspora, both literal and metaphoric, as an islander and as a lesbian, in terms of her mother.

In Ada Griffin and Michelle Parkerson's documentary film, *A Litany for Survival*, Lorde talks of growing up through multiple invisibilities, coming to writing with no precedents for her subject matter and with no presses that would welcome her work, and having cancer, first diagnosed in 1978, altering her priorities. Her activism, of course, made her visible as she worked to insert black people, black women, poets, lesbians, and then cancer patients into the discourses of power that had excluded, marginalized, or controlled them.[18] In terms of diaspora, however, Lorde's quite literal return is marked at the end of *a burst of light*, with the date August 1987: "*Carriacou, Grenada, Anguilla, British*

West Indies, St. Croix, Virgin Islands" (1988, 134). *A Litany for Survival* includes extended scenes of Lorde in African robes and headdress responding joyfully to this island world of sea and sky and rich vegetation. Connected to centers of political activism in Europe, Africa, and the States, she comes into her own fruition as her mother's daughter returning home.

The metaphor of lesbian sexuality that parallels this geographical return is sexual and sensuous and has, of course, its own literal component. Lorde comments on what she posits as the literal in *Zami*: "I believe that there have always been Black dykes around — in the sense of powerful and woman-oriented women — who would rather have died than use that name for themselves. And that includes my momma" (15).[19] She then develops her own sexuality as a composition of her mother and her island "origins" in an extended narrative of her mother's mortar and pestle — what Watson, nicely capturing the passion and significance "incorporated" in the daily female routine, calls "Lorde's kitchen erotics" (155). Lorde recalls the occasion of her first period, her mother's happiness, complicity, and comfort for her expressed by the ritual form of letting her choose the evening meal, and her own deliberate and equally ritual choice of "souse." Unlike the "forbidden [american] foods" that her sisters choose in their turn, souse involves use of her mother's mortar and pestle, "and this in itself was more treat for me than any of the forbidden foods" (73). Like the wily choice that involves more than is apparent, and like the notion of foods that are not allowed, Lorde's repeated use of the phrase "my mother's house," to describe the Harlem apartment in which their father also lived, establishes a mythic framework for the practical task of pounding garlic and herbs for a meal.

In ritual fashion, her mother complains on this occasion about finding "'time to mash up all that stuff,'" and Lorde's offer to pound the garlic "would be [her] next line in the script written by some ancient and secret hand" (73). Her sensuous pleasure, furthermore, in the mortar and pestle, in "the mingling fragrances" of garlic, onion, black pepper, salt, celery, and green pepper, and in the "anticipated taste of soft spicy meat" invoke and blend with pleasure in her own fully sexual body and her mother's love. "I would have a fantasy of my mother, her hands wiped dry from the washing and her apron untied and laid neatly away, looking down upon me lying on the couch, and then slowly, thoroughly, our touching and caressing each other's most secret places" (78). The mortar and pestle, mystical and suggestive agents in this merging of the two women, is no mere Puerto Rican contraption available from the market under the bridge, but a special one, fragrant and carven, mysterious in origin but surely from "the vicinity of that amorphous and mystically perfect place called 'home'" (71).

Lorde's multiple positioning in multiple margins creates repeated isolations, so she uses writing to fabricate community. Browdy de Hernandez discusses Lorde's "biomythography" as the constructing of a myth or model larger than her own life in order to guide other black lesbians. Even though I feel this biomythography is not sustained, this dense and metaphoric narrative relaxing into sequenced events empty of narrative tension, nonetheless Lorde's evocation of her mother and her mother's homeland demonstrates the significance of metaphor in the creation of diasporic space. Trinh dislodges singular or literal meaning as quickly as it is posited with her constantly shifting medium and perspective. What Lorde achieves is, in one sense, more traditional — not a refusal of interpretation but, rather, a doubling (at the least) of every reading. Permeable borders in Lorde's narrative, as with Kingston's alternative versions of one story, replicate the experience of multiple positions and plural possibilities. Even with her apparent "return" to "origins," in other words, Lorde creates in autobiography that diasporic space in which new cultures and new identities continuously emerge.

CROSSING BOUNDARIES

This emergence of the new becomes possible when traditional boundaries transform into permeable membranes. Like metaphor, mythography creates a reality by means of imagined possibility. Both metaphor and myth provide clear circumstances that overlap or blur with one or more alternatives, and each alternative radically shifts the grounds for interpretation of all the others. Like the rose-colored wall through which the pyramid of Ondaatje generations melt, or Trinh's surrogation of one woman for another, Lorde's desire for the uncharted Carriacou in terms of her mother's body serves to define specific meaning and simultaneously to destabilize meaning in its singularity. The specific or literal establishes the boundary that melts and transforms into diasporic spaces. For Blaise and Mukherjee, Hinduism models combination of the literal and the metaphoric, the simultaneously rigid and fluid, the insistence on tradition and the acceptance of change. Blaise describes his two small sons joining their grandfather in prayer.

They too wear *poyta*, the sacred Brahmin's string that Dodoo has tied and blessed and put over their necks, though they are not strictly Brahmins. Strictly speaking, because I am *mleccha*, outside the pale of brahminical civilization, they are untouchable. But that's all right. Hinduism is as flexible as it is rigid. They are honorary Brahmins.

And so our children sit beside Dodoo on the bed, one broad brown back and two frail white ones, all three with sacred strings, all with their hands cupped to their foreheads, two trying to repeat ancient prayers and Bernie content to pray with a phrase of his own, "Lufthansa, Lufthansa, let down your hair," and that too is all right. Dodoo will laugh and repeat, "*Lufthansa, Lufthansa, no mostu . . .*"; nowhere but here does one encounter such insistence on formal ritual and such delight in diversion from it. (38)

Astonished by "moment-by-moment inventiveness *within* the rigidity" (161) in the elaborate ritual of a cousin's wedding, Blaise realizes: "Of course there was order, even precision, to the ritual, but it was the order and precision of oriental carpetry, of intricate design endlessly repeated and varied, without a clear vanishing point or center of attention" (159). Emblematic of space absorbing difference and time, Hindu rituals absorb all the contradictions of this composite travelogue.

Days and Nights in Calcutta contains two narratives, parts one and two, of the same journey from Canada to India, by a married couple, both writers, who undertake these parallel and interrelated accounts as a sabbatical project. As researchers, they are keen to pursue all possible avenues of experience and information, but the focus of their attention, like their understanding of what they learn, is determined by differences in their original positions within languages and cultures and their own experiences of the past. What in practical terms is a double journal becomes in interpretive terms two voices. Male and female, white Canadian and Bengali Canadian returning to her original homeland, they establish both the sympathies and the conflicts and contradictions of plural positioning. Both are displaced as writers: Blaise unable to write about North America in these circumstances, Mukherjee received with acclaim as a distinguished Bengali but locating herself with difficulty in terms of subject matter and reading market. For Blaise, time in the East exposes his own Eurocentrism even as he dismisses it ("Europe bored me now" [9]), and it enriches his understanding of his wife of ten years. For Mukherjee, intense recognition of aspects of her original home, and disturbing ambivalences in response to Eastern family and

Western husband, bring the West into clear focus.[20] Center and periphery shift, providing critiques for each other.

Also emblematic for the whole text, also both literal and metaphoric, is the permeating sense of danger in this journey — danger to personal safety both physical and psychological, but danger also to the social, economic, and political fabric of the wider communities in India and in Canada. As with Chow's definition of the Chinese *wieiji*, however, danger or crisis also means opportunity, in this case for definitions both of difference and of diasporic identities. Danger begins with a series of accidents in Montreal, including the destruction of their house by fire and its subsequent incarnation as distorted fragments in ice. Danger is constant on the streets of Bombay and Calcutta, in the warnings of family and friends and in their memories both of the great Bengal Famine of 1943–44 and of Naxal insurgency. Mukherjee herself remembers violent strikes in her childhood, and other strikes, with curfews and rumors of street battles, impinge upon their visit both in Bombay and in Calcutta. The question for them, as for family and friends, is how to position the individual and the affiliated self in relation to stasis and change, in particular when these are expressed in threatening forms. Both narratives engage repeatedly with Hindu recognition of fate (to which people respond with intelligent resourcefulness), in contrast to the Westerner's sense of independent choice (which may be determined by elements beyond one's control). Repeatedly Blaise asks whether he is to understand particular situations in terms of Marx or of Hinduism.

For an example of multiple contrasts in a scene of high risk, both Blaise and Mukherjee tell of one particular incident when their wealthy Hindu host takes them to a Muslim neighborhood in Calcutta at two in the morning and begins provoking a rickshaw driver by challenging his credentials (147). Blaise thinks: "*Spanish Harlem* — what if this were Spanish Harlem? We all deserve to die because of this crazy stunt, right here, now" (147–48). Mukherjee, in her turn, begins by recalling how chic and liberal it had been for a Hindu woman to eat "in such unflinchingly Muslim surroundings" (249). She continues, however, with a double response, informed by experience of both East and West. She hates her host "because I knew I ought to get out of the car and tell the rickshaw puller to ask Anil for *his* credentials. Because the rickshaw puller . . . was suddenly not just a Muslim resident of a Calcutta slum, but he was also me, a timid, brown naturalized citizen in a white man's country that was growing increasingly hostile to 'colored' immigrants" (250). This experience of controlled conflict between people of distinct religion, ethnicity, and class stirs equivalent practical fears in both narrators, but otherwise positions them distinctively from each other. Neither of them is able to determine how their host and his victim have understood their roles. Blaise, however, responds as a white man among people of color, and Mukherjee as a woman of color identifying not, in this case, with her own kind but with its oppressed other. The space of experience includes memory, associations, and the cumulative effects of past conditioning for each narrator, as well as their meeting ground on what both see as an abuse of power.

The title of this work echoes that of Satyajit Ray's film, *Days and Nights in the Forest*, which Blaise describes as "realism of so high an order that it sustained all types of interpretation" (121). Indeed, Ray as an artist becomes an emblem for this joint project. Like Joyce, Ray "had to adapt foreign traditions to express a native reality" (127). Accused by some Bengalis of bowing to Western viewers and admitting cultural impurities into his work, Ray seems to Blaise "an instinctive synthesizer of cultures" (122). He responds to Professor Bhattacharya's insistence on cultural purity, for fear that adopting foreign elements leads one to surrender one's native culture, by creating "a *third* thing that is neither hybrid nor bastard, and that too will be unique" (122). Not only are Blaise and Mukherjee as narrators enmeshed in elements foreign to each, both displaced and merging, continuing and beginning anew, but their story also includes repeated examples of the accommodation between cultures evident around them. In particular, apart from the precise differences of caste, class, and gender within the Hindu community, and apart from recurring distinctions to be made among Parsis, Goans, Marwaris, Muslims, and visitors from all parts of the world, the history of the British Empire affects Canada as well as India and critiques the ethnicity of the British who also inhabit hybrid or diasporic spaces. Like Hindu ritual, and like Ray's "*third* thing," varieties of accommodation discriminate difference even while accepting it.

For example, Mukherjee packages medicine for Mother Teresa's lepers in the flat of an Englishwoman whose furniture, deportment, and speech "suggested the endless adjustments she must have made so that Britain and India could coexist in her life" (241). In contrast, Anjali's brother, with whom Mukherjee had once been prepared to fall in love, was now living in England with an English wife and unlikely to be singing Raj Kapoor songs any more (247). India's colonial past is most clearly symbolized by the Bengal Club, which had taken down its sign during the Naxal riots, and the Calcutta Turf Club, where rioting brings the races to an early conclusion. Mukherjee observes that "[n]o Englishman need feel lost, even now, in the owners' enclosure of the

Calcutta Turf Club" (261). But she notices, also, that the Englishmen who have returned from England to Calcutta for the winter season are distinguished by "leathery masks of tropical service" which "probably branded them in England as surely as they did in India" (261). Feeling, in the Bengal Club ("that spot forever green") that she ought to be reading "*Indian Alps and How We Crossed Them* by 'A Lady Pioneer'" (260), Mukherjee also finds its Reynolds Room "uncannily reminiscent . . . of the dated elegance of McGill's Faculty Club" (260). Colonial history still carries traces of the empire on which the sun never set. Despite Mukherjee's irony about finding no time for pioneers of the past because she is so engaged with pioneers of the present, she incorporates into her narrative these continuities of displacement: the English in India, the Indians in England, the adjustments her old friends are having to make to changing conditions, and her own oscillation as a postcolonial subject between colonial remains many thousands of miles apart.

Adjustments between the two narrators also establish each one as the critical reader of the other. When Blaise assumes too easily that Chattopadhaya "must be alienated from Calcutta, still nostalgic for the west" (103), he includes his wife's response: "*here I was*, as Bharati would later remind me, a foreigner in Calcutta asking a native-born Calcuttan who had come back to his home in order to rise to the top of his profession, about his disappointment and dissatisfaction" (104). Berating himself for making such crass assumptions, Blaise continues by demonstrating similar recognitions at work in his marriage: "And for me to have snickered, during the ten years of our marriage, when visiting Bengalis would ask the same of Bharati in Montreal. 'What have you given up? Is it worth it?' For the next year, I was to hear her answers, and it has shaken our marriage to its core" (104). Just as this journey calls into question the cultural securities of the Western white man, requiring him to listen in new ways to his Bengali wife, so too the qualities of narrative, shifting significantly from part one to part two, function responsively, pointing up both harmony and dissonance. Mukherjee cites arguments with Blaise, in which she defended the authoritarian sense in which her friends construed democracy: "I wanted to show him," she writes, "how thinly spread had been my acquisition of liberal sentiments, and how fast the the process of unlearning could become. To defend my friends was to assert my right to differ from him" (202). Like her husband cringing at his own inadequacies, Mukherjee takes the blame here, attributing what she calls her "self-gratifying, vicious game" to her anxiety about ambivalent loyalties. Neither one casts stones at the other as, reflexively, they adjust themselves in terms of what the other sees.

Mukherjee's narrative acknowledges the possibilities of "tribal differences in our narrative structures" (209), as she listens to a friend's story, which omits specific causes and conclusions. Similarly she, in contrast to Blaise, begins by collapsing time and distance. She takes as her emblem the temple relief from Deoghar of the god Vishnu asleep on a multiheaded serpent and surrounded by a panoply of figures human and divine. "My years abroad," she writes, "had made me conscious of ineradicable barriers, of beginnings and endings, of lines and definitions" (171), whereas the Deoghar sculpture posits simultaneity of experience and the merging of contrasts. When Blaise tells her parents about their fire in Montreal, Mukherjee comments: "He separated the peripheral elements from the central, then forced such a swift, dramatic pace on the haphazard event of our fire that hearing him recount it moved me in ways that the event itself had not" (177). In contrast, Mukherjee's mother narrates yet another version of their fire, which Mukherjee, for all her time in the West, acknowledges is right for her; many thousands of miles away, her mother had had premonitions and a telepathic recognition that they were unhappy: "Though we had been oceans apart, she had shared our misery. That was the point of her story. Drama and detail did not concern her. Nor causality, nor sequence: What mattered was her oneness with our suffering. It was as though we were figures in the same carving and the oceans that separated us were but an inch or two of placid stone. This is, quite simply, the way I perceive as well" (177).

Mukherjee begins also with an ironic collapsing of crises in India and Canada into one overview, as if anticipating her own crises — both that her Bengaliness has not been erosion-proof and that Canada is not her home. "It was not yet a time for emergency measures," she begins (167), and goes on to list crises of varying dimensions all over the subcontinent. Emergency measures being not yet timely in the India of 1973–74 implicitly contrasts with Pierre Elliott Trudeau's recent invocation of the War Measures Act in Quebec, establishing the precarious nature of distinctions and the ironies of this writer's diasporic spaces. Mukherjee understands her own separation and move toward the West as beginning in crisis. Merge, says the Deoghar sculpture, but her parents initiated separation from their extended family to form an individual unit and took their daughters to Europe for nearly three years.[21] Returning to India then, to live within the compound of her father's pharmaceutical factory, Mukherjee recalls the factory taking over the estate of "a refined Bengali gentleman after whom a street had been named in happier times. . . . His botanical gardens — full of imported rarities — were cut down and cleared, the snakes scared away, the pools filled, the immense Victorian house converted into a production plant for capsules, syrups, and pills." She also recalls that she "saw the conversion as a triumph of the new order over the old, and felt no remorse" (183). All these years later, she is not so sure. She and her sisters had walked in those orderly gardens, safe from the life of India around them, dreaming of "westernized" husbands. "We had preoccupied ourselves with single layers of existence . . . and we had ignored the visionary whole" (185). Critique of her Indian past begins here as Mukherjee blends the happier days of the Bengali gentleman, her own happy days in a new era, and her present recognition of choices as crucial to future trajectories.

Mukherjee also explores the impulses to her own move westward as a woman and the implications for her own life of the Hindu marriages to which she returns. In her 1995 epilogue, she corrects her own first impressions of this project: "I thought I was setting out to write a communal autobiography of the women of my age and my vanishing class who had stayed on in the riot-pocked hometown and made their survivalists' peace with Marxist revolution. . . . But the 'real' story that I ended up writing — in spite of myself — was about North America, not India" (301–2). Mukherjee's interviews and casual conversations with old friends and with friends of friends expose both the rigid structures of possibility for women and the permeable nature of boundaries encountered by the talented, the beautiful, the rich, or the lucky. She recalls stories of humiliation, suicide, and suffering. And she recalls her own mother's angry determination that her daughters be well educated so that no one could make them suffer (227–28). "My mother had loved us enough to risk the wrath of elderly relatives, and through the perversities of love, I had squeezed more selfish pleasure out of life than she could ever have dreamed, but I had also lost belief in the self-sufficiency of Calcutta and made a foreign continent my battleground for proving self-worth" (229).

Like her friends in Calcutta who, Mukherjee feels, lead "craftily welded lives," she herself has worked with the multiple strands of her own possibilities, wrested her "fate" out of its likeliest directions, and sought to "prove self-worth" in what she now sees as estrangement from her homeland, her *desh*. The real story, as she puts it, is not about leaving but about staying away. "Leaving is easy in our new diasporic age, but staying away and fashioning 'home' among hostile people in a

strange landscape was . . . my urgent subject" (302). Mukherjee echoes
Kingston's poignant sense of the necessity and the paradox of self-
creation "among hostile people and in a strange landscape." Kingston
tells the story of the "icicle in the desert" (1975, 208–9), the high note
of the barbarian flutes, to which the Chinese poet, Ts'ai Yen, responds
with "a song so high and clear, it matched the flutes. Ts'ai Yen sang
about China and her family there. Her words seemed to be Chinese,
but the barbarians understood their sadness and anger. Sometimes they
thought they could catch barbarian phrases about forever wandering.
Her children . . . eventually sang along when she left her tent to sit by
the winter campfires, ringed by barbarians" (209). To stay away is to
embody in one's person the languages of one's past and to blend one's
voice with the barbarian pipes.

Together, Blaise and Mukherjee frame their experience of India both
in time, with his prologue and her epilogue written in 1995, and with
their further migration from Canada to the States. This move, too,
has to do with varieties of imperialism, with "race," and with writing. Mukherjee has envied Blaise his Canada, which accepts him so
nicely (136), and struggles with her own problem of straddling cultures. Apparently irrelevant in Montreal, her mother tongue being
neither French nor English, Mukherjee describes herself as "a late-
blooming colonial who writes in a borrowed language (English), lives
permanently in an alien country (Canada), and publishes in and is
read, when read at all, in another alien country, the United States"
(170). Writing her novel *Wife* during her time in Calcutta, Mukherjee
wonders: "[H]ow could I explain this anger [of the women who tell
her their stories] to critics in New York or Montreal who did not know
that a young Bengali woman could rebel by simply reading a book or
refusing to fast?" (268).[22] Recognition in Calcutta does not provide
the readers of the West for whom she writes. Privilege of caste and class
in India, even elevation of her status to that of honorary man, does not
translate to Montreal, where she becomes "a despised and discrimi-
nated-against minority in a race- and color-conscious society" (302).

The family move from Canada to the States, which uproots the
contentedly Canadian husband and sons, follows a sequence that explains once again why diaspora in the West is so often a matter of color.
Writing in 1995, Blaise mocks himself for having "confidently projected the collapse of a whole subcontinent" but "failed to see the
collapse of the only world — my fragile and constructed Canadian identity . . . —that had fed my sense of purpose" (xiii). What he refers
to as "the distant rumble" in 1973 "of Canadian racism" becomes in

Mukherjee's conclusion experiences of "racial harassment in increasingly crude forms" (302). With Canada at that time still a Dominion of Great Britain, without a constitution of its own or an enforceable bill of rights, racism belonged on no official agenda. Mukherjee's move to the States involves once again deliberate choice in preference to yet another inheritance. She calls this move a building for their family of a "homeland" made "of expectation, not memory" (303). Both prologue and epilogue to a book ostensibly about India focus on Canada, on the limited and colonial culture that does not embrace the Indian and calls into question, accordingly, the ethnic affiliations of the white husband. A work whose whole burden is interpretation and analysis of the familiar and the foreign concludes with yet further migration, a process that shifts in emphasis but does not end.[23]

More keenly and self-consciously than most autobiographers, immigrants acknowledge in their work the processes of what Eakin has called "self-invention." Quite explicitly they make their own realities from a kaleidoscope of possibilities. These possibilities, furthermore, of memory, necessity, experience, and choice, their baggage for travel, enable autobiographers of diaspora to construct their homelands not as stable and singular, as for purists, but as protean and plural because constructed in relation to each other. They engage with what Mercer has called "the collision of cultures" (56), and with what Brah has called "*locationality in contradiction*" (204). Less brittle, more expansive, Chow's concept of diaspora describes a process of "*multi-locationality across geographical, cultural and psychic boundaries*" (194). Like Griffiths's "passing" in the Métis community, or like Meigs's alarm at being defined as "a sort of Lesbian," double seeming leaves the migrant neither here nor there, the boundaries of the mind remaining permeable even in those cases in which political boundaries have closed. Identities constructed in diaspora tend, therefore, to be liminal, and to avoid taking the step that could be construed as final.

LIMINAL IDENTITIES

Growing up Chinese in Malaya, Shirley Geok-lin Lim describes the risks attached to finality for a liminal identity. As a child, she carried an ID card, which she frequently had to produce at gunpoint, pervasive violence threatening her own experience of identity in terms of "race," language, education, and culture. Born to a "peranakan" mother, an assimilated Chinese born in Malaya, and a Hokkien-speaking Chinese father, her own heritage crossed boundaries from the beginning. Named Shirley, for Shirley Temple, by her Chinese grandfather, who preferred the films of Hollywood to those from Bombay, Lim's identity came from a mixture of sources and carried a range of possibilities. She grew up as a British subject (35–36) in a country controlled during her girlhood by British, Japanese, and then again British powers. She was aware as a child of the atrocities the Japanese inflicted on Chinese men and of violent deaths within her own family (37). She was aware, also, of possible confusion, both in appearance and affiliation, between the Chinese Kuomintang and Chinese communists, who were enemies of the British and to be suppressed (39). Waving her flag as a schoolgirl, to welcome Sir Gerald Templer as the new British High Commissioner in 1951, she had learned to hate Chinese communists as the enemy ("men with faces like my father's or my uncles'" [40]). She also knew that both Kuomintang and communists were hostile to peranakans, "whom they looked down on as degraded people, people who had lost their identity when they stopped speaking Chinese" (40). Lim's own rejection of Hokkien and her comfort with Malayan and with English result from family politics and eager Westernization. Not only did her grandfather name her for Shirley Temple because they both had dimples, but her father subscribed to English and American magazines and played Western songs. In his photographs, he "is almost always smiling. . . . In this way his image is already un-Chinese" (20). (Kingston also contrasts "that far gaze" in Chinese photographs with pictures of her father "smiling and smiling in his many western outfits" [1975, 59].) Despite the permanence and authority of British citizenship, it is small wonder that young Lim, challenged to produce her identity card, heard "I.C." both as "'I see (you)!' and as 'Ai sei!' or 'You are dead!' in Hokkien" (40).[24]

Lim's conscious and continuous activities of translation continue with her education. Learning the song of the Jolly Miller on the River Dee (64), Lim knows nothing about millers or about larks, but is even more engaged by the foreign concepts of the individual and of choice when the miller declares he cares for nobody and nobody cares for him. "Caring denoted a field of choice, of individual voluntary action, that was foreign to family, the place of compulsory relations. Western ideological subversion, cultural colonialism, whatever we call those forces that have changed societies under forced political domination, for me began with something as simple as an old English folk song" (64).

British colonial education included Scottish and Irish ballads in the music curriculum, prompting Lim to wonder "why Indian, Eurasian, Malay, and Chinese children should be singing, off-key, week after week . . . the melancholic attitudes of Celtic gloom" (67–68).[25] For Lim herself, as for Rodriguez, agile appropriation of all that school had to offer enables escape into new opportunities. Lim does not choose radical separation from her past but freedom from "that other familial / gender / native culture that violently hammered out only one shape for self" (65). Translation from East to West completes her diaspora. Like Kingston and like Mukherjee, Lim embraces the dangers and the opportunities of diaspora to open up plural identities. The limited gender identity provided by her original culture propels each of these women into what Mukherjee has called an alien country.

Because Lim has chosen linear narrative, however, *Among the White Moon Faces*, so rich in perception and analysis of her early years in Malaya, relaxes, like Lorde's *Zami*, into less discriminating, more sequential narrative that is less concerned with mediating her experience of diaspora. Certainly, *Zami* and *Among the White Moon Faces* are engaging and richly rewarding texts. What matters here, however, is some distinction between their stated subject matter (transformations and plurality of self) and the genres that enable them to "realize" these issues.[26] Retaining the spatial narrative that recreates (instead of declaring) one's layered identity depends on a sustained use of fictive techniques. Liminality, in Victor Turner's thinking, belongs "in the 'subjunctive mood' of culture, the mood of maybe, might-be, as-if, hypothesis, fantasy, conjecture, desire," and is best described, perhaps, "as a fructile chaos, a fertile nothingness, a storehouse of possibilities, not by any means a random assemblage but a striving after new forms and structure" (295). Transitions and overlap, boundaries and their permeation, simultaneous inside / outside instabilities, hybridity, hyphenation, cultural creolization, are not experienced as linear and find fullest expression in narrative that is permeable, polygeneric, and significantly free from the constraints of time. Autobiographers who begin in one mode are distinctly changing horses when they move from work that is conceptually spatial to work that is conceptually linear. On the one hand, as with much aboriginal autobiography, they may be concerned with having their story read. On the other, they may also be shifting their focus from the situation in which they find themselves to an exploration of identity, which relies so heavily on narrative time (see Eakin 1999).

Kingston's *The Woman Warrior* and Ondaatje's *Running in the Family* push the limits of what critics have been happy to consider autobiography precisely because they invent new forms of narrative to suggest both the range and the instabilities of diasporic identities.[27] They achieve the fluidity of their cultural experience in equivalently fluid narrative, blending fiction and whimsy with research, analysis, memory, family stories, history, memoir, and the mythic components of cultural identity. Like Blaise and Mukherjee, they establish readers within their texts, and situate themselves as readers in relation to family lore. Like Trinh, they reject singular statement, subverting each possible meaning with numerous alternatives. Like Lorde's, their works are rich in metaphors that function like prisms to refract the many meanings of the self. Like Lim and Mukherjee, they position themselves across conflicting cultures, liminal and therefore particularly self-inventive. What they achieve, above all, with their uses of the fictive and fabulous is transformation of their reader, who experiences these particular liminalities as if in a first language, forgetting to translate.

Born in the United States, identifying herself with her husband's English name, Kingston works across a generational divide. Her most urgent task is to use her Chinese heritage for an American life — to make an ancient culture, its language, and its stories work for her in the new world. *The Woman Warrior*, accordingly, focuses precisely on transition and translation: between languages, between oral and written forms of expression, between cultures and their values (particularly problematic for a Chinese girlchild), between her parents' experience as Chinese Americans and her own, and between the stories she has received and the forms in which they can make sense of her own experience.[28] So *The Woman Warrior* focuses on forms of narrative and reflects explicitly upon its choices. The most serious obstacle it must overcome is silence, either imposed from outside or inflicted from within. Its most serious challenge is to make narrative sense for the narrator. "Insane people," she knows, "were the ones who couldn't explain themselves" (186). Or, as her mother, Brave Orchid, says when identifying her sister Moon Orchid as deranged: "'The difference between mad people and sane people . . . is that sane people have variety when they talk story. Mad people have only one story that they talk over and over'" (159). Having behaved as if halt, clumsy, and defective through her young girlhood, in order to avoid the miseries she anticipates of slavery or an arranged marriage, Kingston, as narrator of a story for new generations to grow up on, needs to ensure her credibility.

To explain in her American life the ancestral Chinese stories inscribed upon her body (45), Kingston resorts to multiple stories, not just numerous but layered and polyphonal. Malini Schueller describes *The Woman Warrior* as a dialogic text because it "subverts singular definition of racial and ethnic identity and . . . valorizes intersubjectivity and communication" (421).[29] She refers also to the necessity in this text "of maintaining and creating multiple ideological positions, of always letting the numerous voices echo in [Kingston's] own articulations" (427). Gender and "race," she suggests, are not defined as transcendent and true categories but as dialogically interactive (433). Couser describes *The Woman Warrior* as figuratively collaborative: Kingston writes autobiography through the biographies of her parents, in particular that of her mother.[30] Like her mother needing to be talked back into her present situation after her encounter with the Sitting Ghost, Kingston also needs to look for her descent line, Couser suggests, but "in a deliberately improvisational and bicultural fashion" (1989, 235). Constantly accepting plural perspectives, acknowledging the impossibility of any secure knowledge, Kingston foregrounds the activities of listening and narrating, and the processes of translation that both listening and narrating involve. So the community life of New Society Village funnels into the individual life of this "outlaw knotmaker," and the ancient myths of that community translate into narratives appropriate to Kingston's new situation.

Kingston's narrator receives the secret story of No Name Aunt as a warning, mother to daughter, when she begins to menstruate. She is not to shame her family and risk the punishment of being forgotten, no longer named. For the American child, however, No Name Aunt is more a mystery than a threat. Her haunting, not always well intentioned (16), stirs the imagination of the woman-writer, who identifies with the transgression of seeking individuality. "The villagers punished her for acting as if she could have a private life, secret and apart from them" (13). Unable to figure out what was her village (45), the narrator receives this story not for its communal construction of reality (13) but for its personal value to her and because it establishes modes of reception and translation. Imagining the various possibilities for her aunt's story, the narrator looks for the ancestral help this aunt can give her, recognizing that this aunt "crossed boundaries not delineated in space" (8). Receiving her secret warning against sexual transgression, the narrator is concerned only with how to achieve the narrative transgression that will enable her to cross the boundaries, also unmapped, between the old world and the new.

No Name Aunt, the father's onetime sister, becomes pregnant while her husband is away in America, the Gold Mountain. On the mother's side, Moon Orchid has also been abandoned in China, her husband no longer a "sojourner" but settled in America with a new wife. The story of her arrival in America moves the mythology of past situations into the present tense of the narrator's life. In contrast to No Name Aunt, Moon Orchid does provide a terrible warning. "Brave Orchid's daughters decided fiercely that they would never let men be unfaithful to them. All her children made up their minds to major in science or mathematics" (160). Whereas No Name's story had come directly from the narrator's mother, "a story to grow up on" (5), the narrator receives Moon Orchid's story at several removes, from her sister, who had received it from their brother, who had driven the two elderly sisters down to Los Angeles to confront the husband of thirty years before (the fairy-tale element of their story compounded by their mutual astonishment that the other one has aged, "two old women with faces like mirrors" [118], "two women over whom a spell of old age had been cast" [152]). "His version of the story may be better than mine," she suggests, "because of its bareness, not twisted into designs" (163). Such speculation, associated with dangerous and forbidden knot-making, and with extended analysis of silence and storytelling, comes after the event. It foregrounds narrativity and complicates reception but does not affect the crucial information that this aunt, too, has "crossed boundaries not delineated in space" (8); her punishment is not death but insanity. She has, in her sister's words, "misplaced herself" (157). No longer anchored to this earth, she speaks in a monotone, not even interrupting herself to ask questions, reduced to one single story with no explanatory power.

Brave Orchid, "a champion talker" (202), has tried to create heroic possibilities for her sister, casting her as the good Empress of the East come to release her husband, imprisoned by the conniving Empress of the West (143). When Moon Orchid "misplaces herself" after her husband's rejection, Brave Orchid tries to talk her back to her new address. Neither the heroic tale, however, nor the calling of the poor woman's spirit can help her overcome the transition between East and West that has been, in her case, too violent and absolute. Where she has begun by translating everything that she observes, from the children's activities to the workings of the laundry ("She could describe it so well, you would think she could do it" [142]), she has been unable to make sense or use of any of what she describes. From the beginning, she is literal, unable to fashion matters of fact into narratives for living. The warning she provides, therefore, is indeed of ancestral help, not because husbands might be unfaithful (a literal fact) but because stories need to absorb multiple possibilities, to distort the straight rope into twists and turns for new and difficult knots. Stories to live by need to adapt to new circumstances.

In refashioning ancestral myths, furthermore, Kingston is working well within the tradition from which they come. Sau-ling Cynthia Wong tells of different versions of the Fa Mu Lan story in the Ting, Ming, and Qing dynasties as well as in the modern period. Its genres, furthermore, range from the ballad, novel, and opera libretto to the *baihua*, or vernacular play (1991, 28–32). Elsewhere, Wong suggests Fa Mu Lan is already prone to variations, some of which include a sister and a cowardly cousin (1992, 275). King-Kok Cheung reads Kingston's version of the Fa Mu Lan legend as conflated "with that of Yue Fei, a male warrior, whose mother carves words on his back before he leaves for battle" (151). Certainly, her training draws on the martial arts novels and their modern incarnation in cinema. She is not, says Bobby Fong, "transportable" to American soil (120). When Moon Orchid includes Fa Mu Lan among her gifts of exotic paper cutouts ("'She was a woman warrior, and really existed'" [120]), she is highlighting the association that a number of critics observe among the narrator's lineal and cultural ancestors. Translating Mu Lan as Wood Orchid or Sylvan Orchid, they place this untransferable hero in the same generation as mother and aunt (Wong, 32; Lee, 59) — a symbolic sisterhood whose guidance for an American girl is of limited value and therefore in need of variation. A young American girl, for example, reacts with anger and fear to the Chinese sayings that disparage girls. Accordingly, her Fa Mu Lan avenges, in Schueller's words, "not only the wrongs to her village but the hierarchical genderizing she has been subject to" (426). The patriarchal moral about filial piety in the story she receives becomes incidental (432), with the result that a myth of clear directives becomes problematic and unstable.

Alternatively, myth provides a constant paradigm whose explanatory powers can absorb new circumstances. Or, to put it another way, some situations recur with variations for which the ancient stories remain adequate. For example, Couser sees interesting parallels that Kingston does not make explicit between the ancient legend and the American situation. He associates the mythical emperor's conscription of Fa Mu Lan's father with the U.S. president's drafting of Kingston's brother for Vietnam, and the offenses committed against Fa Mu Lan's family with the abuses inflicted by the Red Guards on the family left behind in China. Certainly, in *China Men* Kingston associates Fa Mu Lan, her armor soaked with blood, with the images of war that permeated her childhood and recurred during the Vietnam War in which her brother fought (268). Her confusion, furthermore, about images of Chinese men in American uniforms in conflict with Japanese, Chinese, and Vietnamese men bears comparison with Lim's anxiety that the enemy looks like father and brothers. Certainly, too, the second communist five-year plan finds her parents spending their fare home on furniture to replace the orange and apple crates which they have been using so far. Kingston's narrator expresses relief ("May the Communists light up the house on a girl's birthday" [191]) at her receding chances of returning to China and being turned into a wife or a slave. Ironically, she reverses the dangers encoded in these stories as enforced displacement from China and fears most intensely for herself an enforced removal from America.

The narrator's terrible fears, manifest in her brutality to the silent Chinese girl whom she desperately wants to see as an opposite rather than as a mirror image, culminate in her shouting match with her own mother, who actually has to explain that derogatory comments are intended to protect and that the Chinese "'like to say the opposite'" (203). Not until her mother shouts at her the things that she herself had intended to say does she discover her significant inheritance of "talk-story" transcending her confusions between truth and falsehood, lies and evasions, ghosts of elusive and frightening meaning. Stories of suicide, abandonment, and madness have proved strong contemporary alternatives to stories of the woman warrior and of Brave Orchid's own exceptional past ("[s]he had gone away ordinary and come back miraculous" [76]), creating intense ambivalence in the narrator about the Chinese "invisibilities" that her mother continuously placates and a continuous anger and fear about the fate of Chinese girls, which she expects to share. Recognizing her own role in talk-story connects Kingston's narrator both with her mother's tradition and with the younger "ghost" generation of American women of Chinese ancestry.

Kingston's final translation, accordingly, is of a story her mother begins for which she herself provides a new ending. As with the stories of No Name Aunt and Moon Orchid, this story also begins with that of another aunt, the youngest, Lovely Orchid, who barely escapes kidnapping by bandits. Whereas No Name Aunt transgresses invisible boundaries, exciting the young listener with the transgressive possibilities of an individual's story, and Moon Orchid provides a terrible warning to the woman who cannot find the variant stories with which to make the necessary transition from East to West, Lovely Orchid initiates the original and symbolic Chinese moment in which a daughter of the Han people is snatched away from her community to live among aliens. She herself is released when the bandit sees "'[a] prettier one,'" and lets her go (207), but her possible story, feeding into the mother-and-daughter narration, turns into that of Ts'ai Yen.

Like Fa Mu Lan, Ts'ai Yen is an historical figure reported to have lived as a captive to barbarians for about twelve years. Schueller sees her as representing Kingston's mother, a stranger among the Americans, a woman who fights when she needs to, and whose children do not speak her "language." In the original telling, however, Ts'ai Yen leaves her barbarian children behind, returns to the Han people, and bears children to her father's line, her time among barbarians no more than an interlude. For the American daughter a new ending is required. Just as this narrator transforms the Fa Mu Lan story to incorporate uncertainties, so Ts'ai Yen becomes a story of intercultural understanding rather than a story of ethnic superiority (Schueller, 432). In this version, Ts'ai Yen does not leave her barbarian children among the barbarians while she herself returns to China but transforms the Chinese poet into a new kind of artist. In completing her mother's story, Kingston is concerned with turning the interlude among barbarians into continuing time. She is also eager to blend the music of barbarian and Chinese. Where the Chinese girl she had abused could not move into their new culture, silent as a plant, wheezing into her flute, the narrator now has the barbarian pipes draw the Chinese poet into concert in "a song so high and clear, it matched the flutes" (209). As in Kingston's version of Fa Mu Lan, who inspires her army with the glorious songs that "poured out and were loud enough for the whole encampment to hear" (37), Ts'ai Yen's singing is clear both to her children and to the barbarians. Whether played on barbarian pipes or with Chinese instruments, it "translated well" (209).

In an interview with Arturo Islas, Kingston implicitly connected her mother's great power of talking-story with the necessary liberties she herself has taken with the stories she received (Kingston, 1983). Notably, her mother's dialect is not a written language. While deploring the finality and permanence of print, Kingston points out that the oral tradition "changes according to the needs of the listener, according to the needs of the day, the interest of the time, so that the story can be different from day to day" (18).[31] She works against stability in print

not only by introducing variants and speculation in every account but also by foregrounding her own activities of translation. "'Let it run,'" says the old woman of Fa Mu Lan's menstrual blood. "('Let it walk' in
Chinese)," the narrator explains parenthetically, adjusting the meaning in the process, or pointing out at the very least the inadequacies of translation (31). Alert to the impression her children must be making upon the aunt newly arrived from China, Brave Orchid deplores the greed they show for presents in front of the giver. "How impolite ('untraditional' in Chinese) her children were" (121). Or, "'I'm not a bad girl. I'm not a bad girl,'" the narrator screams at her mother, and then offers her childhood translation of this outburst in cultural terms: "I might as well have said 'I'm not a girl'" (46). Or the child, both understanding and appreciating nuances in two languages, notes the interchange between an American customer and her mother working as a Chinese laundress: "'No tickee, no washee, mama-san?' a ghost would say, so embarrassing. 'Noisy Red-Mouth Ghost' she'd write on its package, naming it, marking its clothes with its name" (105). In a work about transition and translation, the autobiographer moves from the problematic ideographs of "I" and "here" to her own most important achievement: "Nobody in history has conquered and united both North America and Asia. A descendant of eighty pole fighters, I ought to be able to set out confidently, march straight down our street, get going right now. There's work to do, ground to cover. Surely the eighty pole fighters, though unseen, would follow me and lead me and protect me, as is the wont of ancestors" (49).

Notably, Kingston's conquest of North America and Asia is achieved not in one linear narrative that moves through time but in a collage of narratives, each one combining personal and community experience, Chinese histories and present circumstances, Chinese legends and their contemporary American translations, with the result that this work, too, is spatial, its maps to be determined in memory, dream, and the languages of talk-story. Foregrounding its own processes, *The Woman Warrior*, like Michael Ondaatje's *Running in the Family*, slips among generic categories but is captured by Linda Hutcheon's term "historiographic metafiction." For autobiographers who have listened to oral histories that they have not entirely understood, or heard contradicted, or heard differently each time, writing about the act of writing becomes the autobiography. Ascertaining any truth remains a matter of desire. For Kingston, who has discovered that her village dialect is so local that she has ceased to identify herself as bilingual, her work creates all the maps she has of place, of languages, of memory, and of imagination.

"I'd like to go to New Society Village someday," she concludes, "and find out exactly how far I can walk before people stop talking like me. I continue to sort out what's just my childhood, just my imagination, just my family, just the village, just movies, just living" (205). For Ondaatje, such return becomes, at one level, a reality, but he too writes about writing as discovering the maps in his own mind.[32]

The frontispiece for *Running in the Family* is a line map of Ondaatje's Ceylon, now Sri Lanka. With its compass pointing north, with its graph of kilometers and miles, it is not, as an island, identified by any name at all. (One needs to note, however, that the absent father is the narrator's "north pole" [172], the magnetic field of this work.) This line drawing, however, with place names on it that anchor in space the stories of the text, is elaborated with variations within the language of the work. The very existence of Ceylon, for example, originates in the narrator's emotions of loss and desire: "Ceylon falls on a map and its outline is the shape of a tear" (147). He refers to "false maps" on his brother's wall in Toronto ("The shapes differ so much they seem to be translations — by Ptolemy, Mercator, François Valentyn, Mortier, and Heydt" [63]), situating his own mapping as also subjective, his "tabula Asiae" just one "tabula" among many. Even the apparent progress in these maps "from mythic shapes into eventual accuracy" remains fantastic: "Amoeba, then stout rectangle, and then the island as we know it now, a pendant off the ear of India" (63). The island as we know it now is the site and source of the narrator's lost childhood. In place of "blue-combed ocean busy with dolphin and sea-horse" and "naive mountains" with their "drawings of cassowary and boar who leap without perspective across imagined 'desertum' and plain" (63), he peoples his own map with relatives and family friends, memories and lost stories. His beasts are wild boar, thalagoya, cobra, gecko, and ant. His purpose, like that of the mapmakers of the past, is to find his own bearings, to locate his self. "This pendant, once its shape stood still, became a mirror" (64) reflecting each new adventurer, including the original Ondaatje: "Here. At the centre of the rumour. At this point on the map" (64). "This is the colour of landscape," he says at another point in his exploration, arriving in tea country, "this is the silence that surrounded my parents' marriage" (167).

Ondaatje's mapmaking becomes a metaphor for interpretation, for his own efforts to understand what he hears, to locate what he has lost, and to ascertain his own place. In the chapter "Lunch Conversation," for example, speakers are not identified (just as the frontispiece map is not named). Narration therefore adds a level of chaos to the assumptions and hypotheses with which conversation begins. "Wait a minute, wait a minute!" the chapter begins. "When did all this happen, I'm trying to get it straight" (105). Here, as so often, Ondaatje's ellipses mark unidentified spaces, his narrator as original reader confused by a babel of voices telling two stories—no, three—across some fifty-six years. "No, *one*, everybody says laughing. One when your mother was nine. Then when she was sixty-five and drinking at the wedding lunch" (108), except that no one is sure whose wedding this was, just as the narrator cannot receive as single a story in which his mother is both nine and sixty-five. "No story is ever told just once," he explains at an earlier point. "Whether a memory or funny hideous scandal, we will return to it an hour later and retell the story with additions and this time a few judgements thrown in. In this way history is organized" (26). As is the blended life of boy and man. At a formal dinner, for example, Ondaatje's sister Gillian tells a story she had heard from Yasmine Gooneratne, once a prefect at Bishop's College for Girls, about the brutal bathing that the little boys received every second night. The narrator wonders why he has no memory of this experience. "It is the kind of event that should have surfaced as the first chapter of an anguished autobiographical novel" (138). But he moves on to the Wilpattu Jungle lodge where he and family and friends throw a bar of soap around like a foaming elixir as they bathe in the monsoon rains. Listening to shifts in tense and perspective, and to shifts from memory to rumor, gossip, scandal, and tall tale, the narrator incorporates these into his own mapmaking, including also shifts from his parents' past time to his present-tense Canadian family, including the photographs that he receives as documents and the poems that he creates in response to his experience.

With materials of so many kinds and from so many sources, speculation is the only possible procedure and space the only comprehensive dimension in which to imagine it. Distinctions between then and now, before and after, become irrelevant. Causality is never an issue because no event can be identified as the result of another. Crawling across the stones of St. Thomas's church, measuring the chiseled lettering of the Ondaatjes' name with his own body, the narrator finds the personal eliminated. Being named in so spacious a way maps the individual in the long history and the extensive storying of his family. He is breathless with smallness: "It makes your own story a lyric" (66). Not an aria from the "frozen opera" of his parents' generation that he wants to touch into words (22), but an intensely realized moment. Mapping fits this lyric into the romantic yearning for an exotic origin: "*Asia*. The name was a gasp from a dying mouth. An ancient word that had to be whispered, would never be used as a battle cry. The word sprawled. It had none of the clipped sound of Europe, America, Canada. The vowels took over, slept on the map with the S" (22). Realizing the map in language creates the sounds of this romantic whisper, of the voices that narrate with their shouting and laughter, of the frogs that provide a background chorus to peacocks. The narrator receives all this varied information, his own perception playing a small part among many others, his task to chart what he discovers.

As with Kingston's variations on any possible story, which foreground the activity of story-making, so Ondaatje's processes of mapmaking figure largely in this text. Not only is he the traveler, aware in his thirties that he "had slipped past a childhood [he] had ignored and not understood" (22), and the listener to memories, gossip, rumors, and tall tales that are embellished with each telling, but he is also the scribe, his hand pushing the pen across the page, wondering what sense his words will make. The making of text, then, which begins with his own activity, *"Half a page — and the morning is already ancient"* (17), spreads to encompass his parents, his past, and the history of Ceylon. So he notices that the signature of Simon Ondaatje, "the last Tamil Colonial Chaplain of Ceylon" (67), is very like his father's. He notices his mother's handwriting, which changes from the thirties on: "It looks wild, drunk, the letters are much larger and billow over the pages, almost as if she had changed hands." Her writing turns out, however, to be the result of serious effort, "as if at the age of thirty or so she had been blasted, forgotten how to write, lost the use of a habitual style and forced herself to cope with a new dark unknown alphabet" (150). Her writing marks her transition from the Gatsby days of her youth to the terrible responsibilities she faced with a paranoid and alcoholic husband and four small children.

Ondaatje himself, caught in that transition which began his own long absence from Ceylon, recalls the Sinhalese alphabet and the lines he had to write out as punishment at "St. Thomas' College Boy School." Like Kingston's woman warrior, Ondaatje's narrator figures this script as embodied: "The bones of a lover's spine . . . the small bones in the body" (83). But the Sinhalese alphabet, moving "east across the page as if searching for longitude and story, some meaning or grace that would occur *blazing*" (84), also connects with fifth century B.C. graffiti poems on the rock face of Sigiriya, and with the poetry written on the walls and ceilings and in hidden corners of the Vidyalankara campus of the University of Ceylon by defeated insurgents of 1971 held there as prisoners. The body contains history and is the map of experience.

Just as the alphabet of the narrator's childhood becomes small bones, so Ian Goonetileke, who has known the poets and recorded their words, embodies the suffering and the resistance for which Ondaatje himself was not present. "He is a man who knows history is always present, is the last hour of his friend Lakdasa . . . , is the burned down wall that held those charcoal drawings whose passionate conscience should have been cut into rock. The voices I didn't know" (85). He himself, prodigal returning, is not unlike the British who slept through the crazy journey when Ondaatje's drunken father commandeered the train, a problematic but telling association. No one imagined waking them up. "They slept on serenely with their rage for order in the tropics, while the train shunted and reversed into the night and there was chaos and hilarity in the parentheses around them" (154). The space empty of consciousness, like the spaces of the frequent ellipses, becomes the center oblivious to all the meaning (*"blazing"*) in the margins. One painful aspect of this personal mapping is Ondaatje's sense that that central space is the one he cannot complete. Reaching for his father, he concludes: "There is so much to know and we can only guess. Guess around him" (200), like active parentheses again enclosing empty space.

On rock or wall or document or the present page, these alphabets that provide clues to meaning in their syntax and their punctuation represent not only the absence of their writers but also the tendency of all such mapmaking toward decay. The "coming darkness makes it necessary to move fast in order to read the brass plaques on the walls" (65); the narrator washes his hands and anticipates "that eerie moment when [he will] see very clearly the deep grey colour of old paper dust going down the drain" (68); or he is "[r]eading torn 100-year-old newspaper clippings that come apart in your hands like wet sand" (69). Ink in church ledgers has turned brown with time, "[t]he thick pages foxed and showing the destruction caused by silverfish, scars among the immaculate recordings of local history and formal signatures" (66). Silverfish also "slid into steamer trunks and photograph albums — eating their way through portraits and wedding pictures" (135–36). This work in process fares no better; in a surreal fantasy, the narrator's father, as desired reader, watches the ants carry away the page we are reading but which he himself has not yet reached (189). Kneeling on the red tile, like his son on the gravestone in St. Thomas's church, he forgets about the mirror he was looking for and surrenders the page that might show him to himself.

But the prodigal returning is also the invader, the plunderer of his own past. He is the one devouring documents and photographs, absorbing them into his body like his aged aunt, who no longer needs to see the photograph she talks about: "She has looked at it for years and has in this way memorized everyone's place in the picture. . . . It has moved tangible, palpable, into her brain, the way memory invades the present in those who are old, the way gardens invade houses here, the way her tiny body steps into mine as intimate as anything I have witnessed and I have to force myself to be gentle with this frailty in the midst of my embrace" (112). Either the narrator will remain an alien invader, or he will absorb the people and the materials that have themselves absorbed his history. He is like "the gecko on the wall waving his tail stiffly his jaws full of dragonfly whose wings symmetrically disappeared into his mouth — darkness filling the almost transparent body" (70) — the center now filled, no longer a gap between parentheses. Greedy for the riches of the spice island, this plunderer comes away, in effect, empty-handed but retains on his body and in his senses the identifying (but very delicate) fragrance of cinnamon.

Ondaatje records his search for his father but arrives at no conclusions. He wants to say, "Look I am the son who has grown up" (180). He wants the password ("Sweet Marjoram") that will enable him to write "when [he is] least sure about such words" (180). But in the end "the book again is incomplete. In the end all your children," he writes, addressing the absent father, "move among the scattered acts and memories with no more clues" (201). And the mad, drunken song so frequently repeated remains, unlike Kingston's collaboration with her mother, "that song we cannot translate" (201). As Kingston negotiates her mother's powerful act of cutting her frenum (either hampering or releasing her speech), so Ondaatje's prenatal "first memory" of kabaragoyas is similar but not equivalent to being fed the magically inspiring thalagoya tongue. Instead, Ondaatje's search for his "father tongue" makes an imaginative reach into the silence of his father's "final days," and, indeed, into the end of his own journey.

DIALOGUES OF DIASPORA

Stuart Hall articulates most succinctly why dialogism is so central to autobiographies of diaspora. Practices of representation, he reminds us, always implicate the positions from which we speak, but who speaks and the subject that is spoken of are never identical, never in exactly the same place (222). While this observation holds for all forms of autobiography, the diasporic experience foregrounds the conflict of cultures, languages, memories, and desires in the processes of self-invention and self-construction. The "dialectical interplay between the individual and his or her culture" that Eakin identified in *Fictions in Autobiography* (256) and then elaborated in *Touching the World* is both foregrounded and intense when the autobiographer, positioned between cultures, is able to critique both and to choose, accordingly, what complex of hybridity to embrace. Who speaks and who is spoken in these works may put a girdle round about the earth — and yet find no resting place.

The narrators of these autobiographies position themselves with more confidence in relation to other people. Parents are important to Lorde, Kingston, and Ondaatje not only in terms of personal relationships but also in terms of their ability to define the other or originary half of diaspora. Whole families and communities populate Lim's memory, Trinh's film, Ondaatje's journey, Lorde's lesbian identity, Mukherjee's sense of narrative. Each text constitutes its reader as responsive; Trinh's film is again a case in point, but Ondaatje and Kingston consult their families, and Blaise and Mukherjee co-respond in recognition of mutual bond and mutual displacement. Rodriguez and Lim, whose voices are the most public among this particular collection of texts, perhaps not least because both find some resting ground in the United States, some clarity about the constituency they address, still position themselves most articulately in relation to a range of liminalities.

If interaction between speaker and spoken, between individual and culture, and between narrator and correspondent contributes to dialogic discourses in these autobiographies, their distinctive contribution to generic innovation has to be the narrative focus on space rather than time. Certainly the visual arts and other narratives of crisis share this preference for space over time. Comics, film, and photography deploy visual and spatial relations to provide subjective depth without reference to any timeline.[33] In distinctly bitter circumstances, Breytenbach evolves a spatial narrative to articulate his crisis. Diasporic space, however, invites the imagination to work with memory and desire and to create maps of identity that shift in kind and are both mythical and precise, enabling the journeys of self-invention to move among multiple cultures without abandoning one place for another. This tension of competing possibilities lies outside the scope of linear narrative or memory related in linear terms. Eakin's convincing analysis of narrative in the service of identity (1999) therefore suggests that the autobiographer of diaspora is more concerned with the situation than with the self. Moving among the graves and ghosts of ancestors, the lost and incomprehensible stories, and the balancing act of cross-cultural marriages and families, autobiographers of diaspora privilege space over time in order to retain all their possibilities. Space, as realized in these narratives, enables plural identities to coexist simultaneously despite their being contra-dictory.

5

Refractions of Mirror Talk, or the Historian in Hell

The Case of Primo Levi

In a memorable phrase, Irving Howe has referred to survivors of the Nazi Holocaust as "captives of history" (14); they are the necessary scribes for this caesura in civilization. No experience in Western history has been more important to record than that of the death camps of the Third Reich, and none has presented its chroniclers with more difficulty. Apart from the pain of remembering such experience, and the burden of responsibility to all who did not survive, Holocaust autobiographers risk intense solipsism. They deal, after all, with their own anonymity in crowds of tens of thousands, with surreal situations for which no comparison exists, with experience that is often incredible for narrators to recall and that challenges the imaginative range of readers who were never there. Their witness, of course, contributes significantly to the historical knowledge that Nazi strategists aimed to suppress. Whereas other histories can map the wider picture of this assault upon humanity, survivors alone can vouch for the nature and extent of their personal devastation. Again and again in personal accounts of incarceration in the death camps, this devastation afflicts the whole person. So extreme was the suffering, so unremitting the personal danger, so absolute the disconnection from sustaining relationships that survivors describe radical isolation and a void in their selves, a black hole from which they derive no sense of historical authority. Their histories, accordingly, are intense but necessarily impressionistic and limited in scope.

Readers of a later generation glean what is possible from remnants and signs: from the camps that are now museums,[1] from photographs, film footage, drawings, and writings in various genres. These materials, however, can signify in two directions simultaneously. As used by the oppressor, language and image become significant means for destroying humanity both before and as human beings are destroyed; as used by the survivor, these same signs can reconstitute the humanity and the human being that were intended for destruction. Focusing on language in this chapter, I propose to examine some of the strategies common to Holocaust autobiography as survivors take the tools once misused for oppression into their own hands. In the process, I suggest that Primo Levi's ingeniously multiple interactions—personal, linguistic, narrative, and generic—amount to strategies for resisting extinction both in life and in the text. Levi's writings clearly demonstrate the connections between an assault on language and an assault upon humanity. In their exploration of moral chaos they expose satisfaction or meaning as chimerical yet, in more personal terms, they also enable this survivor to reconstitute in language the multifaceted human being that the fascists set out to destroy.

I know of no other literature in which the gap between a fact and its narration has proved so problematic. The first and ongoing failure for the autobiographer is that of language; as it tries to approach the atrocity of the Nazi genocide, language falters, reveals its inadequacy. The very fact of so much suffering and death becomes radically incommunicable; for the survivor, the event seems to burst the constraints of language. What needs to be said seems to exaggerate and so to devalue words or distort meaning. Adam Epstein provides a clear example: "As the word 'genocide' became debased, the term 'holocaust' was adapted in the mid-sixties to try to explain the uniqueness of the Jewish fate." Not only, however, does "holocaust" suggest a purposefully religious sacrifice, it becomes familiar in this new context and "trivialises to an even greater degree the atrocity it purports to describe" (37–38). Levi himself avoided the term "holocaust"; wishing to "erect a dike" in the fatal slide of the imagination "toward simplification and stereotype," he uses only the word "Lager," or prison camp (1989a, 157). George Steiner has identified complex disturbances to a writer's sense of responsible authority when distinctions between the imaginary and the literal collapse. "It is one of the daemonic attributes of Nazism (as of sadistic literature)," he writes, "to taint those who accept its imaginings as literally feasible—even when they reject them with loathing—with an element of self-doubt and unbalance" (159). Both Nazism and survivor witness depend on language for literal information and for meaning, which is culture-bound; if the Nazis employed one set of meanings, what can survivors make of the same words? Or how take the same information and translate it back into human terms? If the SS counted their human cargo as *Stücke*, pieces, how does the autobiographer reintroduce the notion of *Menschen*, or human beings?

At the apparently simplest level, then, language handicaps the autobiographer. Holocaust autobiographers resort to a number of common strategies with varying degrees of effectiveness. They depend heavily on synecdoche, a trope that allows the specific experience to represent a much wider phenomenon, often extending its use to epiphanic metaphor. Elie Wiesel's character, Moché the Beadle, is one example, as is his painful rendition of the child on the gallows, or his image of the violin smashed in the snow. Viktor Frankl connects his subjective experience of hope with his vision of a light "in a distant farmhouse, which stood on the horizon as if painted there, in the midst of the miserable gray of a dawning morning in Bavaria '*Et lux in tenebris lucet*' — and the light shineth in the darkness" (64). Similarly, the bread that is shared near the end of *If This Is a Man* specifically represents the return of desperate people to some remembered state of community, "the first human gesture that occurred among us" (Levi 1979, 166). For Levi, precise rendition of particular moments serves this synecdochic purpose, but he also works repeatedly with individual characters. He claims that his curiosity as a scientist has meant he is never "indifferent to the individual that chance brings before me. They are human beings but also 'samples,' specimens in a sealed envelope to be identified, analyzed, and weighed . . . food for my curiosity" (1989a, 141). His writings are studded with memorable characters who also, in many instances, represent a type or a common response to shared or recurring circumstances.

For the most part, however, even the most eloquent find that language fails them. Charlotte Delbo, able to conjure up specific and terrible details of physical suffering, is defeated by shoes: "No description can give an idea of the shoes that we had" (86). Fabio Girelli-Carasi has explored what he calls the "Anti-linguistic Nature of the Lager [or camp]," and he refers to the privative prefixes that define the actual only in terms of negatives: the unspeakable, the incredible, the inhuman, and so on (40). Epstein uses the term "negative understanding," suggesting that description "depends on a negative comparison with this world for its representation" (37). Careful use of literary tropes and the failure of positive comparisons both point to the gap, so problematic for survivors, between language literal or metaphoric and the reality of their incomprehensible experience. Indeed, this apparently insurmountable gap suggests the weighty connections between vocabularies and their culturally assigned meanings, and the confounding of such meanings by abuse both to people and to words.

PROCESSES OF DEMOLITION:
LANGUAGE IN CONTROL OF MEANING

The SS claimed that no story of the Lagers would survive because it would rest only with the Nazis to tell. One serious difficulty for survivors is the possibility that the SS were right. At one level, no witnesses were expected to survive. At another, the SS had taken control of the language uses on which any witness would depend. Levi makes what he calls "an obvious observation that where violence is inflicted on man it is also inflicted on language" (1989a, 97). If the Third Reich both found and created the language "to express," as Levi puts it, "this offence, the demolition of a man" (1979, 32), then, in Gail Gilliland's words, "Levi can only . . . retain his integrity as a human being by continuing, within the written text, to insist that the Lager is unspeakable, beyond description. . . . [H]e cannot allow this expressibility to take place in his text" (203). He cannot admit what Steiner so colorfully calls "the habits of hell into his syntax" (100), the distortions that alter meaning at the profoundest level of words like good and evil, just and unjust, man and non-man (Levi 1979, 92).

Levi's writings elaborate the many and significant connections between language and life: first, because he demonstrates the profound damage caused by language that is stripped of human and imaginative references; and second, because his narrator resists the torpor that this damage includes in order to recreate human interaction. Levi suggests that the notion of Aryan purity, creating a Germanic Self and an alien Other, is essentially monologic, allowing for only one voice. Denying plurality, this monologism led to the Lager, whose main function was the elimination of the alien Other. This monologic notion of Aryan purity had a lasting effect on particular vocabularies, radically disconnected language and meaning, and destroyed millions of individual people. Indeed, it began with the burning of books, went on to the burning of synagogues, and concluded with the burning of human beings. The people of the book were destroyed, from word to body, in a process that Alvin H. Rosenfeld, borrowing from Wiesel, calls a double dying: the dying not just of human beings but of the very idea of human beings.

This double process, manifest in the commodification of human bodies and body parts, finds expression in the reductively literal nature of Nazi-Deutsch. Brutal atrocities were enabled by brutally literal language that collapsed the imaginative space between sign and referent, admitting neither question nor causal connections nor any vestige of meaning. Levi refers to this warped and literal language as the *Lager-jargon*. *Häftlinge*, or prisoners, for example, did not eat like men but fed like beasts; the word was *fressen*, not *essen*, "devour," not "eat." Use of the crude term *krepieren*, "to croak," meant their deaths were also as brutal or inconsequential as those of animals. Pervasive, apparently, in all the camps was the term *Muselmann*, or "Muslim," an oddly non-literal term to describe the Jew who had lost the will to resist fate and was therefore sure to die soon. A similar linguistic twist substituted the effect for the literal fact when the rubber truncheon, for example, became known as *der Dolmetscher*, the interpreter. "If anyone hesitated," Levi writes, "(everyone hesitated because they did not understand and were terrorized) the blows fell, and it was obvious that they were a variant of the same language. . . . [T]here was no substantial difference between a scream and a punch" (1989a, 91). Ironically, in the total separation of the Lager from any civilizing human context, *Morgen früh*, tomorrow morning early, was camp slang for "never" — a new day that may not be lived and that certainly will not mean a new beginning.

Demolition of meaning as of human beings was not only brutal and direct but also insidious and pragmatic. The poison of fascist ideology, as pervasive in tone of voice as in thought-suppressing slogans and clichés, seeped into the languages of Eastern Europe that in turn loaned vocabulary to the *Lagerjargon*. It was also manifest, of course, in the behavior of civilian informers and of the separate national police forces, of Jewish police in the ghettos, and of Kapos in the camps. It bespoke alignment with power and the literal erasure of alternatives. Emmanuel Ringelblum's terrible anecdote of the little child in the ghetto makes this point with great poignancy. The eight-year-old goes mad, in his telling, screaming repeatedly: "I want to steal, I want to rob, I want to eat, I want to be a German" (39). All of Levi's writings pay sensitive attention to meaning, translation, and subtle nuances of interpretation in several languages. His use of the German language, however, is as uncompromising as the child's vision of German identity. In *If This Is a Man*, in particular, Levi's use of German literalizes the power and survival that this young child understood as fact. Levi's text is "intensely aware," as Epstein puts it, "of how the German of the camp deprives language of its meaning" not only because it distorts experience but also, one might add, because it erases alternative languages and peoples (33).

Steiner once argued that the uses and effects of this tainted and debased language had damaged German irreparably. He modified this position in his study of Günter Grass, but he questions, for example, whether one can use the word *spritzen* in a sane way after it has signified the "spurting" of Jewish blood from knife points (99). Levi's German friend, Mrs. Hety S. of Wiesbaden, tells him long after the war: "[F]or many among us words like 'Germany' and 'Fatherland' have forever lost the meaning they once had: the concept of the 'Fatherland' has been obliterated for us" (1989a, 191). From the notorious sign *Arbeit macht frei*, to the daily use of words that reversed previous experience of meaning, new vocabularies emerged that confounded traditional understanding.[2] In the translation of Oswiecim to Auschwitz, for example, the Reich created a word that means a previously unimaginable atrocity. Specific words such as *volkisch* or *fanatisch* remain unusable. Certainly, Hans Mayer, who changed his name to Jean Améry, felt compelled to abandon his native language altogether. "Améry-Mayer also affirms that he suffered from the mutilation of the language . . . in a way . . . that was spiritual rather than material. He suffered from it *because* German was his language, because he was a philologist who loved his language, just as a sculptor would suffer at seeing one of his statues befouled or mutilated. . . . [I]t was a barbaric jargon that . . . scorched his mouth when he tried to speak it" (Levi 1989a, 135).[3]

The suppression by Nazi-Deutsch of all other forms of language affected life and death. Recognition of basic information, for example, connects dramatically with survival. Levi writes that almost all the Italians died within the first two weeks because they did not understand German and therefore could take no measures, such as prompt obedience, to protect themselves (1989a, 93). Jean Samuel, who appears in *If This Is a Man* as "il Pikolo del Kommando 98," attributes his own survival to his knowledge of German, saying "[he] could understand all the orders that were barked at us constantly" (Tarrow 1994, 102). Levi worked at his German. "I soon understood that my extremely meager *Wortschatz* had become an essential factor of survival. *Wortschatz* means 'lexical patrimony,' but, literally, 'treasure of words'; never was a term more appropriate. Knowing German meant life" (1989a, 95). Language used as Nazi-Deutsch was used means suppression of the very idea of humanity insofar as suppression of unauthorized language involves suppression of whole categories of thought. Levi makes this clear when he understands his chemistry test in German but fails to know how to take leave of his examiner. Elsewhere he writes of the risks of not sharing a common language: "[I]f you don't find anyone, your

tongue dries up in a few days, and your thought with it" (1989a, 93).
Resisting this monologic oppression is also key to survival, and Levi's
work includes wonderful stories of prayer, song, and conversation
achieved beyond the limits of the possible and enjoyed for their power
to renew life. Years later, he claims to remember one Hungarian song
he traded for a song in Italian because those few moments of exchange
were moments of such intense joy (Thomson, 16).

Just as individual words acquire new meanings, so meanings themselves become inconceivable or hazardous to try to conceive. For example, Levi writes of his arrival at Auschwitz in a convoy of Italian Jews in
February 1943. Showered and shaved, they were transformed from
individual men to anonymous, interchangeable *Häftlinge*. "When we
finish, everyone remains in his own corner and we do not dare lift our
eyes to look at one another. There is nowhere to look in a mirror, but
our appearance stands in front of us, reflected in a hundred livid faces,
in a hundred miserable and sordid puppets. . . . Then for the first time
we became aware that our language lacks words to express this offence,
the demolition of a man" (1979, 32). Suffering in his own person the
"demolition of a man," and seeing this demolition replicated all around
him, Levi identifies the body as the site of presence and language as
its necessary fabricator. His use of the present tense, here and often
throughout his work, implicates the reader in an immediate predicament, imitates the activity of precise recall, and establishes the use of
language for reconstitution of the self.

Just as the whole convoy mirrors Levi's personal appearance, so
other documents of this period echo particular features of his narrative
and verify the individual as simultaneously unique and symbolic. Recording his experience of the Warsaw Ghetto, for example, Chaim A.
Kaplan, in a diary note for November 18, 1939, makes a similar comment about Jews being ashamed to look at each other. Truly, they are
cattle in the eyes of the Nazis, and have now reached the desperate stage
of looking on themselves as inferior beings, lacking God's image (74).
Not being a religious man, Levi lacks the spiritual affirmation that
might counter the Nazi contempt, but he shares Kaplan's sense of the
hazard to the whole person of violence inflicted on the body.[4]

Levi's convoy is reduced to naked bodies with shaved heads, suffering the most basic deprivations of food and drink, and stamped with
numbers that replace their names. (Wiesel describes himself as becoming just a body: "Perhaps less than that even: a starved stomach. The
stomach alone was aware of the passage of time" [60].) The literal
details of Holocaust autobiographies begin with such violent uproot-

ings and dislocations, distortions of time, forceful separations from all the equipment required for self-identification — friends, personal belongings, clothes, hair, names — and an intense focus on physical needs. Then they seek through recall of these specific deprivations to re(dis)cover and re(in)state an original version of the self. Clearly, experience and memory of the concentration camp are so profound as to affect even the likelihood of self-re-cognition. Levi's refractions of narrative and tone provide an ironic perspective that prevents the possibility of recognition becoming singular.

These hollow men, "reduced to suffering and needs" (1979, 33), have escaped the first selection for the gas chambers but run the risk of repeated selections. Levi tells of his admission to the infirmary: "The nurse points to my ribs to show the other, as if I was a corpse in an anatomy class: he alludes to my eyelids and my swollen cheeks and my thin neck, he stoops to press on my tibia with his thumb, and shows the other the deep impression that his finger leaves in the pale flesh, as if it was wax. . . . He turns to me, and in near-German, charitably, tells me the conclusion: '*Du Jude, kaputt. Du schnell Krematorium fertig.*' (You, Jew, finished. You soon ready for crematorium)" (1979, 55). But this most common and most feared conclusion is, in Levi's case, not conclusive. His narrative recreates the instability of experience and of meaning in the Lager, demonstrating at the same time the stresses between that harsh reality and the uses of language that can recast it in communicable form.

New arrivals were bewildered by the violence of incomprehensible orders and appalled by the crowded and unsanitary conditions of huts and lavatories. Over time, hard labor and the elements also became their enemies. Plagued by scabies and lice, they succumbed to infected sores and wounds, the lack of food, drink, and adequate clothing, and died from their wounds, from starvation, or from scarlet fever, diphtheria, or typhus. Of the 650 people crowded into the train with Levi at Fossoli (some were elderly people from geriatric wards, and some were children), 525 were sent to the gas chambers on arriving at Auschwitz. Of the 125 who were retained for hard labor, only three returned home at the end of the war.

Levi attributes full survival, "without renunciation of any part of one's own moral world . . . only to very few superior individuals, made of the stuff of martyrs and saints" (1979, 98). For most, physical suffering and psychological trauma disconnect them from their own previous humanity and from the sufferings of those around them. Both Wiesel and Isabella Leitner describe the salvation that comes from remaining connected to family and the intense burden of that connection. From inside the Warsaw Ghetto, Ringelblum lists appalling atrocities and comments sadly: "There is an evident and terrible slackening of the sentiment of compassion" (225). Frankl describes the removal of a corpse: "[F]irst the feet, then the trunk, and finally—with an uncanny rattling noise—the head . . . bumped up the two steps. . . . The corpse . . . stared at me with glazed eyes. Two hours before I had spoken to that man. Now I continued sipping my soup. If my lack of emotion had not surprised me from the standpoint of professional interest, I would not remember this incident now, because there was so little feeling involved in it" (34–35). Similarly, Levi recounts the two-day-long dying of Sómogyi, an Hungarian chemist suffering from typhus and scarlet fever. Dying in the night, he hurls himself to the ground: "I heard the thud of his knees, of his hips, of his shoulders, of his head. . . . On the floor, the shameful wreck of skin and bones, the Sómogyi thing" (1979, 178). Both Frankl and Levi illustrate their emotional exhaustion in terms of previous and subsequent expectations, the extreme being most clearly visible in terms of its opposite. Levi also demonstrates his own implication in Sómogyi's death. Surprised by the arrival of the Russians, while carrying Sómogyi outside, Levi "overturned the stretcher on the grey snow" (1979, 178). The "very light" body and its sick and starving bearer experience different stages of the same assault upon humanity.

Inured to suffering and death, the survivor has escaped only by chance and is burdened with the responsibility of having done so. His life is most visible in terms of multiple deaths now realized in all their magnitude. He fears that his life continues at the expense of others, that his capacity to survive cost others their lives. Haunted by the dead, the survivor cannot return fully to the world of the living. His task, to represent the dead, is complicated, moreover, by the likelihood that the dead in fact represent him. In a poem titled "The Survivor," dated February 4, 1984, Levi's speaker addresses his ghosts:

> Stand back, leave me alone, submerged people,[5]
> Go away, I haven't dispossessed anyone,
> Haven't usurped anyone's bread.
> No one died in my place. No one.
> Go back into your mist.
> It's not my fault if I live and breathe,
> Eat, drink, sleep and put on clothes.
> (1992, 64)

For a writer whose prose is so eminently reasonable, poetry becomes the medium for the enactment of nightmare and the surreal. As just one of Levi's genres, poetry also suggests his multiple cultural moorings and their varied capacity to present nuggets of experience. Mirna Cicioni, reading another poem that I shall explore later in this discussion, remarks on his continuous reference to Dante. Here, Cicioni suggests that the last line of the poem recontextualizes the last lines of Canto 33 of the *Inferno*. Where Dante describes one sinner (Frate Alberigo) who, for his wicked deeds, has his soul already awash in Cocytus though his body still dwells on earth, Levi suggests by association that the survivor, too, is actually in hell though his body goes through the motions of everyday living (132–33).[6]

Reducing both men and language to mere skeletons, the SS severely curtailed opportunities for independent behavior or insurrection. The role of dialogue in general and of questioning in particular disappears. Indeed, the reality-testing function of language has been eliminated, or rendered superfluous. Particular facts present in their own monolithic existence an absolute obstacle to comprehension of any meaning beyond the factual. Girelli-Carasi points to the incident when Levi, reaching for an icicle to suck, has it snatched from his hand by a passing guard and asks "'Warum?'" or "why?" The guard's answer expresses the monologic character of Auschwitz: "'*Hier ist kein warum* [here there is no why]'" (1979, 35). Recreating the situation that brooks no question, Levi builds a supple dialogue between then and now, between two men who could not talk, between writer remembering and reader needing to comprehend. He engages in continuous discussion of crucial distinctions. Of one detail, an incident in which the Kapo "slammed [him] to the ground with a violent slap," Levi writes: "But there: as I write this sentence today, and as I am in the act of typing the word 'slap,' I realize that I am lying, or at least transmitting biased emotions and information to the reader. Eddy was not a brute" (1987, 30–31). The languages in which the one would have told the other that both their lives were in danger were useless, "out of tune, and much too roundabout. For this very reason, punches and slaps passed among us as daily language, and we soon learned to distinguish meaningful blows from the others inflicted out of savagery, to create pain and humiliation, and which often resulted in death" (1987, 30–31). So incredible is the difference between the writer's subject position, both before and after the Lager, and the submissive object of abuse in the camp that Levi repeatedly discusses his own uncertainty that what he has actually experienced could indeed have happened—his previous life when he was in the Lager and the Lager itself after his return to Italy. So total was the disconnection between one part of his life and the other, between incontrovertible event and the habit of meditation, and so apparently unbridgeable in terms of language.

What Lawrence Langer has called "the language of atrocity" disintegrates into blows, into abuse both physical and verbal, and into signs with no civilized referents. Levi recognizes the arbitrary nature of all signs and the non-referential nature of all language, and so demonstrates both the humanly degrading nature of these signs and the human activity of interpreting them. They form, after all, just part of the Babel problem for which the narrator is interpreter. Babel, in this sense, means the radical disconnection between words and the meaning they convey, which depends on cultural context. So Levi studies the signs of his new context not for explanation, since he quickly gives up on questions, but in order to understand how they construct the meanings that matter to his survival. He recognizes the *Muselmann* Null Achtzehn, a non-man with no life, as "a sign from which language has been expelled" (Girelli-Carasi, 51). He comes to understand physical blows as a comprehensible language. He has to work to understand the role of the tattoo.

A brutal sign of separation from humanity, and particularly offensive to Jews, to whom such branding is forbidden by religious law,[7] the tattoo is not unreadable. These numbers under the skin conveyed a "funereal science" to the old-timers: "[T]he period of entry into the camp, the convoy of which one formed a part, and consequently the nationality. Everyone will treat with respect the numbers from 30,000 to 80,000: there are only a few hundred left and they represented the few survivals from the Polish ghettos. It is as well to watch out in commercial dealing with a 116,000 or a 117,000: they now number only about forty, but they represent the Greeks of Salonica, so take care that they do not pull the wool over your eyes. As for the high numbers they carry an essentially comic air about them, like the words 'freshman' or 'conscript' in ordinary life" (1979, 34). This visible branding serves a cultural purpose within the camp, distinguishing among men whose appearance is otherwise uniform. But it is not only visible; Levi describes internalizing, ironically, not his own number but that of his predecessor in the queue for soup: "a tangle of sounds that ended harmoniously, like the indecipherable counting jingles of children, in something like 'stergishi steri' (today I know that these two words mean 'forty-four')" (1989a, 94). The Polish sounds for numbers branded on an unknown man ahead of him came to mean "soup" for the survivor; reading and translating signs takes many forms so that their referents become means for survival in the face of destruction.

Confused by indirect references to the dangers they all run, Levi receives a lesson about the tattoo numbers when he spends time in the infirmary. Working from Levi's own number, 174517, Schmulek struggles to make himself understood in Yiddish ("I understand him with difficulty, only because he wants to be understood");[8] if only about 30,000 *Häftlinge* currently live in the camps, why is Levi's own recent number so high? "*Wo sind die Andere?* Where are the others?'" (1979, 58). Levi is unable to imagine. Schmulek's answer, like so many signs in the Lager, occurs not in words but in literal fact: in this case, his own selection for the gas. "In [a] discreet and composed manner, without display or anger, massacre moves through the huts . . . every day, touching here and there. When Schmulek left, he gave me his spoon and knife" (1979, 59). The literal experience conveys unequivocal meaning where language had allowed the imagination to be evasive.

Physical suffering and death are absolutely literal; "'*Du Jude, kaputt. Du schnell Krematorium fertig*'" is no figure of speech. Names, which connote family, sex, and cultural context, are replaced by numbers that are inseparable from the body and essentially associated with that body's durability. So, too, Babel is a literal fact even though it also connotes the judgment of God and the confounding of human communication. Babel signifies the brute power of the Nazi forces and the incomprehensibility of Auschwitz. The Carbide Tower in the middle of the Lager, erected by the inmates, is the new tower of Babel over which hangs a curse "not transcendent and divine, but inherent and historical" (1979, 79). Built with "*Ziegel, briques, tegula, cegli, kamenny, mattoni, téglak*, and . . . cemented by hate," this "insolent building [is] based on the confusion of languages and erected in defiance of heaven like a stone oath" (1979, 79). The prisoners call it *Babelturm, Bobelturm*, symbol of the insane dream of the Nazi Self and its domination over the nonhuman laboring Other. Using the languages that have been so profoundly controlled, working precisely with his doubts about meaning, the survivor's task is to reconstruct a multifaceted presence.

FROM DEMOLITION TO RECONSTRUCTION

From that Babel has emerged the postwar labor of reconstruction, in various forms of autobiography, of sane and recognizable selves defined in many languages and resistant to the monolithic language of demolition. To reconnect body and soul, to release himself from the past and claim the future, Levi turned to writing. In "Chromium," in *The Periodic Table*, Levi describes the "things [he] had seen and suffered . . . burning inside of [him]; [he] felt closer to the dead than the living and felt guilty at being a man, because men had built Auschwitz, and Auschwitz had gulped down millions of human beings" (1985, 151). Survival, accordingly, concerns the body and the mind and a coherent sense of moral integrity. Writing, which began as an urgent purification, became an exercise in reintegration. For nearly forty years, Levi explored the central components of his Lager experience: the possibilities that constitute a man, the nature of serious threats to his integrity, and the means by which he can reconstitute himself.[9] He does not allow atrocity to speak for itself but invariably contextualizes brutal experience in his consideration of human nature, as manifested in specific situations, and of his own ability, in particular, to resist the annihilating consciousness of Nazi officialdom. Recognizing his experience of Lager atrocities as fundamental to his life and his writing (1984, 13), Levi repeatedly and consciously combined life and text in his understanding of himself.

What Levi does is distinctive in my experience of Holocaust autobiography. He insists on language as a tool for comprehension not only by telling his story, as so many do, but by telling it in terms of multiple layers of dialogue. He counters the monologism of the Lager with the polyphony of his texts. He includes, for example, the cacophony of Babel in order to demonstrate the complete breakdown in ordinary communication, the confusions of cause and effect, the substitutions for civilized signifiers and referents — all the processes for the demolition of human beings. In his using, however, even Babel gives voice to the silenced multitudes and produces extraordinary moments of human interaction, reminders and restorers of what a man is.

For example, Levi tells the story of his exchange with the *Zugang*, the newcomer, Kraus from Hungary (1979, 138–41). Kraus, clumsy and incapable of walking in line, works too fast and apologizes in "a miserable German" for his mistakes. Levi, the seasoned inmate, is impatient: "[H]e has not yet understood where we are, I must say the Hungarians are really a most singular people" (1979, 140). About to reprimand Kraus, Levi suddenly sees the eyes of the man behind the glasses, a transforming experience that removes them both from the context of the Lager. In "bad German, but slowly, separating the words, making sure after each sentence that [Kraus] had understood," Levi begins inventing a dream he has had; Kraus had visited him in

Italy, bringing a large loaf of warm bread, and had been welcomed into the Levi household. Kraus's emotional, voluble response to this dream "in a flood of outlandish Magyar words" has the interesting effect of closing down the narrator's own emotions, possibly indicating his own strategies for survival at the time. "Poor silly Kraus," he says, does not know the story is not true; he is the foolish type that cannot survive long.

During the telling of the dream, however, both men are involved in an intense exchange that incorporates the dream of comfort within the nightmare of the Lager. By home in Italy, Kraus assumes Naples, and Levi accepts Naples because "this is hardly the time to quibble." Within the dream, furthermore, both men are wet, as now, at work in the rain and the mud, both the man who arrives from outside and the man who welcomes him in. Both enjoy the wonderful warmth that enables them to dry. Kraus's interjections in the narrative indicate the difficulty both men experienced of understanding German and form Kraus's own contribution to the dream that translated them into visitor and host, from Budapest to Naples. Clearly, Levi, "explain[ing] to his parents who [Kraus] was," explained not the clumsy *Zugang* struggling through the mud but the man Kraus behind the eyes. To conclude the exchange by suggesting that nothing is real "except the hunger inside and the cold and the rain around" is to frame in its context of exhaustion and despair a warm moment of exchange that roused both men to life.

Levi's decision to build layers of interaction into his narratives is both resourceful and explanatory, perhaps, of his exceptional power. Working in poetry continuously after his return home, Levi went on to produce two central autobiographical accounts, then essays, short stories, a novel, and that magical amalgam of genres and languages, *The Periodic Table*, in which chemistry provides the linguistic, imaginative, and interpretive tools for extended meditations on family history, Jewish identity, and the Holocaust. These works in different genres intersect like pieces of a puzzle. They reproduce the same episodes from different but overlapping perspectives. Each one is independent but together they compose a conversation of voices. Levi was closely involved with the translation of his works but unable in every instance to protect the subtlety of his Italian expression even in the titles that foreign publishers assigned to his works.[10] It is necessary but also appropriate, therefore, that the texts discussed here can be considered only in translation. Given their subject matter, they already incorporate vivid semantic fragments from several languages. The *Lagerjargon* to which so many survivors refer, this "new, harsh language," provides their imaginative context. Reading Levi on the subject of Auschwitz is, accordingly, a matter of moving among genres, among languages, and among varying intentions and interpretations that originate in the texts themselves and contribute to Levi's particular variants on mirror talk.

Levi creates multiple versions of self and others with deliberate mirroring techniques; outrage, suffering, and resistance take no single form and are best apprehended from multiple angles of sight, of language, and of interpretation. Levi's first deliberate interaction, indeed, takes place between the event, "a too ferocious reality" (1989a, 143), and the problems of its narration. Many Holocaust autobiographers refer to the ghetto, the trains, the camps, and the forced evacuation marches as versions of hell but have difficulties conveying what hell means. Quite apart from the conventional understanding of hell as part of a moral universe, since they experienced pervasive moral chaos, survivors themselves find their own stories incredible and fear not being heard, understood, or believed.[11] They suffered a common dream in the Lager of telling their stories to people who did not listen or did not understand (Levi 1979, 66). Taking a chemistry exam for special work within the Lager, Levi reports having "the definite sensation of not being believed, of not even believing . . . myself" (1979, 112). In fact, "[t]oday, at this very moment, as I sit writing at a table, I myself am not convinced that these things really happened" (1979, 109). "I have often been reproached for remaining silent," says Levi's friend Jean Samuel, "but the words wouldn't come. And who would have believed me?" (Tarrow 1994, 106). Radically dispossessed of reference and meaning, Holocaust survivors find words inadequate. Many survivors also refer to the experience of being invisible as human beings to the authorities that controlled their daily lives and surviving only as ghosts, invisible also in the realities to which they return, and therefore ineffectual.[12] In particular, no one of the genres of history-making, from chronicle to poetry to high drama, can meet the narrative needs of this experience. Levi refers to the "essential inadequacy of documentary evidence" and the need for dramatist or poet to convey the depth of such characters as Hitler, Himmler, or Goebbels (1987, 99–100). Kaplan asks who will immortalize extreme and particular abuses, the troubles of the ghetto, feeling that newspaper reports cannot be equivalent to religious poetry (79). By November 19, 1940, however, he writes: "If it were said that the sun has darkened for us at noon it would not be merely a metaphor" (225).[13]

Sharing such trauma with his fellow survivors, Levi meets these difficulties of narration by voicing a multifaceted antiphon to Nazi monologism, with two particular results. Not only does he diminish the controlling Nazi perspective to make room for others, but he also defers the possibility of explanation through a continuous activity of investigation, resisting thereby any chance of simply replacing the enemy voice with his own. Understanding, for Levi, is not reached by opposing polarities but by a process like chemical analysis — serious and honest attention to material that may or may not yield up its secret. Repeatedly, therefore, Levi's writings engage in varieties of dialogue that position the hostile and overwhelming force of Nazi language and action as just one among many voices for the man who does not succumb. Levi creates dialogues among languages, to which he was keenly sensitive: dialogues within language about the failure of language to make sense of atrocity; dialogues about interpretation and meaning in situations where language is debased; and dialogues of identity for Levi himself — as a chemist, a detective in the material world; as a Jew, despite his lack of faith; as an Italian, specifically through his reliance on Dante; and, with increasing certainty, as a writer, committed to the multiple tasks of translating experience into language.

Repeatedly, Levi stresses the need to be clear. Impatient with both Philip Toynbee and George Steiner for suggesting that syntax, language, and reason all fail this genocide, Levi told Ian Thomson: "I believe it is the task of every writer to describe what he sees in plain language" (Thomson, 18). Plain language, however, is quite complex. His own Holocaust writing stays close to literal information but parodies in its supple inflections the literal nature of Nazi-Deutsch.[14] Fully aware that autobiography is not an autonomous work of art but is securely grounded in empirical reality, Levi uses the language of chemistry as his cognitive paradigm, the language evolved for investigation of the material world.[15]

Clarity or plain language therefore involves a complex recognition that one's verbal inventory is a raw and incomplete language, that imaginative engagement with etymologies reveals layers of possible meaning, and that typographical convenience may efface distinctions between variable and imprecise meanings (1989a, 100–103). "Now," he writes, connecting chemistry with writing, "my trade is a different one, it is the trade of words, chosen, weighed, fitted into a pattern with patience and caution" (1989b, 106). Drawing the same analogy between chemistry and writing in *The Periodic Table*, Levi refers to his chemistry as "a mess compounded of stenches, explosions, and small futile mysteries" in which one learns to "distrust the almost-the-same . . . the practically identical, the approximate, the or-even, all surrogates, and all patchwork. The differences can be small, but they can lead to radically different consequences, like a railroad's switchpoints; the chemist's trade consists in good part in being aware of these differences, knowing them close up, and foreseeing their effects. And not only the chemist's trade" (1985, 60). Working, then, with the raw material of experience that challenges both survival and understanding, Levi's clarity of language begins with precision and an imaginative sense of resonance to achieve its single end, which is communication. In this instance more urgently than in most, responsible communication is a political act both personal and far-reaching. "By attempting to give language its communicative value," Epstein suggests, "Levi is committing an anti-fascist act" (38). He is also reconstituting the personal perception that was effectively silenced and erased during his time in the Lager.

Urgency also takes Levi's writing beyond its grounding in the literal and into polyphonies that include faith and culture and the voices that died around him. First, his role as survivor and witness empowers this speaker with a new *Shema*; he transforms the prayer of remembrance, the cornerstone of the Jewish liturgy, into a terrible warning against readers comfortable in their homes who ignore or forget what these stories tell them.[16] "If the Lagers had lasted longer," Levi writes, "a new, harsh language would have been born" (1979, 129).[17] Even worse is the inability to speak at all. In *The Truce*, Levi tells the story of three-year-old Hurbinek, a child of Auschwitz, unable to speak: "[H]is eyes, lost in his triangular and wasted face, flashed terribly alive, full of demand, assertion, of the will to break loose, to shatter the tomb of his dumbness" (1979, 197). To tell one's story is to open dialogues among unequal forces, but to die in silence, as Hurbinek does, is to disappear.

> [T]he enemy was all around but also inside, the "we" lost its limits, the contenders were not two, one could not discern a single frontier but rather many confused, perhaps innumerable frontiers. (1989a, 38)

These dialogues begin with the common problem of stereotyping an enemy, of identifying an "other" to which the "self" is superior. In *The Truce*, Levi tells of watching an Austrian film from the First World War in a transit camp on his long journey home, and of his dismay that the

Italians were depicted as the enemy, both evil and ridiculous. "We Italians," he writes, "so little accustomed to seeing ourselves cast as the 'enemy,' odious by definition, and so dismayed at being hated by anybody, derived a complex pleasure from watching the film — a pleasure not without disquiet, a source of salutary meditations" (1979, 336– 37). He elaborates on such meditations in his preface to *If This Is a Man*: "Many people — many nations — can find themselves holding, more or less wittingly, that 'every stranger is an enemy.' For the most part this conviction lies deep down like some latent infection; it betrays itself only in random, disconnected acts, and does not lie at the base of a system of reason. But when this does come about, when the unspoken dogma becomes the major premiss in a syllogism, then, at the end of the chain, there is the Lager" (1979, 15). By identifying specific peoples as *Ausländer*, or aliens, the Nazi project of racial purification opened a monologue in which the other could not be heard.

In a late and whimsical story, "The Mirror Maker," Levi develops another aspect of this problem. Timoteo, the protagonist, comes from a long line of conventional mirror makers but is constantly experimenting with unexpected reflections. One of his inventions is a metaphysical mirror which "does not obey the law of optics but reproduces your image as it is seen by the person who stands before you." The narrator claims no originality for this idea. "Aesop had already had it, and who knows how many others before him." For the purposes of his narrative, however, "Timoteo had been the first to realize it" (1990, 49). The size of a calling card, flexible and adhesive, this Metamir attaches to the forehead and shows the self perceived as various kinds of other depending on who is doing the perceiving.[18] When the SS does the perceiving, the inmate is reduced not only from subject to object but also from visible to invisible, and is threatened with becoming a non-man. "Their life is short," Levi writes of these non-men, "but their number is endless; they, the *Muselmänner*, the drowned, form the backbone of the camp, an anonymous mass, continually renewed and always identical, of non-men who march and labour in silence, the divine spark dead within them, already too empty to really suffer. One hesitates to call them living: one hesitates to call their death death, in the face of which they have no fear, as they are too tired to understand. They crowd my memory with their faceless presences" (1979, 96). Effectively invisible and inaudible, these are the victims in whom personality has been defeated before the physical death that must inevitably follow.

Of these ghosts, Null Achtzehn, or Zero Eighteen, is both specific and symbolic and relates significantly to the narrator himself. Null

Achtzehn seems to have no name and is identified only by the last three numbers of his tattoo, 018.[19] The empty cipher precedes the 18, the *chai*, the Jewish symbol for life, to indicate that this non-man has no life. He is accordingly a dangerous partner with whom to work. Not only clumsy and unresponsive, Null Achtzehn also cannot measure his ability or his exhaustion, and he drops a beam on Levi's foot, causing a literal "impediment" that could cost Levi his life. When his wound turns out to be "a good wound," not dangerous but justifying rest, Levi rejoices with Chajim, whose name means unqualified life. "Chajim is experienced in these matters. . . . Chajim is my bed-companion, and I trust him blindly" (1979, 53). We cannot know what liberties Levi might be taking with numbers and names, but we can recognize in this story an exchange between death and life that implicates the narrator himself. Beyond the extreme issues of life and death, this narrative engages with the hazards of approximating the hollow man and with the rejoicing, even over the lesser of evils, with the man who is still very much alive.

Inserted into this story, furthermore, is a brief episode in which the narrator and Null Achtzehn, before the accident, are interrupted in their work by a goods train. To all appearances two *Muselmänner*, "bent and in rags, we wait for the wagons to pass slowly by" (1979, 49). What the narrator perceives at this point not only establishes his subject position but also connects language and storytelling with the rejoicing with Chajim. Stopped by the train, the narrator sees lettering on the wagons: "*Deutsche Reichsbahn. Deutsche Reichsbahn. S. N. C. F.* Two huge Russian goods wagons with the hammer and sickle badly rubbed off. Then, *Cavalli 8, Uomini 40, Tara, Portata*: an Italian wagon" (1979, 49). Seeing first fragments of foreign codes and then fragments of Italian, the narrator is transported into a fantasy, kissing the Italian earth "as you read in books," and telling his story, in Italian, to a woman who understands and believes and feeds him. Waking from fantasy is painful, and some ambiguity remains: does this desire to reach through words to life constitute a quality necessary for life, or is such dreaming a weakness that exposes the narrator to the accident that follows? Levi's methods of narration balance, like the beam he carries, between possibilities that he does not resolve: on the one hand, the literal — non-men ("tired beasts"), train, beam, foot — and on the other the sources of animation — words, desire, story, and recognition. Maintaining that balance, not allowing it to fall, distinguishes between one-sided, singular meaning and the continuous effort of multiple possibility.

Levi's sense of the threat to his own personality surfaces again in his shame when he stands with the crowds of *Häftlinge* at the hanging of a man who had taken part in the destruction of the Birkenau ovens. This story sets up a series of dialogues that enact the narrator's own struggle for survival. On the one hand, the narrator is thinking his own thoughts through the long, angry, and incomprehensible official speech about this man's crimes. "[P]erhaps the Germans do not understand," he thinks, "that this solitary death, this man's death which has been reserved for him, will bring him glory, not infamy." The actual question, however, "*Habt ihr verstanden?* [Have you understood?]" is asked by the raucous official who stresses ignominy here, and not glory at all. "Who answered '*Jawohl*'?" the narrator asks. Who accepts the official version? "Everybody and nobody: it was as if our cursed resignation took body by itself, as if it turned into a collective voice above our heads." By contrast, "the cry of the doomed man . . . struck the living core of man in each of us: '*Kamaraden, ich bin der Letz!*' (Comrades, I am the last one!)" (1979, 155).[20] The contrast between the raucous official and the cry of the doomed man, like the contrast between the internal and public response of the crowd, is part of the dynamics that define for the narrator himself how much ground he has lost as a man. If the last man capable of resistance has died on the gallows, the destruction of the many is apparent in the apathy of the masses.[21] To hear all these voices is to refuse both the official version of this experience and the numb apathy with which it is received, and to ensure that the telling is not singular.

Apart from such episodes of internal and narrative dialogue, Levi's writings repeatedly seek to reconstitute the situation and its protagonists by means of dialogue. Certainly, the reader is implicated: "Would you not do the same?" Levi asks (1979, 21). More important, perhaps, the narrator repeatedly addresses particular men who were complicit with the policies of the Third Reich.[22] As Gilliland puts it: "The dialogic text must of necessity interact so that there is both Self and Other, both speaking and hearing" (192). Silenced and erased by the authorities of the Reich, Levi positions his Self as interlocutor, and looks for a *Mitmensch*, a co-man, with whom to exchange perspectives. Jean Samuel told Susan Tarrow he thought Levi had asserted something of a balance even within the camp: "I think Primo succeeded in establishing a more or less correct relationship with a few German citizens—and I never did. . . . Primo speaks of this experience of being invisible, but I think that he nevertheless managed in some cases to interact on a human level with the Germans" (Tarrow 1994, 104).

Levi himself, on the other hand, tells the extraordinary story of the chemical examination in which he is prevented from interacting by the Kapo Alex and by Doktor Pannwitz. Even as Levi is rediscovering the "German names of compounds and laws" and recalling his status as a chemist, his Kapo expresses disgust at his jacket and beret, exclaiming, "*Was für ein Muselmann Zugang*.' What a messy recruit!" (1979, 110). The same Kapo, after the exam, having fouled his hand on a greasy cable, "wipe[d] his hand on [Levi's] shoulder, both the palm and the back of the hand to clean it" (1979, 113–14). Disgusting or non-existent to the Kapo, Levi, whose self-disgust makes professional quali-fications seem absurd (B. Sc. Turin, *summa cum laude*), is essentially invisible to his Nazi interlocutor. Levi stages an internal exchange that complicates his narration of the chemical exam, which does not itself form part of this text:

> One felt in that moment, in an immediate manner, what we all thought and said of the Germans. The brain which governed those blue eyes and those manicured hands said: "This something in front of me belongs to a species which it is obviously opportune to sup-press. In this particular case, one has to first make sure that it does not contain some utilizable element." And in my head, like seeds in an empty pumpkin: "Blue eyes and fair hair are essentially wicked. No communication possible. I am a specialist in mine chemistry. I am a specialist in organic syntheses. I am a specialist." (1979, 112)

Pannwitz may not perceive Levi, but Levi resists being unperceived. Moreover, Levi complicates the counterassertions of this non-dialogue with his suggestion that he has often thought of Pannwitz, wondering how he functioned as a man: "[A]bove all when I was once more a free man, I wanted to meet him again, not from a spirit of revenge, but merely from a personal curiosity about the human soul" (1979, 111). Excited by a projected translation of his work into German, Levi writes of Pannwitz's descendants: "Before they had been oppressors or indif-ferent spectators, now they would be readers: I would corner them, tie them before a mirror. The hour had come to settle accounts, to put the cards on the table. Above all the hour of colloquy. I was not interested in revenge. . . . My task was to understand them" (1989a, 168). Levi rejects Jean Améry's perception of him as a forgiver and reiterates his desire not to tip the balance but to restore it.[23] (This balance, so crucial to dialogue, motivates surprising reversals in many Holocaust auto-biographies. So Jack Kuper, finding two Germans frightened and caked with mud, writes: "The enemy suddenly didn't look like the enemy at all. The two Germans reminded me more of myself and my Uncle

Moishe" [178]. Similarly, Kitty Hart, foraging for food after liberation, cannot kill a family hidden in a basement. "If I committed murder," she writes, "the S.S. would have succeeded" [201].) Dialogue, like mirroring, risks collapsing distinctions into recognition and so requires self-assertion.

Levi constructs two overlapping accounts of later communication not with Pannwitz, the SS official, but with a civilian businessman who had profited from the slave labor of the camps. He appears as Mertens in "The Quiet City" (1987, 99–105), "an almost-me," Levi writes, "another myself, turned upside down" (1987, 100), and as Müller in "Vanadium" (1985, 211–23). The former story is an imaginative telling of how this good citizen could account for his collaboration during the war. "Vanadium," on the other hand, reads like a painful dialogue that troubled both participants and satisfied neither. In his postwar incarnation as an expert in varnishes, Levi is troubled by an imported resin that fails to harden when ground up with lampblack. His complaint to the German supplier produces two letters from a Doktor L. Müller, whose name, profession, and writing style all persuade Levi that this man was at the Buna factory with him. Curiously, the detail that confirms the connection is an idiosyncrasy of language; both Müllers mispronounce and, accordingly, misspell compounds with "th," using "naptenate" for "napthenate," or "Naptylamin" for "Naphthylamin." Levi remembers this Müller as an inspector at the rubber plant who had, in fact, treated him with courtesy, expressed some concern about his well-being, and authorized a pair of leather shoes for him and an extra shave each week. He had even asked Levi-the-*Häftling*, "'Why do you look so perturbed?'" "I," writes Levi, "who at that time thought in German, had said to myself, *'Der Mann hat keine Ahnung'* (This fellow hasn't got an inkling)" (1985, 214).

The story of this latter-day dialogue, involving identification, discomfort on both sides, evasions, and a planned meeting prevented by Müller's death, is a complex story through which the narrator continues to feel that Müller still has "keine Ahnung," but in which he himself is forced to imagine "a colleague varnish maker" (1985, 217). Müller hastens to resolve the international commercial dispute between their two companies, but he writes and speaks on the phone in German, whereas Levi writes "on [his] own terrain" in Italian. Their ability to recall the same man, Goldbaum, like their "shared" experience of being recognized as chemists after the war, does not enable the two men to understand the same realities.[24] Narration from experience rather than invention exposes irresolvable complexity: "[I]f this story were invented, I would have been able to introduce only two kinds of letters: a humble, warm, Christian letter, from a redeemed German; a ribald, proud, glacial letter from an obdurate Nazi. Now this story is not invented, and reality is always more complex than invention: less kempt, cruder, less rounded out. It rarely lies at one level" (1985, 218). It is also less satisfactory, one might add. For the writer who opens dialogue hoping for resolutions, only the issue of gloss or protection is resolved, only the matter of the varnish. Gilliland writes, "Language . . . is only possible between two beings whose human experiences and ethical patterns align" (206). Levi's faithfulness to the complexity of his experience prevents him from arriving at resolutions available only in imagination.

Language, the maker of meanings, becomes simultaneously polyglot, iconoclastic, and inadequate in the Lager. Through language, nonetheless, Levi constructs his own multifaceted Lager identity. He explains his survival as a matter of chance, but also of good luck. He was lucky to be selected to work in the chemistry lab. He was lucky in his friendships with Lorenzo, who brought him food and even a letter from home, and Alberto, with whom he shared everything. He was also lucky to be so ill that he was abandoned in the infirmary when Alberto and all who could walk were marched to their deaths through the snow in the German retreat from the advancing Russians. These narratives of luck all work on the principle that the inmate-survivor-narrator Levi is part of a series of relationships. Even the processes of reflection and commentary contribute to the narrative patterns of interaction — between people, between languages, between incidents — and to a balance and tension that create the illusion of immediacy, avoid singularity of perception, and arrive at no judgment or conclusion.

Similarly, Levi represents himself as a man and connects this man in the Lager with the young prewar student and the postwar chemist and writer, not in any continuous narrative but in apparently random vignettes that fit together out of sequence or in apparently causal connections through the body of his work. He is both a Jew and a nonbeliever; assimilated as Italian, his status is complicated by race; as a writer, he draws on the long traditions of the Jewish people and on his own training and avocation as a chemist. Levi presents himself only in multiple faces, not, one feels, to be elusive, though he does protect the private life of family and friends, so much as because the multiple faces are all simultaneously valid and make most sense when balanced one with another, no single one given the status of "truth."

Selected for the Lager because he was Jewish, Levi refers to himself as a "nonbeliever, and even less of a believer after the season in Auschwitz" (1989a, 82). Jean Samuel talks of Levi's intellectual honesty and courage in his relationship to Judaism. On the manuscript, for instance, of his conversation with Ferdinando Camon, at the point at which he had said " 'There is Auschwitz, so there cannot be God,' he had added in the margin: 'I don't find a solution to this dilemma. I keep looking, but I don't find it' " (Tarrow 1994, 108). In *The Periodic Table*, in which he identifies parts of his life and chemical elements each in terms of the other, Levi elaborates on his cultural Judaism. Argon, an inert gas considered rare even though it is significantly present in the air we breathe, summons up Levi's ancestors. They "arrived in Piedmont about 1500, from Spain by way of Provence. . . . introducing there the technology of making silk" (1985, 4). Their unspoken history, dependent for recognition on the wider historical map into which Levi fits them, includes the expulsion of the Jews from Spain and their insertion as a minority into an alien culture. Their particular blending of words from Hebrew roots and Piedmontese endings formed a minority jargon of some human interest, Levi suggests, "as are all languages on the frontier and in transition" (1985, 9). Speaking to Sodi in 1988, Levi agreed that he had done a mitzvah (in this case, honoring his parents) in "Argon," in his rendering of the half-Jewish, half-Piedmontese dialect that his own mother still used. He finds in this mixture "an admirable comic force, which springs from the contrast between the texture of the discourse, which is the rugged, sober, and laconic Piedmontese dialect, never written except on a bet, and the Hebrew inlay, snatched from the language of the fathers, sacred and solemn, geologic, polished smooth by the millenia like the bed of a glacier" (1985, 9). This collapsing into one of the oral vernacular and the ancient literature creates what Levi later calls the "holy tongue," marked by a distinctive vocabulary peculiar to the family histories of a small band of people.[25]

Levi's Judaism, then, belongs to a pocket of the diaspora that he describes in terms of its impurity. Whereas he had begun "within [him]self and in [his] contacts with [his] Christian friends" by considering his origin "as an almost negligible but curious fact, a small amusing anomaly, like having a crooked nose or freckles" (1985, 35), racial legislation and publication of the magazine *Defense of the Race* (1938) persuade him to value his difference. Studying zinc in the chemistry lab, Levi discovers the curious fact that zinc resists change only when it is pure. In an internal dialogue with himself, the student concludes in favor of impurity, which he now defines in chemical, historical, and personal terms as the crucial component of flexibility and change: "In order for the wheel to turn, for life to be lived, impurities are needed, and the impurities of impurities in the soil, too, as is known, if it is to be fertile. . . . Fascism does not want them, forbids them, and that's why you're not a Fascist; it wants everybody to be the same, and you are not" (1985, 34). He has "begun to be proud of being impure" (1985, 35).

While one component of Levi's self-identification originates in the family history of Piedmontese who are also Jewish, part of his self-identification, even at this early stage, stems from his own experience of fascism in Italy before deportation. In "Nickel," he tells the story of his first job in a nickel mine, an unexpected job because discrimination was by then entrenched in legislation. "I had in a drawer an illuminated parchment on which was written in elegant characters that on Primo Levi, of the Jewish race, had been conferred a degree in Chemistry, summa cum laude. It was therefore a dubious document, half glory and half derision, half absolution and half condemnation" (1985, 61). (He had been able to complete that degree only by virtue of beginning at the university before Jews were forbidden to attend.) Just as graduation and Jewishness doubled his identity, so too his brief role as a partisan added another component. When captured, however, he ate his false identification papers ("the photograph was particularly disgusting" [1985, 131]) and said only that he was a Jew. "I admitted to being a Jew: partly because I was tired, partly out of an irrational digging in of pride" (1985, 134). Levi's acceptance of Jewishness results, modestly enough, from opposition to fascism; by choosing to honor what the fascists despise, Levi takes back their perception of him for his own uses.[26]

The strand of Levi's identity that seemed at first, and while he and his family controlled it, an amusing anomaly, was gradually made central to his identity, first by the enactment of racial laws, then by the experience of Auschwitz, and finally by his realization in Eastern Europe that racial discrimination did not begin and end in the Lager, that he would continue to be constructed from the outside as a Jew. (Similarly, he tells Sodi, he became a Jewish writer by dint of being called a Jewish writer, particularly outside Italy [Sodi 1987, 360].) Levi tells the story of his arrival after the war at a small place in Poland where he, in his "zebra" clothes, was surrounded by a curious crowd. Aided by a friendly lawyer who emerged from the crowd, "the messenger, the spokesman of the civilized world, the first that I had met," Levi poured forth his story about Auschwitz, but soon "realized that the [lawyer's] translation of [his] account, although sympathetic, was not faithful"; the lawyer had described him not as an Italian Jew but as a political prisoner because "'*C'est mieux pour vous. La guerre n'est pas finie*'" (1979, 226–27). Italian Jews had been so assimilated before the fascists came to power that, as Levi told Thomson, "most of us felt more Italian than Jewish, so it was hard to come to terms with being persecuted for one's religion" (Thomson, 16). Like the tattoo on his left forearm, this branding by an apparently inescapable history, in particular by the anti-Semitism that had already given Polish Jewry so strong a sense of identity, nonetheless remained only one strand in Levi's construction of himself. When Sodi asked him on what he based the fact of "feeling Jewish," he replied: "It's a cultural fact. I can't say that Judaism has been my Pole star. I'm also a chemist and also a writer: there are lots of things that interest me and Judaism is just one of them" (Sodi 1987, 360). As with his treatment of the Lager, Levi's treatment of his Jewishness begins with fact, balances fact with the combination of circumstances that adjusts simple facticity, and then sets that nuanced fact in relation to other elements of the same whole.

Sander Gilman has described the idea of language as inherent to the Jewish self and written of the assimilated Jew after the Holocaust, "condemned to deal with the Jew in those languages in which a pejorative idea of the Jew and the Jews' language was embedded" (1989, 139). Levi's recognition of languages as central to dignity and identity both personal and cultural pervades his work, as does his repeated interest in being able to use both German and Yiddish. In a chapter called "Communicating," Levi regrets his inability to understand Yiddish, not only because it "was de facto the camp's second language," but also because he "should have understood it" (1989a, 100). Recognized for political reasons as a German dialect in World War I, Yiddish became a degenerate language in the terminology of the Third Reich. Closely related to German and yet distinguishing its speakers from the pure Aryan race, signifying both murderers and victims, "Yiddish is that tongue both unknown and known too well, the tongue of the Other and of the self" (Gilman 1989, 143). Levi applied himself to both languages at Auschwitz and afterward, refusing as incomplete the roles of self and of other.

So it is that Levi tells the story of Lilith or recasts the Hebrew *Shema* for the new and terrible purposes that Auschwitz brought about. The narrator in both cases is a Jew but not simply or wholly a Jew. He receives the Lilith story as a lesson in Judaic lore from an explicitly alter ego, a believing variant of himself. And he writes his *Shema* in terrible, secular parody of the Biblical prayer that lies at the foundation of Jewish faith and culture.[27] In both cases, the speaker's explicit recognition of his source, of his role as current narrator, and of his audience speaks of tradition and of exceptional circumstances. It also acknowledges the relations between oral and written traditions and the responsibility of the narrator — whose present narration, however, is just one among many suitable to different people and different times.

Levi receives the story of Lilith, Adam's first wife, from Tischler, who may or may not have been a carpenter, when the two men had climbed in at different ends of an iron pipe to find shelter from a downpour. They even meet partway with language, despite the fact that Tischler's first language is Yiddish, because Tischler's father had been interned in Italy during the First World War, somewhere near Turin in fact, and had passed on some Italian to his son. Tischler also shares a (surely symbolic) half-apple with the narrator, the only fruit he receives during a year of imprisonment, so that they can celebrate what turns out to be their shared age and shared birthday. But then their twin identities diverge in a very particular way. Tischler is mockingly indulgent that Levi does not know about Lilith: "[E]veryone knows that western Jews are all Epicureans — *apicorsim*, unbelievers" (1987, 40), so he prepares to tell the story. Levi recognizes the situation that is developing, typical of traditional storytelling "and a game that I liked: the dispute between the pious man and the unbeliever who is by definition ignorant. . . . I accepted my role" (1987, 40). The story of Lilith, like the dialect of Piedmontese Jews or the initial stories from the Holocaust, is oral, and in danger of being lost. Furthermore, after he has received it, this story of God's lechery and the resulting blood and trouble on earth becomes, in due order, Levi's to tell. "It is inexplicable," he writes, having completed the double narrative of the story and of the circumstances in which he received it, "that fate has chosen an unbeliever to repeat this pious and impious tale, woven of poetry, ignorance, daring acumen, and the unassuagable sadness that grows on the ruins of lost civilizations" (1987, 45).

The unbeliever, however, is also burdened with the role of prophet in dangerous times. Where the Hebrew God is recorded from the beginning as requiring His people to "Hear," the poet after Auschwitz turns to his readers, "you who live secure / In your warm houses," and demands that we consider whether the degradation of men and women in the Lager stripped them of humanity. In the sternest tones, we are enjoined to "[c]onsider that this has been." To avoid the moral delinquency of denying, forgetting, or allowing repetition, we are, as in the divine command, to bear these words within us and through every part of each waking day. Notably, the unbeliever not only depends on the terms and the rhetorical cadences of the Torah but also addresses this injunction to a world of unbelievers. He is like the Ancient Mariner, another favorite analogy for Levi, who has a terrible story to tell and is determined to be heard. In other words, Levi approaches what Gilliland has called "the language of inexpressibility" (205) by means of this serious but partial alignment with his chosen people, whose history was "so ancient, sorrowful, and strange" (1987, 82). Levi told Thomson that American Jews had been his most hostile critics, accusing him of having a "tin ear" for religion (Thomson, 17). These particular uses of his religious inheritance, however, are crucial to his moral authority as a narrator of the Holocaust and to his project of implicating the reader in the constitution of what is and what is not human. Levi rejects the possibility of God but works with the multivoiced histories that enable human beings to assess and determine their relations to each other. In the process, he responds to and corrects the Nazi perception of him as Jewish by defining his own complex perception of that significant strand of his identity, acknowledging his Judaism with a pride that avoids simplicity.

LEVI AS ITALIAN: DANTE AT AUSCHWITZ

Dante's *Inferno* contributes details, associations, and verbal resonances that are present throughout Levi's first Holocaust narrative, *If This Is a Man*, establishing Levi's credentials as an Italian beyond all the ifs and buts that attach to his Jewishness. This foundational component to his sense of himself tends to be flattened or erased in translation into English—both his immersion in Dante, and his own pellucid use of highly educated Italian (see Gunzberg, 28 n. 22, and Clive James). Thoughtful critics have struggled with the role of literature in relation to the Lager, from Adorno's repugnance at associating the Holocaust with literature, to Steiner's discussion of silence in relation to appalling truth (46–54), to Langer's suggestion that Dante spoke for an ordered and comprehensible world, which Holocaust writers could not do (17). Levi, however, absorbs the *Inferno* into his text by deliberate choice to provide another perspective, indeed plural perspectives, from which to contemplate and render the necessary narrative.

Most critics refer at least in passing to Dante's presence in Levi's work. From Levi's early suggestion that the Lager is hell, to his central chapter on the Ulysses Canto, allusions to Dante are evident even in English translation. Serious discussion of Dante's role, however, has been relatively recent, and I am indebted to three critics in particular. In 1986, Lynn Gunzberg identified Levi's need for a universal language that would restate collective understanding of unimaginable atrocities, and she suggested that parallels between the *Inferno* and *If This Is a Man* fall into specific categories: "factual analogies, spiritual analogies and the protagonists' progress" (14). When Risa Sodi's book appeared in 1990, she called Levi a Dante of our time, comparing *If This Is a Man* and *The Drowned and the Saved* with the *Inferno* for their treatment of three particular issues: justice, memory, and the morally gray or neutral zone so prevalent in both versions of hell. More recently, in 1993, Zvi Jagendorf has associated Levi's use of Dante with Benjamin's understanding of storytelling as a crucial passing on of wisdom (32). All three critics emphasize the moral weight of the Levi-Dante alliance, and the leverage that Dante provides for the telling of an impossible story.[28]

Levi works with certain obvious associations: between one hell and another; between the sign at the gate of Auschwitz, *Arbeit macht frei*, and the sign at the gate of hell, "Lasciate ogni speranza, voi ch'entrate" (3.9), a comparison that accentuates the irony of the Lager sign; between Dante's breathless, anxious journey in acquisition of extraordinary wisdom and Levi's own journey, particularly within the camp to collect soup in the Ulysses chapter; and between the accompaniment of adventure in both texts by continuous exploratory discourse. To an Italian audience in particular but also to a culturally literate audience, these associations will be easy to make. They ground Levi's work in classical European civilization in terms of literature and language that predate and transcend Auschwitz, providing an authority like that of the Torah because it is familiar and shared, and establishing certain relations between writer and reader. As with the Torah, however, Levi seems also to challenge that which is familiar in order to point up the differences that lie beyond the scope of any shared language. He enters into dialogue with Dante in order to proliferate meanings — sources and corrections and even failures of meanings. Even while the *Inferno* seems to anchor this story from outside human experience, Dante serves also to destabilize and call into question any final truth or certainty.

Levi's attempt to recount the Ulysses Canto to Jean, the Pikolo (or messenger) of the Kommando, provides a sustained example of multiplying voices. As the youngest member of the Chemical Kommando, Jean is the messenger-clerk who, in this instance, selects the narrator to help him fetch the vats of soup. A warm day, a bright young companion who has already demonstrated his quickness of wit in the politics of survival—Levi undertakes a lesson in Italian as they walk: "The canto of Ulysses. Who knows how or why it comes into my mind" (1979, 118). And he tells the story of Vergil addressing the twin flames of Ulysses and Diomedes, and of Ulysses's story of his final voyage past the Pillars of Hercules and into the open sea where he and his men all perished (*Inferno*, 26). Jean Samuel remembered it well. "It was a beautiful spring day, with no Kapo, no SS, no German boss on the scene, an extraordinary instant of freedom, a breathing space. Even today, I relive that shining moment with deep emotion. But you needed two or three days to get over such a 'human' experience" (Tarrow 1994, 103). The friendship between the two young men, which outlasted the war, provides the initial interaction. Levi wrote one version of this episode on February 14, 1946, before he knew that Jean Samuel had also survived, and sent him a copy in May of that year.

Another significant drama in this chapter consists of Levi's struggle to remember, recite, and explain. Due to gaps in his memory, fragments and lacunae appear in the narrative with all its ellipses, false starts, and fragmentary sentences. Meanwhile, Levi is also translating between Italian and French ("Disastrous," he exclaims. "[P]oor Dante and poor French!" [1979, 118]), and he resorts to prose as he loses rhymes. But Pikolo helps with suggestions for translation, and Levi himself comes to understand certain phrases for the first time, recognizing their particular audacity and their echoes within the passage: "As if I also was hearing it for the first time: like the blast of a trumpet, like the voice of God" (1979, 119). Jagendorf refers to the resonance of connections in this effort of memory—between the camp, Levi's writing, Dante's Ulysses, and the *liceo*, or high school classroom, in which this episode must first have been vivid to the narrator (35). Even though Pikolo has chosen a leisurely route to the *essenholen* (or food collection), time is short and the opportunity is fleeting. The hour of urgent recall is also an hour of instruction—in language, in literature, and in the inspired wisdom that literature can impart.

The struggle to remember and recite and to translate and explain, always in relation to the friend who listens and responds and wants to know, is contained within the camp. The chapter begins with Levi's Kommando scraping and cleaning an underground petrol tank. Pikolo takes Levi from the dark and the damp into the spring day, where they carry poles for the soup, reminiscent of the beam Levi carries with Null Achtzehn and a counterpoint to that dangerous experience. As they walk across the camp, furthermore, they meet others to whom they need to respond, an SS man, Limentani from Rome, Frenkl the spy. Then Levi's sudden flash of intuition, of illumination, "perhaps the reason for our fate, for our being here today" (1979, 121), coincides with their arrival at the soup queue and the babel of recognition that today's soup is cabbages and turnips: "*Kraut und Rüben.* . . . *Choux et navets. Káposzta és répak*" (1979, 121). Levi's struggles with memory, languages, and meaning, and his efforts to demonstrate the significance of this material to his friend, are compounded by the inescapable conditions into which they are introducing Dante.

Or, as Jagendorf puts it, "the scene of food-fetching . . . becomes a scene of memory, or word-fetching" (34). The questions with which the Kommando greets Pikolo, about the Kapo's mood, Stern's twenty-five lashes, the weather, and so on, are transfigured into major questions about fate and free will, God's justice and the nature of sin, and the serious adventures of the human soul. The integration of Dante into Auschwitz offers the (failed) hope of explanation. More certainly, it arouses the deeply spiritual hunger which is like the hunger for the mountains of home that Dante also triggers, a hunger for acts of contemplation and reverence. ("I would give today's soup to know," Levi says at one point when his memory fails on a detail.)[29] The sordid, weary crowd of soup-carriers is made up of men like those whom Ulysses addresses in his story of final daring and disaster. In what little is left of their lives, Ulysses tells them, they need to venture beyond what is known to men. Consider, he says. They were not born to live like beasts but to pursue honor and wisdom.

> Considerate la vostra semenza:
> fatti non foste a viver come bruti,
> ma per seguir virtute e canoscenza.
> (*Inferno*, 26.118–20)

Ulysses's contrast between brutishness and human aspirations sounds through the rhythm and alliteration of the second line, and through the opulently cadenced rhymes that connect origin and destiny in "semenza" and "canoscenza." What Levi chooses to recite, apparently without any sense of why it came into his head, is Ulysses's call to the inner man, his romantic aspiration, indeed, that had landed him in hell for daring to undertake more than God allowed.

Tension between the two texts is apparent in the failure of the *Inferno* to provide a prototype for the Lager. Contrasts between Dante's hell and the Lager elaborate what Levi has called the "useless violence" of Auschwitz (1989a, 105–26). For example, although Dante, too, is lost and terrified, and although he is alarmed by much of what he sees and hears, he enjoys the protection of a powerful guide, who can control the dangers they face and make sense of their experience. If Levi is turning to Dante as a Vergil for his own experience, then his guide is too orderly and meaningful to make sense of the chaos of the Lager. Whereas Auschwitz points to a moral void of absolute godlessness, entailing deliberate confusion, random suffering, and punishment where no crime has preceded, Dante's hell is a feature of divine order and justice in which punishment is matched to crime. Unlike Vergil's guidance of Dante's understanding, Dante's guidance provides Levi a moment of illumination which he can neither express nor retain. The end of Dante's journey, furthermore, is the revelation of absolute truth. Even within this one part of the *Commedia*, the travelers begin in the starless dark (3.23) and emerge "a riveder le stelle," to see the stars again (34.139). For Levi and Pikolo, the end is the *essenholen*, which submerges their aspirations as Ulysses and his men are submerged by the sea.

Gunzberg suggests that Levi felt "a sense of kinship with Dante, whose poem reflects the bitter experience of exile and expropriation resulting in uprootedness and precariousness," and that he used the *Inferno* as "a conceptual grid" with which to make sense of his incomprehensible world (26–27). In my reading, however, the conceptual grid is more problematic than Gunzberg indicates. Although Levi feels an undoubted affinity with the preeminently Italian poet who brings back to him the richness and beauty of a world now lost, stimulating that fervent intellectual life of which the Lager deprives him, the Ulysses Canto actually orchestrates the conceptual framework that Levi has in place from the beginning. Auschwitz, the "*anus mundi*, ultimate drainage site of the German universe" (1989a, 65), remains incredible and unimaginable even when refracted from many angles, repeated and altered and questioned from shared and conflicting perspectives. Where Dante posits a universe created and ordered by God, the "universe concentrationnaire" defies both order and meaning. Tension between Dante's *Inferno* and Auschwitz, which contradict or merely approximate each other, establishes Levi's negative pole for positive construction and, simultaneously, his refusal to arrive at a final picture.

Like the verbal echoes of Dante throughout Levi's text, the focus on

Ulysses highlights the resourcefulness of all three narrators: Ulysses himself, Dante, and Levi. Dante's suggestion that a physical and spiritual journey precedes its narration in verse is reversed in Levi's text,

in which he turns to literature to make sense of an immediate living experience, which we as readers, however, receive only as text. Word-fetching in both texts involves continuous interplay between the oral and the written, between the immediate situation and the power of literature, and the effort involved in crossing from one mode to another. Word-fetching can also be dangerous (as Jean Samuel indicates when he mentions the time needed for recovery). It can be seditious; Gunzberg argues that Levi is deliberately instructing Pikolo in material applicable to their condition (21). It also opens the mind to defiance of God (for Ulysses) or, in Levi's case, to multiple meanings in place of the controlling monologism of the Lager. It involves, for example, intense and elevated conversation: Dante with Vergil and both of them with the souls of the damned; Levi with Pikolo and other characters in the camp; and Ulysses with other men he addresses in his narrative. It suggests role playing; is Levi the Vergil to Pikolo's Dante, or is Pikolo to become an adventurous Ulysses? (These alternatives do not exclude each other.) Nicholas Patruno suggests Pikolo as Ulysses for curiosity and daring (22). Sodi believes Levi is actually talking to himself, that he is his own Dante and Ulysses.[30] In both versions of hell, other characters seem eager to tell their stories, which affirm their own understanding, of course, of who they are, but which also reach past the narrator to the reader — to the world of the living beyond the text. By virtue of extraordinary circumstances, these stories are also secret; Dante is burdened with knowledge familiar only to God, and Levi, like so many Holocaust survivors, is a *Geheimnisträger*, a secret-bearer. "I am one of those people," he writes, "to whom many things are told" (1985, 68). Both Dante and Levi, accordingly, reflect the anguished characters with whom they speak.

Ulysses is centrally important to Levi as narrator, furthermore, because his final sin was an act of will, which places him deep in the Christian hell — in the eighth Bolgia of the eighth Circle. In the Lager, where, as Gilliland suggests, the sin of the Jews is their difference from the Aryan self of the Reich (204), survival depends upon such deliberate will. Hollow *Muselmänner* like Null Achtzehn cannot survive, whereas the passionate intellectual engagement that Levi and Pikolo share increases their chances of physical survival by enriching their sense of who they are as men.[31] Curiously, for Levi as for Dante, Ulysses also represents an ancient enemy; Vergil can conjure him to speak on the strength of favorable mention in the *Aeneid*, which suggests some of the power the writer enjoys to explore wisdom even from hostile sources. For Levi, the whole framework of the Christian hell is also hostile. Whereas Dante, the Christian, can take hope from Vergil's witness to the harrowing of hell and Christ's redemption of the patriarchs (4.52–63), Levi, the Jew, is part of an "ancient" and "sorrowful" history (1987, 82) in which present suffering is only one chapter; Judecca, a name commonly used for Jewish ghettos, appears as the final stop at the very bottom of Dante's hell (Halpern, 199).

For Levi, the narrator who lacks both adventures and sins to recount, narration itself becomes a powerful act of will. Levi makes his strongest and clearest connection with Ulysses when he begins his recitation not at the beginning of the canto but at the effort that Ulysses makes to speak through the flame that envelops him (1979, 118–21). The flame itself shudders, murmuring, "Crollarsi mormorando," as if shaken by a wind. Sodi describes "the physical violence that permeates Ulysses' recounting" as paralleling "the mental torment involved in remembering" (Sodi 1990, 65). The fire itself seems to speak, the tip of flame moving like the tongue that brings forth words. The efforts of memory and speech are in themselves heroic. Levi cannot recall the lines about Circe, but struggles then with the richest possible meaning of "misi me per l'alto mare aperto." Ulysses did not "set forth." Rather, he hurled himself into adventure on the open sea, beyond the pillars set by Hercules to limit men's wandering, until smitten by the whirlwind that submerged them all: "infin che 'l mar fu sopra noi richiuso (until the sea closed over us)."

These perilous waters in which none can survive, narrated by the voice that speaks through fire, become potent images for the Holocaust autobiographer who resists the demolition of a man. Destroyed by water, consumed by fire, struggling with memory and speech, Ulysses recalls his challenge to his sailors, which is none other than Levi's own question of conscience: What is a man? Not a beast, but a mind capable of exhilarating experience of beauty and thought. Using Ulysses, Levi demonstrates the intense yearning of the two young men on their way for soup in the Lager and the capacity of language to raise them above the squalor of their physical conditions — to themselves, to each other, and to the reader. He juxtaposes, furthermore, the romance of heroism with the inglorious fate of each narrator, swinging a bucket of cabbage soup from a pole being easily the more sordid.

Levi himself talks of multiple tellings of his stories from Auschwitz.
He refers to "haphazardly scribbled notes" even in the lab in the Lager (1986, 28). He told Thomson that his first two books were "the written forms of oral stories which [he had] told countless times" (Thomson, 15). He told Sodi that he paid no attention to style in his early writing but "wrote . . . without giving it a second thought: at night, in the lab, on the train, wherever [he] happened to find [him]self" (Sodi 1987, 366). As a captive of history, he writes from his need (Howe, 14). By writing, he claims, he also "found peace for a while and felt [him]self become a man again, a person like everyone else, neither a martyr nor debased nor a saint: one of those people who form a family and look to the future rather than the past" (1985, 151).

Reintegrating his life across the chasm of Auschwitz, connecting past to future, Levi has also ensured that Auschwitz itself, with its complex of forces for the "demolition of a man," will be as real to the imagination of others as words can make it. As an historian, he approaches many facets of before and during and after, many characters involved in different aspects of the experience, many angles on his own perspectives, as if, through repeated attempts at narration and interpretation, to catch in the round a grotesque but elusive set of memories. In the end, Levi, like so many other survivors, bears witness because he fears for the future. Proteus-like and hard to recognize, this horror can recur. The dimension to Levi's work, then, that is not present in his narrative of the past comes only in the occasional warning that he fears the past conveys. Aligning himself and his readers with Chaim Rumkowski, corrupt and unheeding elder of the ghetto in Lodz, Levi fears that "we too are so dazzled by power and money as to forget our essential fragility, forget that all of us are in the ghetto, that the ghetto is fenced in, that beyond the fence stand the lords of death, and not far away the train is waiting" (1987, 172). The very fact of Levi's own survival, in other words, offers no completion. Refraction continues beyond what he can remember or narrate into dimensions of time and possibility he has not lived to see. This future dimension to Levi's historiography, furthermore, is inherent in the endings he provides for stories from the past. Just as memories cannot be stilled, so no story simply concludes. Mirror talk involves two-way reflection. So Levi dreams in *If This Is a Man* of returning to the comforts of home and trying, but failing, to tell his story; and he dreams in *The Truce* a dream within a dream — that being finally at home, in the comforts of his own bed, is not the reality, that he is still in the Lager and nothing else in fact exists. So his wanderers at the end of *If Not Now, When?* conclude with a childbirth and with news of Hiroshima. Using the same narrative strategies with which he establishes his own human dignity, Levi also narrates refracted visions of a perpetual and nightmare present that dismantles hope through irony.

Death and Its Points
of Departure

Death asks us for our identity.
— Fulton, *Death and Identity*

Inevitably, my subject is death. I do not apologise for
feeling the need to speak of it.
— Woods, "AIDS to Remembrance"

Given the political concerns of much recent autobi-
ography, it is not surprising that terminal illness, the process of dying,
and the facts of death have taken on, so to speak, a new life. Remarkable
numbers of people living in the shadow of death have begun to speak
out on issues that have, for a long time, been considered entirely private if not actually shameful, and to insist on being heard. So dying has
become a significant point of departure for life writing. Furthermore,
its impact on the genres of autobiography is likely to be far-reaching. If
death is both a singular and a universal experience, how can one gener-
alize from the particular? Given, furthermore, that one cannot record
one's own death in retrospect, how are such texts created? How far can
a dying person go in telling this story? How does one represent the
unrepresentable? And why? And what strategies are autothanatographers discovering that will serve the purposes of other forms of life
writing?[1] I propose to look briefly at this relatively recent literature,
this rediscovery of death, in order to contextualize it. Context necessarily engages questions both of social taboo and of medical practice. It
also enables us to see this writing, like much other contemporary autobiography, energetically engaged in the politics of representation —
with interesting ramifications for discussion of the relations between
life and text.[2]

Next to birth, death is the most absolutely singular experience of disconnection (no one can die for us or even, truly, with us) and, at the
same time, the most entirely universal: no one can avoid dying. Like

birth, which separates each infant from a(m)other's body into its own solitary identity, death is a powerfully separating experience, because it is singular, and because the living try so hard to avoid it. For these reasons, death has been a taboo subject in the Western world for many generations, hidden behind euphemisms, the dying hidden behind hospital screens, medical practitioners — dedicated to life-saving — hiding behind life-extending technologies. But death will not die and cannot be ignored. The specter of death hovers over all autobiography, usually unnamed,[3] providing serious impetus to the activity of setting records straight, clearing old scores, avoiding misinterpretation, taking control of the absolutely uncontrollable — the "end" of the story. These forms of control make sense, however, only for so long as "the story" retains explanatory power; for the more sophisticated of contemporary autobiographers, narrative completion, like famous last words, can seem inappropriately romantic or contrived.

The postmodern reaction to formalism includes a recognition, even an embrace, of mutability, or a desire, as Bauman puts it, to efface the opposition between the transient and the durable (10). Therefore, even as religious and cultural systems of explanation and consolation have eroded, various strategies have become available to the autothanatographer whose narrative is specifically about fragmentation and uncertainty. These writers deromanticize their expected ending. They want to name their fear and helplessness, their exact experiences of pain and degeneration, even their failures of character and charm. Crashing the barriers of tradition and taboo becomes for many of them a profoundly personal need. Harold Brodkey, for example, produced sections of *This Wild Darkness*, the story of his dying, in the *New Yorker* while he was still alive, and inserts into the final text his doctor's reservations about publicity: "Barry still wishes I hadn't been so public. He doesn't want me to advise anyone else to go public. . . . Barry had warned me that if I made my condition public, the condition would become the overt center of my life. I had told him it was therapeutic not to lie. That truth is a form of caress. That lying is, among other things, conservative" (113–14). In cases of resistance to medical control, public perception, or government opportunism, writing also becomes part of an urgent political agenda. One thinks of the large AIDS literature in this context, but also of Audre Lorde's refusal to wear a prosthesis after her mastectomy, or of Terry Tempest Williams's tracing of the cancer epidemic in her family to years of nuclear testing in Nevada, when her family was among the "virtual uninhabitants" of the test area. If these writers can call it as it is, then they introduce the possibility of change; at the very least, others will follow a trodden path and die in company.

By virtue of their numbers, if for no other reason, autothanatographers are affecting public, medical, and political consciousness. Their reading public, however, has its own fear to contend with and its tendency to avoidance or denial, self-protective forms of resistance that say "not me," "not really," "not yet." Philippe Ariès refers to contemporary attitudes to death as "sauvage," or "wild," by which he means that death is considered shameful, embarrassing, excluded, forbidden. Denial, William Gavin suggests, is not natural but violent. Writing in 1995, he quotes Geoffrey Gorer, writing thirty years earlier, on the "pornography of death" (21). For the dying subject, accordingly, strategy becomes a pressing issue: How does one connect representation of living persons to representation of their dying bodies so as to persuade a reading public that this profoundly disturbing experience is not obscene? How to make narrative sense of a body that is intrusive because often in pain and a time whose anticipated trajectory has been radically foreshortened? How to make sense, in other words, of a life that is both physical and interrupted? The physical and the sensory lack narrative traditions and are accordingly problematic for narrative interpretation. Similarly, the drastic interruption of a life story by imminent death is also scriptless. As lived experience, furthermore, one's anticipation of death is dominated by contingency, and therefore resistant to the meaning-making tendencies of narrative. Terminal illness, finally, posits the primacy of experience to subsequent understanding. We might see an ironic twist here to notions of the self under erasure. Reduced by pain and disability, limited by place and time, the person who faces imminent death certainly knows about the self as a suffering and particular body. Significantly, therefore, these writers, who know they are dying, insist that they are also living—from moment to moment, in definitely foreshortened time, in unreliable bodies, and in circumstances that are dramatically, often suddenly, altered. Lacking any *ars moriendi*, very often lacking any spiritual comfort, the "dier" uses this ultimate crisis of disconnection to reconnect, to constitute a living presence that precedes narrative and forces recognition.

DYING AND DIALOGISM

Given the contingency that precedes any attempt at narrative, it is not surprising to find that mirror talk in these texts takes place primarily between people even when specifically interactive genres come into play. Because dying is a process forcing intimate recognitions of what living has been about, dialogic forms of autothanatography seem well suited to dramatizing the undoing and remaking of the body-self and of the relationships that attend it. Anne Hunsaker Hawkins refers to the practical need for very sick people to work with someone close and thus "override the conventional boundaries of self and other or biographer and subject" (3). Arthur W. Frank refers to the "inter-human," which "opens when suffering becomes the call and response implicating self and other" (178). Arthur Kleinman describes the meaning of illness and death as transactional, or negotiated. "[D]eath is an awesome process of making and remaking meaning through which we come to constitute and express what is most uniquely human and our own" (157). Dialogic forms of narrative juxtapose the disappearing act of lived experience and the production of the record so that the auto-thanatographer is restored from fading body into the community of text even at that most singular moment, "in the face of death."[4]

Forms of dialogism reconstitute the self that is threatened with iso-lation *in extremis*. They also constitute the living companions who both validate the dying self and, as subjects in their own right, simulta-neously establish the fact that they are alive now but will also, someday, die.[5] Whereas the dier responds "in character" to the absorbing experi-ence of a failing body, the surviving perceiver of death suffers all that the living can know of death: observation of another, the emotional pains of support and loss and grief, and complex forms of identifica-tion — of the self as alive and also of the self as destined, in the end, to die. This reflective companion differs from the conventional biogra-pher, of course, in being so implicated in the process — even to the extent of knowing the end of the story, living beyond the death — but not yet knowing the effects of that death on the surviving self. Told by the doctor that nature respects the brain of a dying person by numbing it, Gerda Lerner writes of her husband's death: "But I'm watching it happening and writing it down. So nature's not kind to me" (188). While the title of her book, *A Death of One's Own*, describes her wish that her husband die in his own way and not according to a medical script, it also describes her struggle to support Carl without controlling him. Her own suffering parallels and connects with his but is distinct in character and possibility.

In these dialogic forms, then, the primary autothanatographer is one voice among several, defining the self both in confrontation with annihilation and in relationship with at least one reflective companion, who plays back and so confirms this experience of absolute loss. Nor is the reflective companion by any means exempt from the full range of meaning that these texts create. Georges Gusdorf confirms the value of mirror talk to autothanatography: "Sociology, depth psychology, psychoanalysis have revealed the complex and agonizing sense that the encounter of a man with his image carries. The image is another 'myself,' a double of my being but more fragile and vulnerable, invested with a sacred character that makes it at once fascinating and frightening. Narcissus, contemplating his face in the fountain's depth, is so fascinated with the apparition that he would die bending toward himself. According to most folklore and myth, the apparition of the double is a death sign" (32). In more comfortable terms, dialogism in autothanatography opens up what Norbert Elias, in *The Loneliness of the Dying*, has referred to as *homo clausus*, the hermetically sealed human being, for whom the meaning of life is entirely individual and for whom knowledge of death is appalling (52). Dialogic interactions demonstrate a shared suffering and working toward meaning, but perceiving one's own death in the death of another allows for no easy answers. Despite Gregory Woods's understanding that the elegist is, for the time being, alive, the sharing of a death prevents even the survivor from arriving at satisfaction.

Dialogic autothanatography therefore achieves no more than a momentary stasis in the process of present-tense transition, a recognition of felt experience even as it changes. Frank Kermode's "sense of an ending" is more significant than any particular narrative or physical end in itself. Present moments, intensified by expectation, *are* the story, the "stay" of certain execution,[6] the illuminating *kairos* that punctuates mere *chronos*. These writers vouch for Heidegger's understanding, in keeping with that of all the major world religions, that "being-toward-death" is the only serious form of living. "I do not think about my death as being imminent," writes Audre Lorde, "but I live my days against a background noise of mortality and constant uncertainty. Learning not to crumple before these uncertainties fuels my resolve to print myself upon the texture of each day fully rather than forever" (1988, 127). Full awareness of mortality, from which most of us protect ourselves most of the time, generates a fullness of being to which these texts bear witness again and again.

Because its material is critical to individual lives and to human life experience, and because its methodologies are so current, autothanatography cannot be read as some bizarre offshoot of autobiography studies but is, I suggest, quite central to the larger genre.[7] I suggest that "writing toward one's own death" is neither separate from autobiography nor a new kind of writing that we should all be exploring in place of the old.[8] Rather, this one form of "single-experience autobiography" is crucially, centrally, quintessentially autobiographical—every bit as autobiographical as writing by a woman, for example, or a gay person, or a person of color, all genres based on particular life experiences and all becoming incorporated into the canon since the 1970s. For me, autothanatography does not describe the traditional genre as defined by Gusdorf, by the early work of Lejeune, or by the many distinguished theorists of the 1970s and early 1980s who established this discipline. Its effects are basically similar to those of older forms: the exploration of personally experienced life situations for their moral and political wisdom. But autothanatography is an intensely focused activity and the difficulty of its subject necessarily involves formal variation and even eccentricity. Condensed attention to the one critical issue of "terminal" illness, furthermore, intensifies the rendition of lived experience, the immediacy of crisis, and the revealing processes of self-understanding. The processes of dying do not indicate development of character or strengthen and prepare character for the future so much as they reveal what, "in the end," is there.

THE REDISCOVERY OF DEATH

Each autobiographer who integrates bodily illness and death into interpretation of a whole life raises some key questions: In what way does this experience belong to me? What does this experience add to or subtract from my understanding of myself? And how might my experience be of value to other people? Such questions raise issues of identity and of social context, and are asked most urgently in post-religious times when people are often isolated from communities of meaning. Taking off, so to speak, after World War II, the literature of terminal illness and death has become a boom industry with very practical results, such as the development of hospice care, and with radical cultural implications for societies that may once again face death as a necessary and openly acknowledged experience of life. (As I write, Vancouver's news and entertainment weekly, the *Georgia Straight*, portrays a cozy skeleton in slippers, reading in an armchair. "Death-Defying Words," runs the headline, with the subhead: "Acknowledging death is a central part of our lives. No wonder the theme surfaces so often in our special edition on winter books, the best of which will outlast us all" [November 28–December 5, 1996].) This industry, as the skeleton in slippers makes clear, serves a middle-class population with a keen sense both of "self" and of the "help" to be found in books. Those who write about

their experiences of terminal illness and death are those with the money and time to do so; they seem to come exclusively from a class with sufficient ease and education to ponder the final questions in print. Now, at the end of the century, postwar baby boomers are burying their parents and recognizing their own mortality. Simone de Beauvoir, of course, discovered the symbiotic relationship between herself and her dying mother in *A Very Easy Death* in 1966, but death memoirs have proliferated since then as younger and later writers also find that a parent's illness and death force them to recognize that life and that death as central to their own identity.[9] In addition to this general trend, AIDS and breast cancer activists have contributed political energy to this crisis of identity that originates in confrontation with death.

As part of this postwar preoccupation with death, cultural and academic texts have helped to crash the barriers of taboo. In the sociology of medicine in the 1960s, Elisabeth Kübler-Ross may be credited with making death a public issue and insisting that it belonged with life. In the 1980s, the cultural historian Philippe Ariès produced his histories of the changing cultures of death in Western Europe, contrasting the varied rituals of past centuries with the secrecy, haste, and averted attention of our own. In autobiography studies, G. Thomas Couser introduced a focus on death in 1978,[10] produced a special edition of *a/b: Autobiography Studies* in 1991, and published a book in 1997. Couser's coinage of "autopathography" to describe life writing that focuses on the single experience of critical illness develops Hawkins's suggestion that pathography is the modern adventure story of "essential" experience (1).

Identifying pathography as a post-1950 phenomenon, Hawkins suggests: "Literary critics will want to include pathography as a subgenre of autobiography and examine how it verifies or challenges various tenets of autobiographical theory" (x). Just as writers on death examine terminal illness and death as essential (and essentializing) ingredients of the life story, so they also identify the narrative patterns with which these ingredients conform or the new patterns that they introduce. Frank connects such exploration with his own experience of life-threatening illness in order to identify the body in pain as a bedrock of reality and the stories of that body as falling into identifiable categories — restitution, chaos, quest, and testimony. Only the chaos narrative is sucked, as Frank puts it, into the undertow of illness and its attendant disasters, becoming an anti-narrative of time without sequence, telling without mediation, and speaking without the possibility of reflection (98). Frank's other three categories all support Couser's claim that autobiography depends on the "little-appreciated but quite powerful life-writing convention of the comic plot" (1997, 14); someone, in the end, gets to tell the story. Similarly, Hawkins relates pathographies to conversion narratives and traces myths of battle and journey as recurring tropes. Incorporating illness and death into life, this largely secular generation connects with the oldest story forms in order to find meaning for new, deliberately personalized material.[11]

Whereas storied explanations continue to resonate with the human condition, their apparent ability to make meaning puts at risk the more open-ended possibilities of new understanding. Some interesting texts develop not from narrative literature but from the social and academic disciplines that interpret current discoveries and experiences. Frank's translation of his own life-threatening illness into theoretical analysis connects his work with that of anthropologists who become their own informants. Archie J. Hanlan, in *Autobiography of Dying*, worked through his own experience of Lou Gehrig's disease with his students and as an autobiographical study in social work. In *The Body Silent*, Robert F. Murphy studied his own experience of spinal tumor and increasing paralysis from his professional perspective as an anthropologist. Similarly, Neni Panourgiá responded to her grandfather's death with a remarkable study of time, place, community, and customs, in which she positions herself and her own grief and loss.[12] Such professional perspectives position the suffering narrator as the source of analysis and narrative but neither as alone with the experience nor as the only subject of importance. Using their professional skills to analyze their personal experience, these writers introduce distinctive forms of autobiographical interaction into their dialogics of genres. They demonstrate the public, because profoundly human, value of their work even as they examine the exclusively personal nature of their own experience. They travel to and fro in the divide between the personal and the universal that is so problematic in considerations of death. Refusing both religious wholeness and humanist dualities, they belong with the postmodern embrace of mutability.

In short, autothanatography has taken a central place in the genres of life writing only in the past half century, and bears, accordingly, the trademarks of its time and place. As with so much contemporary life writing from "in the middest" of crisis, these works are shaped in particular by feminist, new historicist, and postcolonial theories, which have decentered authority. Autothanatographers recognize the limited nature of personal perspective and the necessary, indeed constitutive, relations between self and other selves, personal text and other texts. Given also that autothanatography's very subject is the material body realized at its most undeniable, in pain and in the process of dying, and therefore as the positively original site of experience, it requires the tending, witnessing, or confirmation of an attentive other person. Given, too, that autothanatographers want to indicate process and instability rather than narrative and resolution, this recent phenomenon of illness-and-death writing frequently includes varieties of dialogism.

Death is the last and great taboo. (Wilber, 68)

Oh Lord, give each of us his own death. (Rainer Maria Rilke, quoted in Nuland, xviii)

Gerda Lerner borrowed another line from Rilke for her memoir of her husband's death. "It is rare," according to Rilke, "to find anyone who wishes to have a death of his own" (Lerner, 13). Such a death would not be controlled by medical authorities or disguised by technological interventions or conversational evasions. It would not be denied by a repeatedly deferred hope for a cure. It would be a fully acknowledged experience, recognizably "in character," shaped by the life that led up to it and the community in which it took place. "I much prefer to think about how I'd want to die," Lorde writes, "—given that I don't want to die at all but will certainly have to—rather than just fall into death any old way, by default, according to somebody else's rules. It's not like you get a second chance to die the way you want to die" (1988, 110). While most autothanatographers seek cure or remission, not one accepts death "by default, according to somebody else's rules." Peter Noll, indeed, resists both the prescribed treatment that could extend his life on terms he finds unacceptable and the morphine recommended at the end, since he deplores its effects on his self-consciousness. Writing of attitudes toward death, Richard W. Momeyer concludes: "In choosing how to confront death, we choose our very character" (11). That choosing, repeatedly foregrounded in autothanatography, takes the form of resistance to taboos entrenched in medical practice, in social mores, and, inevitably, in language. To arrive at one's own death involves an assortment of strategies both personal and generic.

Despite wars, famines, and various acts of God, death has been imaginatively remote in developed societies in the second half of the twentieth century. Increasing health and longevity, due largely to relative protection from violence and to the medical technology that can intervene before, during, and after the processes of birth and death, result in widespread acceptance of life as sturdy and death as remote or even avoidable. Freud identifies the habitual stress "on the fortuitous causation of the death — accident, disease, infection, advanced age; in this way we betray an effort to reduce death from a necessity to a chance event" (290). In medical terms, each instant of death is postponable; death itself, the natural horizon for life, becomes a curable disease subject to daily manipulations. So advanced are the technologies that take the place of failing body parts or delay the inevitable end that the end is often not acknowledged as inevitable at all.

But when each stage of a terminal illness is treated in isolation, and the medical profession is entirely committed to saving and prolonging life, death becomes ultimate failure for everyone concerned. Not least, the dying person may be lost in the rescue paraphernalia that treats the body but not the human being. Sherwin B. Nuland writes of the important hope "to be oneself to one's last breath" (239). "[T]he *real* event taking place at the end of our life is our death," he adds, "not the attempts to prevent it" (256). Nuland's work, like that of Kleinman on illness, addresses the anxieties of the medical profession and of the general public, which simultaneously longs for medical intervention and fears medical control. Autothanatographers weave their understanding between such ambiguities. They recognize their bodies, and often their diseases, as significant parts of their "selves" but by no means the whole truth; they wish and struggle for life but have faced the facts of death; and they strive above all for authenticity against considerable odds.

These odds are as basic as language, which is complicit with diversionary tactics that give true descriptions of the wrong issues. Susan Sontag describes "the uses of illness as a figure or metaphor" and insists that "illness is *not* a metaphor" but that the "lurid metaphors" prevailing in our language necessarily prejudice one's understanding of the ill (1990, 3–4). William Gavin distinguishes between the medical terms for specific, identifiable kinds of failure, for which language abounds, and the truly significant event, the passing of a person, which cannot be defined, and which ceases to be "a legitimate subject for public discourse" (29).[13] Zygmunt Bauman suggests that collective denial of death's significance as the ultimate in human impotence makes the language of survival the only language available, a language that cannot grasp the condition from which the dying can no longer hide (130). Quite clearly, language reports within a limited circuit of the imagination. More significantly, of course, language creates the truths it seems to report. For the autothanatographer, the task of being true to the self in an unlanguaged situation is important for public and private good alike. As Susan Griffin has put it: "What is so astonishing about putting one's life into words, about telling a story, is that certain aspects of being are not only revealed but come to exist fully for the first time" (358).

These concerns matter for two reasons: first, because so many autothanatographers struggle to recognize their own deaths in the face of medical and social taboos generated in part by the notion of terminal illness or death as failure;[14] and second, because so many autothanatographers resist technological and other interferences that blur their recognition of their own very personal death. If death asks us for our identity, then these writers discover and reveal themselves in terms of their most honest moments of recognizing their changing situation and in terms of the visceral choices they make.

Kleinman has written extensively on the need for doctors to recognize illness within its cultural context and to listen to each individual's explanation of what each illness means. He describes the linguistic rituals of transformation whereby a personal illness becomes a medical disease, a person becomes a patient, and that person's narrative becomes a case history. Harvey Pekar, Joyce Brabner, and Art Stack have vividly captured the subjective response to insensitive medicalization. In the following comic, Doctor Cantor has "scooped out" a massive tumor from Harvey's groin, described it as lymphoma, and hurried away. Joyce, enraged, succeeds in calling him back, but only for another hurried statement, and wheels Harvey away with the word "cancer" framing their two bodies within its terrifying din.

The comics format is particularly efficient here at combining narrative information with multiple subjective responses. Note the snarling circles and curves of Joyce's face, top left, freestanding, controlling the page. The irregularly shaped panels move between rational, public exchange and hysterical impressions that block out hearing and sense. Doctor Cantor, for example, speaks, distantly, from one contained circle and hurries away in the next, leaving the squared-off reality of Harvey struggling into his clothes and Joyce, an outline, moving toward the next exchange. Doctor Cantor's words appear, furthermore, in a ragged balloon in which sentences contain frightening, mostly technical terms. The fearsome cacophony of "cancer" that surrounds the departing couple isolates them in white space in which the one crucial word takes on varieties of form. Kleinman is sensitive to these sub-

jective experiences. He commends one therapist whose records show a
cancer patient working through a terrible realization: "I am the creator
of my own destruction. These cancer cells are me and yet not me. I am
invaded by a killer. I am become death" (148). The therapist, Kleinman
comments, allowed this patient "to build tentative understandings out
of the hafting of words in the face of a final assault on the integrity of his
body-self" (154). Such "hafting of words" is what autothanatographers engage in, a painful project, often very painful to read, but one
that is central to their defining and asserting their own connections
between living and dying.

Nowhere, of course, has this self-assertion by the still living against
the overdetermination of their deaths been more vividly developed than in AIDS literature. AIDS-related autothanatography, indeed, expresses every variation that autothanatography at large can present. For no other group of people, for instance, have the death taboos been more forcefully expressed. In part, the early identification of HIV-related illnesses with gay men explains an often virulent reaction expressed at times under the authoritative cover of medical research. Leo Bersani writes of the "frenzied epic of displacements in the discourse on sexuality and AIDS" (220). Paula A. Treichler makes the more specific point that "[i]n service of [the hypothesis that AIDS is a gay disease] both homophobia and sexism are folded imperturbably into a language of the scientific text" (49). Peter Dickinson identifies the media control of attitudes toward AIDS: "[I]nstead of socializing a discourse on AIDS, the mainstream media have demonized it; instead of contextualizing the issues surrounding AIDS, they have compartmentalized them" (224). AIDS-related autothanatography, accordingly, assumes an assertive political agenda; beyond Paul Monette's immediacy — "Right now you are trying not to vomit dinner" (192) — these texts express solidarity with a whole community in distress, and a concern that the wider public should be more fully educated on gay issues. The existential trauma of facing death attaches, in public perception at least, so completely to manner of life that death writing becomes preeminently life writing, and a bid to take charge of how that life writing is read.

Part of the demonizing of PWAs, or Persons with AIDS, arose, of course, out of the early and much-publicized fears of easy contagion, which assumed inadmissibly porous boundaries between the straight and "therefore" healthy self and the infected other. Popular fears of the "contagions" of sexuality and death mean that AIDS sufferers have been particularly "othered"; quite apart from general and unspeakable fears that death impinges upon life as disease impinges upon the healthy body, reasonable concerns about specific contagion have in this case been heavily overlaid with the sin-and-scourge myths that have scapegoated "others" for centuries.[15] Sontag outlines several ways in which syphilis used to be shifted to another community than one's own, becoming the French pox to the English, morbus Germanicus to Parisians, the Neapolitan sickness to the Florentines, and the Chinese disease to the Japanese. She adds, "[T]here is a link between imagining disease and imagining foreignness" (1990, 136). As Gilman puts it, fear of dissolution contaminates images of disease so that it becomes important to specify an "other" in order to remove the threat from one's self (1988, 1). The gay autothanatographer frequently overcomes this barrier by presenting a partner who completes the cycle of transaction but in the role of lover and in a reflexive relationship.

Sexuality has been taboo in complex ways for a long time, but gay men with AIDS often face the additional problem that their sexuality has been secret until a diagnosis of their illness. When they are faced with bringing sex and death out of the closet at the same time, their revelation of their individuality includes a complex component not required in the heterosexual community. Failure to come out, however, could lead to the eradication of gay men and of gay culture. "If we all died," Monette writes, "and all our books were burned, then a hundred years from now no one would ever know" (228). Autothanatography becomes part of a complex claiming of agency. In Monette's words again, "[W]e figured we had to know and name it ourselves, tell each other what we had become in coming out" (228). To name the self in these circumstances is to reconnect representation to its essential referent, to "know" and reconstitute as integral to "self" the body that illness, sex, and death all make obscene. Challenged by complex crises of representation, these autothanatographers need to reconnect body and language, to reverse "[p]ostmodernism's abandonment of the 'ideal' of the organic, of an assured connection between 'essence' and 'symbol'" (James Morrison, 174). Their ability to reconnect is particularly important when, as Gilman puts it, the symbolic, or what he calls the icon, has such power to shape responses to the disease (1987, 87–107). Only by hafting their own words can these autothanatographers control the space between essence and icon — between the integrity of their body-selves, the experiences that constitute their selves, and the representations that control how they are perceived.

Controlling the comics icons of language and visual art, Gary Trudeau complicated such perception and was both blasted and praised for his treatment of AIDS. Despite the fact that Trudeau's work is not autobiographical, it can be exemplary here precisely for its manipulations of perception. In the following extract, Joanie has been shocked to learn that Andy has AIDS and is in the hospital. Her visit begins and ends with her and Andy's doctor in profile, acknowledging the comics reader as the point of view. Andy consists only of a nose and chin and forelock. He is hidden from view by the technical equipment of hospital care. All but invisible, or reduced to his medicalized self, he nonetheless has the power of introduction between doctor and visitor and

sets the tone with his mordant humor. Framed by oxygen tank, bed rail, pillows, and drip, he jokes about "the original cause of AIDS," but the succeeding frames concentrate on Joanie's silence and the visual evidence of her distress. In conjunction with such visual drama, frame regularity and uniform lettering that is not even ballooned highlight the value of language to these strips; the trauma that involves all three characters contains its ridiculous side, which patient and doctor together persuade Joanie to recognize.

A later sequence, also prompted by a visit from Joanie, but this time to Andy's bedside at home, combines a positive cocktail of emotions with a remarkable economy peculiar to this genre (and to Trudeau's exceptional gifts). Andy is visible this time, working at his zany list of

last things. His first "death," facing outward, is self-dramatizing, un-done by his sudden horror that he has left the oven on. Joanie's relief, her practical assistance in checking on the oven, her fears for him, resolve into his actual death. Note the unframed silhouette of Joanie, bag on her shoulder, ready to go, detained by Andy's failure to respond. The wide open gutters enable Joanie's figure to represent the question she does not ask and the answer she does not receive. Comics creates the shuttle between two subject forces as well as the drama of their sep-aration in death. After the stark economy of the preceding frames, in which pills on the bureau or the kettle on the stove constitute the only scenery, the death scene opens out to the view, a plant beside books and CD speaker, buildings and trees outside, and land and ocean and sky shot through by an ironic line from a song. Andy's death, tidily sani-tized, becomes part of his wider life, a limited but whole "view," con-taining sickness and friendship, the desires of life, and the desires and accomplishments of death as well. It also undercuts Joanie's tension with its ironic sentimentality. Trudeau's comics invite viewer participa-tion as a third party; sharing but not fusing with Joanie's perspective, the viewer's relative freedom of participation enriches the languages available for representation of AIDS.[16]

In part because of the epidemic proportions with which AIDS has hit the Western world, gay activism has achieved a strong and articulate voice. In the public sphere, this lobby has produced rapid changes in social attitudes, in medical treatment, in funding for research, and in a politically effective gay pride extending its influence into wider areas of human rights. All forms of art and autobiography have been affected, but the ACT-UP slogan, "silence is death," suggests that "what is said is far less important than the fact of speaking" (Bergman, 175). For the individual autobiographer, affirming sexuality becomes part of the wider activity of identity politics: controlling public perception of the self, separating the knowable individual self from public construction of disease, and naming the hitherto unnameable in order to place it clearly on the human map. The literature of AIDS is central, therefore, to the politics of choice and self-representation in autobiography at large and to autothanatography in particular.

The fact that AIDS is not an exclusively gay disease, or that gay men also die from many other causes, matters less for present purposes than recognizing what autothanatographers with this background contribute to a genre so centrally concerned with self-identification in the ultimate confrontation with death. For example, *Silverlake Life: The View from Here* first aired on PBS in June 1993 and has become centrally important to my thinking about autothanatography as interactive. This film is also first-personal, as Trudeau's sequences are not, and transgressive in ways that make Trudeau's courageous intervention seem quite anodyne. Kevin J. Harty suggests that film's treatments of the AIDS crisis, beginning in the mid-1980s, lagged behind stage responses. As part of a wider cultural movement than theater, however, film has been particularly important in restoring agency to the perceived victim, enabling forms of protest and self-identification that correct heterosexual hegemony. Treichler addresses this issue when she writes: "The stories we tell help us determine what our own place in the story is to be" (43 n. 21).

Silverlake Life is a film about a gay couple struggling with AIDS.[17] First, in terms of the relations between text and life, the emotional impact of the "reality" displayed in this film prevents any easy evasion; at issue for Tom Joslin and Mark Massi, beyond construction, narrative, or even representation, is what Amos Vogel has called "ferocious reality" (in Sobchack, 283). Second, even if the disease itself represents an overdetermined confrontation with death, these filmmakers have emphatically stressed the then present tense of their "Silverlake Life." Peter Friedman reports: "Shortly after Tom got sick, he said . . . that he was no longer sure of the difference between the word 'living' and the word 'dying.' He said 'I mean sometimes I say to myself, "All these things are happening to me, I'm dying!" and sometimes I say "All these things are happening to me, I'm living!"'"[18] Third, they define themselves very much as a gay couple. They have been together for more than twenty years, and they mirror each other more explicitly and self-consciously than a heterosexual couple would likely be able to. In their earlier, coming-out film, *Blackstar*, Massi challenges Joslin as filmmaker, objecting to the interview format: "How about us?" he asks. "How do we get *us* in film?" He pushes beyond the relationship constructed for film to "the love that has held us together for seven years." In that same film, Joslin's mother says at one point that she has not been able to work out which of them is husband and which is wife; their very relationship blurs conventional constructions. Their challenge to represent "us," and her difficulty in reading their relationship, both seem to underline the mirroring qualities of their interaction.

Silverlake Life was necessarily completed and edited by Friedman, a carefully selected filmmaker and friend, but it is still the very personal project of this couple who explore together their experiences with AIDS and with death. It is, in other words, a collaborative work both at the technical level and at the level of human interaction and self-presentation. It also offers privileged, indeed very painful, access to private territory, enabling viewers poignantly to recognize moments of the autobiographers' most terrible loneliness as still responsive to the creative forces of their relationship. Their involvement of the audience was a deliberate, political move on their part; their dogged determination to film every stage of illness, death, bereavement, and continued illness foregrounds the intimate sources of the autobiographical impulse and its dependence on a cautious and attentive audience.

In a discussion of autobiography, maybe more urgently than in many other fields, one's critical response must acknowledge its own complicity in the autobiographical interaction (see Jouve, 5; Kadar, 10–12). If autobiographers depend on the perception of others to correct and confirm their "selves" in living, so also dying, that apparent closure of subjective self-creation, depends for recognition and possible interpretation on the subject position of others to whom the dead no longer respond, for whom they have become objective. As Sobchack puts it: "[T]he corpse is not perceived as a subject — although it confronts us and reminds us of subjectivity and its objective limits" (299). This is the zero-degree for both life and autobiography; the subject becomes an object entirely exposed to being read, entirely dependent on its reader for constructions of meaning. Dialogic autobiography, in other words, expands inclusively to incorporate participation from the margins into the vortex of the autobiographical enterprise.

Self-representation or virtual performance is necessarily constructed by the autobiographical occasion but need not therefore be invalidated. If we admit of a subject that is chameleon-like in its ability to respond to external pressures, we might consider the autobiographical occasion as one more site of dialogism. When Joslin "plays" himself in his responses to AIDS and to imminent death, he is not performing for continuity or coherence but rather inviting the camera, in direct cinema and cinema verité, to stand by for the crisis. The coherence and continuity of the "character" Tom Joslin emerges from his interaction on film as in life with the partner with whom he lives and suffers and in whose company he dies. They talk to each other, they address the camera alone and talk about each other, they pass the camera back and forth, they even film the camera and the monitor as fixtures in their apartment or by Joslin's bedside. As lovers and partners, suffering from the same disease and facing death simultaneously, Joslin and Massi "perform" in response to each other and to the "gaze" of the camera. Using film as their medium, they can review their "performance" and so look for the coherence that daily living might not reveal. "Perhaps," as Gaye Tuchman has put it, "reflexive self-consciousness is not merely autobiography, but the ability to see ourselves as others see us — as co-present subject and object, as perceiving subject and the simultaneous object of others' perception" (quoted in Ruby, 75). Exchanging these positions between themselves, Joslin and Massi ensure that viewers see them in relation to each other.

Despite the punctuation of familiar cinematic devices (the sun behind trees doubles suddenly for an ambulance alarm light, or the camera focuses on brilliant California blossoms or the visit of a hummingbird), much of the camera work in this film is handheld, sometimes unsteady with emotion, the camera eye still "open" as the camera itself passes from hand to hand. This personalizing of the subject position of the camera underlines the specular nature of viewing *Silverlake Life* and of "the view from here." It turns the lived experience into a way of seeing always from at least two perspectives, those of perceiver and perceived. As if in response to the difficulty Elizabeth Bruss has expressed with this split in subjectivity, Joslin and Massi stress their partnership, their love for each other, their gifts of attention and response to each other.[19] Repeatedly, the one with the camera invites some reaction from the other, a smile, a wave, a commentary, entry into a game, a "sign," as Massi puts it on one occasion, that "we are here."[20] Both of them also articulate their occasional choices not to film. Joslin at one point says he has been very depressed and has not filmed; by sheer necessity, because he has been so weak, we will see him only at his best. Clearly this decision is a matter of emotional energy which can go the other way, as when he films himself at two in the morning, lighted by a flashlight and whispering into the camera about the headache that prevents him from sleeping and his anxieties as he lies awake. Similarly, Massi does not film for a couple of days as Joslin lies dying; he weeps and the camera shakes as he talks about feeling responsible for Joslin's debility after an unsuitable meal that led to vomiting. He has not wanted friends to see the change. Needless to say, the filming process reveals inescapably what visitors in the lived experience also recognize — ocular and emotional proof of Joslin's deterioration. Massi is unstinting, however, in his exploration of the painful lesion on Joslin's eyelid, and the camera holds still for a long time on Joslin's dead body as Massi sobs goodbye and asks, "Isn't he beautiful?"

Although Joslin initiates the project, the autobiography does not conclude with his death; rather, his absence fills the space that his life had filled and alters the dynamics of all Massi's continuing interactions with other people. The camera becomes stable in the hands of Peter Friedman, their chosen editor. Even though their dialogue is probing, Massi's tone and stance in response to Friedman are comparatively formal — a reminder that the private is central to what can be revealed about a relationship and to all re-presentation. Massi's bereavement and isolation are vivid because the gap that he feels in his life is one that viewers see on the screen. He promises at Joslin's deathbed that he will finish the film, that all their friends will finish the film. And as the film continues with the wrapping up and carrying away of the dead body, with the paperwork and red tape, with relatives and the funeral, with Massi getting sicker and weaker, walking down a corridor alone, his voice-over saying that he is really, really beat, he is achieving what no conventional autobiography has ever achieved: the making of (auto)biography beyond the closure of death. "Our journey," Joslin says at one point, "is shorter than we thought it was going to be, but that's life." Massi's death does not take place on camera, but its inevitability is a significant feature of the film, not only in the world external to the film in which he has AIDS, but also because his condition is deteriorating and the film has demonstrated what that means. His solitude in what has been so dynamically a shared place leaves no emotional room for doubt. As Sontag has put it, photography represents "experience seeking a crisis-proof form" (1977, 162). Motion photography, furthermore, is narrational, creating in this case inevitabilities that connect *Silverlake*'s narrative with the narrowing-into-death of "the view from here."

Film provides a "view" and implicates viewers because of the illusion it provides that we are present at an originary scene. Quite apart from any self-reflexive strategies with which filmmakers may choose to iden-tify the processes of their autothanatography and complicate viewers' understanding, a cameraman who shakes with emotion creates our vision and shapes our emotional response. So a film like *Silverlake Life* is dialogic at every level: because it involves two men who respond to each other's needs and mirror each other's condition; because it in-volves the technology that repeatedly involves more than one person and therefore more than one "point" of view; and because this tech-nology involves the combination of picture and language, vision and sound. Such varieties of dialogism are less inevitable or obvious in the printed text, which provides, accordingly, rather different points of departure. Dennis Potter, to be sure, delivered his text, *Seeing the Blos-som*, in dialogue and on film, but I propose to look at its effect as a printed text. Sandra Butler and Barbara Rosenblum's *Cancer in Two Voices* originates, like *Silverlake Life*, in a relationship which involves two people in the illness and death of one. And Audre Lorde's *Cancer Journals* and *a burst of light* both grow, as apparently monologic texts, out of the writer's own terminal illness. Depending on varieties of personal and generic interaction to make the point, these writers faced their deaths with a keen desire to be recognized as fully present.

Cancer and Dialogic Text: Audre Lorde

I begin with Audre Lorde because her texts refuse a singular voice despite the absence in them of any other speaker.[21] In *The Cancer Jour-nals*, published in 1980, Lorde juxtaposes journal entries, commentary, a speech, and an essay in order to integrate her experience of radical mastectomy into the many facets of her life. *a burst of light*, published in 1988, is a collection of essays that connect Lorde's life issues as a black lesbian poet in a patently unjust, judgmental world with her two bouts of cancer. (Lorde was first diagnosed in 1978 and had a mastectomy. She was then diagnosed with liver cancer in 1984, and died in 1992.) "There must be some way to integrate death into living," she says, "neither ignoring it nor giving in to it" (1980, 13). Dying is a life process, causing pain and loss to the physical body. Another entry begins:

I want to write about the pain. The pain of waking up in the recovery room which is worsened by that immediate sense of loss. Of going in and out of pain and shots. Of the correct position for my arm to drain. . . . I want to write of the pain I am feeling right now, of the lukewarm tears that will not stop coming into my eyes — for what? For my lost breast? For the lost me? And which me was that anyway? For the death I don't know how to postpone? Or how to meet elegantly?

I'm so tired of all this. I want to be the person I used to be, the real me. (1980, 24–25)[22]

Elaine Scarry has identified the material body as indispensable to identity and meaning. "The body," she writes, "tends to be brought forward . . . when there is a crisis of substantiation" (127). Lorde identifies her "real me" in terms of her body and in terms of the crises of change. In a retrospective section of narrative, Lorde writes of her surprise that her amputated body did not look like "the ravaged and pitted battlefield of some major catastrophic war" (44). The body figures as battlefield in much autothanatography,[23] posing the conceptual problem that it serves simultaneously for surface and depth; containing hidden dangers, scarred and "transfigured," it becomes "the field of action" both for disease and for reconstruction from the inside out of a still-living self.[24]

The question recurs: How does one imagine a continuing self in these circumstances? How does one resurrect meaning for one's life when reduced to this physical geography with a limited and grim horizon? Christina Middlebrook writes about her experience of extreme treatment: "To save myself, *I*, the me of me, retreated to a far corner above the room. . . . I found a large psychic cloak and gathered my endangered identity within. . . . Without the periodic witness . . . who knew who I was, *I* could not know myself. Not to know oneself is to die" (62). Lorde finds herself an heroic role model. "How did the Amazons of Dahomey feel?" (1980, 35), she asks more than once — and answers by engaging her own particular battle over the prosthesis, which has to do with both the body and the self. Distressed to imagine what the absence of her breast will mean to the pleasures of sex, Lorde listens to the woman from Reach for Recovery, who leaves her with a lambswool form. "I came around my bed," Lorde writes, "and stood in front of the mirror in my room, and stuffed the thing into the wrinkled folds of the right side of my bra where my right breast should have been. It perched on my chest askew, awkwardly inert and lifeless, and having nothing to do with any me I could possibly conceive of. Besides, it was the wrong color, and looked grotesquely pale through the cloth of my bra. . . . I pulled the thing out of my bra, and my thin pajama top settled back against the flattened surface on the right side of the front of me" (1980, 44). This "real me," determined both by physical sensation and by mirror image, is flat on one side but satisfied only with sensual response. It is integrated, one authentic color, every part alive.

Lorde's prosthesis enables her to specify her "real me." "For me," she writes, "the primary challenge at the core of mastectomy was the stark look at my own mortality, hinged upon the fear of a life-threatening cancer. This event called upon me to reexamine the quality and texture of my entire life, its priorities and commitments" (1980, 61). One of these priorities involves recognizing that "it is not the appearance of [her breast that she] mourn[s], but the feeling and the fact" (1980, 65). Another is her commitment to be for other women the role model that she herself has lacked — to speak out where she has heard silence, and to present a brave body in place of an appearance that shelters other people from what she has been through. (Lorde dedicates *a burst of light* "To that piece of each of us which refuses to be silent.") Feeling, ironically, more whole than before her body- and life-threatening crisis, Lorde absorbs acute suffering into her "real me." "[W]ill I ever be strong enough again," she asks, "to open my mouth and not have a cry of raw pain leap out?" (1980, 77).

Lorde's "real me" both internalizes and expresses the pain of her experience in personal, political, and generic forms that ensure polyphony in the printed text. For example, the qualities of oral delivery are frequently important; some parts were delivered as talks, one is a transcript from an interview, one talk includes a poem, and the very processes foreground physical voice. "In playing back the tapes of those last days in the hospital," Lorde notes, "I found only the voice of a very weakened woman saying with the greatest difficulty and almost unrecognizable: *September 25th, the fourth day*" (1980, 45). Furthermore, because Lorde has understood her life as a battle on many fronts, and because her writing makes no distinction between the personal and the political, both of these texts perform a variety of roles. "Each woman responds to the crisis that breast cancer brings to her life out of a whole pattern," she writes, "which is the design of who she is and how her life has been lived" (1980, 9). So the black activist writes about "Apartheid U.S.A." (1988, 27–38); the lesbian poet and activist writes of "The Transformation of Silence into Language and Action" (1980, 18–23), or about "Turning the Beat Around: Lesbian Parenting 1986" (1988, 39–48); and the cancer-stricken black lesbian poet becomes an activist in "Breast Cancer: A Black Lesbian Feminist Experience" (1980, 24–54), "Breast Cancer: Power vs. Prosthesis" (1980, 55–77), and "A Burst of Light: Living with Cancer" (1988, 49–134). Addressed originally to different audiences, some spoken and some written, some originally private journal entries and some public statements, evincing what Couser calls a shifting "back and forth between the proximate and the distant, between the emotional and the intellectual" (1997, 50–51), these pieces interact between the covers of two books to integrate Lorde's dying into her living. Such juxtapositions insistently connect lived experience with life writing, just as they connect racism and cancer and political activism. In her introduction to her essay "A Burst of Light," Lorde writes: "The struggle with cancer now informs all my days, but it is only another face of that continuing battle for self-determination and survival that Black women fight daily, often in triumph" (1988, 49). Generically polyphonic texts reflect a multifaceted life with which political writing is continuous.

Where the essay "A Burst of Light" consists of journal entries from January 1984 to December 1986, *The Cancer Journals* actually repeats material on cancer and prosthesis that was written in different circumstances, on different timelines, and in different modes of address. One significant result is to take the reader from the immediacy of journal entries (chapter 2) to the contextualizing retrospective provided by later commentary and elaboration, and then to the public statement of a formal essay equipped with academic references acknowledging both professional texts and private conversations (chapter 3). Specifically focused on her own experience of cancer and mastectomy, these two chapters play out a narrative fugue; diagnosis, treatment, distress, and accommodation provide only one, very personal strand, the personal experience and the "cry of raw pain," which Lorde then translates into the public statement that is meant to serve the needs of others. The text, in other words, enacts Lorde's lived processes of moving from experience to activism. Disrupting the possibility of any single linear narrative, Lorde demonstrates her multiple roles, conveying her sense of the inadequacy of any one form of writing. By means of such generic interactions, furthermore, Lorde also foregrounds her concern that committing herself to paper is problematic for so multiple a self in such critical times. The unstable body destabilizes perception, recognition, and understanding so that the written texts present Lorde's fears that "the light would change before the word was out, the ink was dry" (1980, 45).

Sandra Butler and Barbara Rosenblum

In contrast to Lorde's solitary but multivoiced venture, Sandra Butler and Barbara Rosenblum responded to Barbara's cancer diagnosis by
embarking on their joint project, *Cancer in Two Voices*, as a map of their
experiences made visible to themselves for the duration, as an attempt
to fix meaning, and as a source of wisdom and experience for other
women. The text reads chronologically but is assembled, like Lorde's
text, from various source materials, in this case daybooks, letters, and
musings that create a sense of random dailiness. The spread of Barbara's
cancer and the repetitions of treatment acquire an exhausting, inescapable quality that retrospective narrative alone could not provide. Entries are separated by writer, sometimes strictly alternating "Sandy" and
"Barbara," often in monologues that respond or take over from the
other's entry, and sometimes indicating one woman for several con-
secutive entries. The continuous effect is of two "I"s and two "she"s,
with names serving both for identification and for reference. This interactive procedure bears comparison with Ken Wilber's *Grace and Grit*.
Presented as "authored" by Ken Wilber, *Grace and Grit* contains large
sections of Treya Wilber's journal, which she kept quite deliberately in
order to be able to serve other people with her own experience. Her
writing interacts with his, the two of them developing a line of thought
or narrative as if in a dialogue. Vertical lines in the left margin identify
Treya's journal voice and distinguish that private expression from her
public talks and letters. Like Ken Wilber, too, Sandra Butler completes
the work they had both begun, taking on the problematic roles of
survivor and therefore of final narrator.[25]

Cancer in Two Voices is a capacious text, including family issues, both
women's return to Judaism, and the personal and professional aspirations of both writers. "In this relationship," Barbara tells Sandy, "each
of us, who had written separately before, found a way to write together,
a way to blend, yet maintain a delicate separation" (118). She identifies
the quality of this collaboration at their formal ceremony of commitment to each other, in which, like Lorde, they combine the lover, the
writer, the suffering body-self, and the public activist into one self-
presentation. Their ceremony of commitment to each other, furthermore, is part of their reconnection with Judaism; attending a New York
commemoration of the Warsaw Ghetto uprising, they honor not death
but resistance. Raised in an assimilationist family, Sandy is at first un-
comfortable with Barbara's sense of witness but is drawn into a retrac-
ing of her own history: "I, too, needed to study, to enter the past

beyond the carefully manicured lives of my parents and their contemporaries and beyond the carefully screened remembrances of my grandparents" (138). The commemoration is held at P.S. 41, the school that both of Sandy's children had attended.

Both in such continuities and in their differences, these two writers are aware of reflecting each other in life and in text, certain inevitable distortions notwithstanding. Hoping for perfect harmony, Sandy opens the text in 1983: "The mirrors that were to reflect us in each other are cloudy and scratched, and we cannot always see where we are going or remember where we have been" (1). To which Barbara's text responds:

> I know she will say it's like a mirror, like looking at yourself in a mirror. It's not that way for me. It's more like two diamonds, each of which is spinning around. Maybe like a *dreydl* or dice, and I don't know which side will be up when it stops moving. Sometimes, only sometimes, does my Jewish or lesbian side match her Jewish or lesbian side. More often, it is a mismatch: my lower-class facet faces her maternal side, or my spare, tight, conceptual, academic side faces her dramatic, flamboyant, emotional side. (1)

From that opening, the text explores and enacts their adjustment of focus so that the dying subject and the supporting subject interact with increasing sensitivity to the needs of each other, neither at any point forfeiting her subject position. One result is even a degree of interchangeability between the two women not only in the rhythms of dialogue but also in the rhythms of their bodies.[26]

Like Lorde's texts, this work focuses necessarily and quite significantly on the body. "She is losing her hair," Sandy writes. "Next month she will lose a breast. It makes the cancer less an intellectual reality and more concrete, more physical" (19). Two years into the process, Barbara writes: "I seem to be getting simpler and simpler to myself, seem to know very clearly what my essence is. . . . The self revealed to the self, observed by the self. Simply. Coming to the essentials" (127–28). This disburdening of clutter brings Barbara to the Heideggerian position that "A dog dogs. The world worlds. Barbara Barbaras. A world where nouns and verbs dissolve into essences" (128). Concluding on her own some two years after Barbara's death, Sandy has been schooled by her own experience, by Barbara's, and by the joint texts on which she has been working; returning home from surgery to remove her own thyroid cancer, she comments simply, "The body bodies" (216).

Many months into her illness, Barbara finds body experiences unshareable. "I grow increasingly aware of the illusion of the intersubjective nature of the world. The world is shattered, language dissolves, and there is only body and its feeling. . . . [I]t is the intrusion of the body sensation that makes loneliness unbearable" (129–30). One impressive feat, accordingly, in the second half of the book, is a chapter entitled "Living in an Unstable Body." Barbara writes at length about the body changes that have followed cancer: chemotherapy, mastectomy, radiation, more chemotherapy, and metastases. She writes of the disruption of body patterns, behavior, and appearance, and her confusion about body signals: "I was thrown into a crisis of meaning," she writes. "I could no longer assess and evaluate what sensations meant. I could no longer measure the intensity of sensations. I was no longer fluent in the language of my body, its signs and symbols, and I felt lost" (164–65).

Writing in isolation, Barbara has left Sandy also isolated at the kitchen table. "She has just begun to write a piece about her changing relationship to her body," Sandy begins, "and has announced quite firmly that she wants to write it alone" (169). Used to writing together, to what Barbara calls making love at the typewriter, Sandy asks herself what she would add if she were asked, but is interrupted by Barbara coming down the hall wanting a reader. "She has just come down the hall," Sandy continues, "carrying the pages she has written. As I read them my eyes fill with tears of recognition. I read how she experiences us making love at the typewriter. How each morning we . . . typed, interrupted, criticized, added, paced, drank coffee, laughed, then grew thoughtful, intense, or joyous with relief when just the right word or image emerged. It was a making of love" (171). Reading of Barbara's physical symptoms, Sandy even recognizes with surprise that she shares many of them in her own body, that she too has gained weight and lost energy. Becoming an extension of Barbara's physical capacities, Sandy finds that "her sexuality has become 'our' sexuality . . . her body has become 'our' body" (172). As Sandy examines her responsiveness to Barbara's needs she discovers the danger she herself runs; the healthy partner does not "reflect" the cancer patient unless her body also ceases to be well. It is also Barbara's responsiveness, however, in her eyes and voice, that enables Sandy to confirm what Audre Lorde's text states as personal discovery: "She is still there inside her changing body" (174).

Dennis Potter in Camera

It seems appropriate to conclude this discussion of autothanatography with a very brief text that is governed quite intensely by its own brevity; Dennis Potter's *Seeing the Blossom* is actually a transcript of a short interview he gave the writer Melvyn Bragg shortly before his death. Potter was so ill when he gave this interview that he could not judge at what point the interview (like his life, indeed) would need to be cut short. Having written so extensively for television, Potter chose to be filmed in a television studio. "[G]rateful for the chance . . . to say [his] last words" (28), he chose his artistic medium as his medium for life-and-death self-presentation.[27] His comfort with the mechanics of television and his interest in a particular audience connect his work very closely with his thinking about life, as does his long practice of working with dialogue. Bragg's introduction makes the working informality of the occasion clear; on film, the cables, lights, and sometimes the crew are all apparent. Every aspect of this scenario, in short, is interactive on technical, professional, and personal levels. When an old and trusted friend asks Potter about his cancer, his childhood, his father, his work, and his thoughts on England, they create between them a voluble, powerful overflow, so to speak, of Potter facing his death.

As soon as Potter knew he was dying, he began writing feverishly, sustained by his doctor, "who has so gently and carefully led [him] to a balance between pain control and mental control where [he] can work" (27). If he can finish the plays that excite him as he and Bragg speak, his final work in what has clearly been an intense vocation, he will go happily: "[M]y only regret is to die four pages too soon" he says, conflating himself and his text;[28] "if I can finish, then I'm quite happy to go. I don't mind, you know. I am quite serene. I'm not . . . I haven't had a single moment of terror since they told me. I know I'm going to die" (28). He is "measuring out [his] days," one might say, in dialogue. This is the story of the story, as Eakin calls it (1998), the complicated self-reflexivity in which relationship figures in both narration and production of narration, which turns in this case toward the corpus of work that will replace the living presence. This consists of two plays, which develop in elaborate metaphor the situation in which Potter finds himself as a playwright performing his own death. *Cold Lazarus* involves cryogenics, "freezing bodies of people, very rich people for eventual regeneration when they can cure whatever it is they died of" (25). In this case, a frozen head reveals, as it thaws, memories of the lived realities of Potter's times. Surprising their "audience" in a time of virtual realities, these memories are seized as a media coup. Ironically, the man with the memories no longer wishes to be healed and restored because he knows now that life is meant to end in death. He is, nonetheless, trapped in the media machine. Cold Lazarus, furthermore, is the central character of *Karaoke*, a playwright, caught up in a terrible series of confusions between his godlike powers of scripting characters, relationships, and events, and the recurring possibility that he himself has neither power nor originality but is imitating life, even being overtaken by live realities. Potter the man is absorbed by the life-and-death issues of Potter the playwright, which are, of course, those of Potter the man, and by the excitement of transmitting in drama the wisdom he gleans from approaching death. Very important, too, is his sense that these plays will be his memorial, his enduring words from beyond his own grave.

Having pointed to the creative interaction that Potter stresses between his life and his work, I need also to stress the intensity of Potter's bodily presence on screen: very frail, very ill, chain-smoking, braced with champagne, coffee, and a morphine flask that he needs quite urgently but is too weak to open. The printed text is a direct (though much abbreviated) transcript, so the physical tension is apparent in sentences that stutter and are incomplete. Such patterns are common in conversation but are also due here to a continuous urgency of articulation. Potter's fragile physical presence, expressed on the page by urgent, broken syntax, once again connects the body under sentence of death with the sentences in which each autothanatographer recreates multiple versions of the self, substantial if only for the time being, and articulate because not all alone.

GENRES OF DEATH AS GENRES OF LIFE

Repeatedly, autothanatographers acknowledge intense living in their processes of self-constitution, and the passing of the baton from living presence to some form of text that contains that intense living and outlives the life. Paul Monette likens the artist's need for a record to graffiti or initials on trees. Sandra Butler and Barbara Rosenblum describe a process of mapmaking that makes them visible to themselves. Audre Lorde "resolve[s] to print [her]self upon the texture of each day fully rather than forever" (1988, 127). Her conflation of person and text includes the crucial connection between the living present and the text that indicates the intensity of living without a future tense. Discussing *Silverlake Life*, Peggy Phelan observes that Joslin "wants to suggest that dying, like living, is an 'is'—its Being fills the present. Dying is not in the future; death is not in the past. Dying is" (392). Peter Noll finds no value in speculating on "how closely, if at all, thought can approach death" (61), and concludes that death does not require such speculation. "Rather, my concern is exclusively with life, life in the face of death, life viewed from the perspective of death. Then everything becomes much simpler and clearer. The limitation in time, the clock ticking away: this I can experience. Death stays the same, but life becomes different" (62). Rosenblum clearly feels the same: "I can even pick my favorite color and favorite ethnic food. I experience my choices and preferences as a step towards clarity, rather than limitation. Simplification, maybe that's what this process is called. It feels more like coming into one's fullest and truest self and simply acknowledging what is" (127–28). Where Treya Wilber knows she may not "live out the year" and exclaims "But just listen to those birds sing!" (280), Potter provides the title for his printed interview, *Seeing the Blossom.* Overriding or penetrating the pain and his own sense of a race against time is his intensity of experiencing the now: "Below my window in Ross . . . the blossom is out in full now . . . it's a plum tree, it looks like apple blossom but it's white, and looking at it, instead of saying 'Oh that's nice blossom' . . . last week looking at it through the window when I'm writing, I *see* it is the whitest, frothiest, blossomest blossom that there ever could be, and I can see it. . . . [T]he nowness of every-thing is absolutely wondrous" (5).

At the point of departure from living, these autothanatographers enact in various ways what Miller has called "the life wish . . . inextrica-bly bound up with the death plot" (1992a, 28). They redeem their lifetime not by narrative, and certainly not by making sense or meaning out of their experience, but rather by a strenuous focus on illness, pain, and imminent death as crucial to the processes of that life. Their texts depend, accordingly, on strategies that deconstruct personal autonomy and continuity — strategies that mirror the unpredictable quality both of the lived experience and of life itself, reaffirming only the moment and that, too, only as process. Such strategies serve to express and to "realize," or make real, identities at the very point of demolition.

Coda: Talking Back
Autobiography as Mirror Talk

Death is life's ultimate crisis, stalking the pages of life writing not only, as de Man would have it, because the text overrides the life, but also, as Couser, Eakin, and Miller understand, because language enables humankind to recognize, anticipate, or live in relation to crisis of every kind.[1] I have focused here on contemporary responses to death but suspect that such attention to consciousness of death could affect our understanding of autobiography from all periods. Contemporary work would then be distinctive not for foregrounding death but for its creative re-culturation of the role of death in our lives. The autothanatographers considered here have been unable to rest on any widely held beliefs about death. They have needed to invent their own ceremonies and explanations. This ultimate crisis has challenged not only their daily living but also, quite crucially, their sense of story or of meaning, which reaches in these genres for final expression. In each case, they have resisted conclusion, opting instead for that ironic ambivalence so common to dialogic autobiography in which each possibility or voice or perspective exists in relation to others that are equally valid. Such ironic ambivalence is determined in part by the absence of master narratives suitable to this largely secular time, and in part by each dying person's dependence on forms of mirror talk that constitute his or her presence.

Like autobiographers of diaspora, who constantly create themselves anew, contemporary autothanatographers create the life of the moment over and over, preferring to mark time as present, liminal space rather than in terms of past or future. Embedding the crisis in the presentation is not, of course, to abandon time, but it does focus inquiry on surface and depth rather than on history or on any teleological drive. Making one's self visible or mapping identity are not only figures of speech but also tropes for recovery of understanding, which is always elusive. Because these genres foreground the plurality and processes of identity and of autobiography, they are also transformative; neither the person nor the text can reveal any single or final truth, but both can provide activities of interpretation, in which the reader is compelled to join. As interpretive subjects, readers, too, find time and its subordinates of beginnings and ends, causes and effects, less valuable than the spatial relations of multiple meanings. We become part of the map of interpretation.

And just as diaspora writing is quintessentially autobiographical, so autothanatography may be seen as the prime synecdoche for all specifically crisis-driven autobiography, which has traditionally been, almost by definition, "obscene": off the stage of cultural acceptance, off the margins of literary canons, marginal even to autobiography studies because its single focus seems to represent "the life" inadequately. The urgent, inventive, transgressive qualities so common to almost all the works examined here have frequently been political in very practical terms: AIDS and breast cancer research need funding, aboriginal peoples need justice, genocide recurs. They have also been political in more personal terms: How can the experience of each diasporic writer enrich and enable whole communities who live in transition between languages and who try to make sense of interrupted or diverted narratives? How can the homosexual experience best navigate in waters ideologically controlled for at least the past few hundred years by heterosexual "norms"? Lived experience that lacks a master narrative is precarious at best, impervious to examination, analysis, or understanding. At worst, such experience is invalid — incredible, invisible, unreal. The crisis that originates in living seeks affirmation and some cultural adjustment in its narration; inviting recognition, mirror talk also adjusts what can be said or seen, vigorously resisting the "obscene."

Mirror talk is profoundly implicated in such resistance. Clearly, it conveys some sense of Lacan's illusion of wholeness received from reflection, but it tends to emphasize mere glimpses or indications of experience and meaning, of relationship and of the processes of narration, rather than revealing some core identity. By virtue of being multifaceted, mirror talk reflects the very indeterminacy of life in crisis. Every reflection examined here has also provided contestation. Crisis, for example, assumes some condition of "normality," or non-crisis. Failed narrative or disrupted processes of narrative posit the impossibility of traditional story. Literatures that provide moments of recognition, like vocabularies that shift in value, like political and geographical spaces that do and do not become part of the past, or like time that is neither linear nor logical, do not provide reassurance so much as they indicate the terms of crisis in which these familiar guides to human experience become inadequate. Even the most supportive of partners or communities presents reflection in terms of what the subject is *not*. Insofar as subjectivity is a central organizing principle in acts of interpretation,[2] subjectivities conflict within each text, producing affirmative but also alternative perspectives, polyphony rather than reiteration. Hemingway's pyrotechnics enable Fitzgerald's perspective to stand independently, controlled in the end, perhaps, only by Hemingway's own choice of an adequate rival. Griffiths and Campbell or, more amiably, Blaise and Mukherjee identify their own experience and understanding as contested. Even Tom Joslin and Mark Massi or Sandra Butler and Barbara Rosenblum, who position themselves as reflections for each other, identify their differences by doing so, and define individual subjectivity in terms of its struggle to exist.

The drama of self-reconstruction, of insisting upon an originary person at a certain point in history, plays out as drama, whether literally on the stage or screen, or in oral dialogues, or within the covers of a printed text — as when Breytenbach sets up numerous elusive narrators, or when Lorde juxtaposes the various genres in which she writes. Mirror talk, accordingly, not only includes numerous genres but also incorporates them into this contestatory space in which plural subjects coexist "for the time being." Technologies of film and photography become extensions of particular perspectives and contribute to the pluralities within each autobiography. They also introduce technical and generic challenges and opportunities for each autobiographer, becoming part of the struggle to establish and insist upon some prior if not autonomous self. As Eakin argues, "the tension between the experiential reality of subjectivity on the one hand and the available, cultural forms for its expression on the other always structures any engagement in autobiography" (1992, 88). Just as traditional autobiography emerged with the novel, so contemporary autobiography turns to the equally flexible and demotic genres of theater, film, photography, comics, quilting, or conversation.

If genre provides a protocol for reading, autobiography's voracious consumption of genres implicates the reader in the polyphony of each text. Clearly, our own subject positions determine our interpretation at each engagement, but these interpretations themselves cannot remain singular because one's engagement with texts like those considered here is always plural and always in process of correction, adjustment, and new possibility. Not only do we step into a different stream each time we read, as we might with a monologic text, but we are stepping into a stream whose currents are already in competition with one another. Our experience of each text becomes part of its instability, part of its unresolved search for meaning or its "impulse towards orientation" (Gunn, 9). Our experience also becomes part of the reflexivity of each text, part of the extraordinary collaboration whereby Cézanne's "famous apples [which] seem about to roll off the table because they are seen from several vantage-points at once" (Ryan, 93) are both precarious and, curiously, despite such crisis, confirmed. The final irony is that polyphony, which serves to replicate the instabilities of the original crisis, serves also to confirm its existence and to secure our ability to believe and to trust in that much.

I have traced deliberate dialogism in autobiography to modernist experimentation. Certainly, we could trace it also to aboriginal story-telling, to marginalized literatures, to developments in anthropology, to film, and so on. I am also open to the suggestion that we could reread traditional, presumably monologic texts positing an autonomous, authoritative self and find unexpected polyphonies. What has engaged me, however, are the connections between crisis, trauma, or extreme marginalization and the genres in which they can be represented. Many of these texts elaborate on a Bakhtinian understanding of the disruption or overthrow of conventional literary forms, pushing at the edges of specific genres in order to bend and blur, combine and recreate. They introduce transformation as a trope for processes of exploration; because neither subjects nor situations stand still, because both time and space serve unconventional purposes, because memory is less the issue than the specific and unresolved predicament, the reader (from Mary Hemingway on) is shaken out of conventional expectations and becomes implicated in emerging identities and the cultures that they and their crises create.

If mirror talk, then, can serve to describe an exploratory process that depends not only on double or multiple voicing but also on oppositionality and the improvisations that emerge in dynamic and reciprocal relations among both people and genres, then I suspect that it will also describe aspects of the oral literatures and the relations between photography and autobiography that are currently receiving so much attention, and that it will apply to work that may be done on web literatures, music, or dance. Just as the politics of autobiography are more than personal and extend into the desire for change beyond any individual life in question, so explorations of the individual life and death seek communal meaning. For these reasons, both autobiography and our attempts to interpret it need to be reborn again and again. They are central to the cultures we inherit and create.

Notes

1 *George Washington Williams: A Biography*, by John Hope Franklin; *Lorelei Two: My Life with Conrad Aiken*, by Clarissa M. Lorenz; and *Terra Infirma*, by Rodger Kamenetz.

2 James Clifford, writing on ethnography in his introduction to *Writing Culture*, includes a vivid story on the partial nature of singular truth-telling. He tells of the Cree hunter coming to Montreal to testify in court about the effect on Cree hunting lands of the James Bay hydroelectric scheme. The hunter is said to have hesitated at the court requirement to speak under oath: "'I'm not sure I can tell the truth,'" he said. "'I can only tell what I know'" (8).

3 See Olney 1972, Fleishman 1983, Egan 1984, and Eakin 1985. Eakin's subtitle, *Studies in the Art of Self-Invention*, denotes what he calls "the auto-biographical imperative" and the tension he details between the self and its creation, focusing on the making rather than the recording of "truth." See also Adams 1990 on the positive (narrative) values of telling lies.

4 See, in particular, Bruss 1976, Gunn 1982, Stone 1982, and Jay 1984.

5 Miller 1996 is a case in point, but for various stages of this autobiographical involvement, see Kadar's call for autobiography as a critical practice (1992, 10–12), Jouve 1991, Freedman, Frey, and Zauhar 1993, and Veeser 1996.

6 Carolyn A. Barros points out that "change, as it is inscribed in autobiog-raphy, has itself changed. The transformation of a self, central to auto-biographical discourse in earlier times, has changed to a consciousness of textual transformation—from the self speaking language to language speaking the self" (22). Sidonie Smith makes the point succinctly: "the subject is now more spoken by language than speaker of language, more product of discursive regimes than explorer of any reified self-essence" (1993, 55–56). I tend to come at this observation the other way around, allowing the speaker more control over the languages in which to be spo-ken. Several of the texts I shall be discussing suggest, indeed, that personal transformation manifests itself as textual transformation, which contrib-utes to the multiplicity of genres now available for autobiography and to the merging and blending that autobiographers frequently inflict on tradi-tional genres. Although the autobiographer may not dare to look for any reified self-essence, s/he certainly discovers new modes in which to be spoken.

7 For autobiographical works, see, for example, Kaysen, Murphy, Nolan, Price, Sacks, Styron, Williams, and Zola. For theoretical discussions, see, in particular, Gilman 1987 and 1988, Goffman 1986, and Eakin 1999.

8 It is surely symptomatic of this concern, and of its "common sense," that de Man's discrediting of an extra-textual self should itself be discreditable not in terms of theory but in terms of the pre-textual life of the theorist — or in terms of his extra-textual uses of texts.

9 See Blake Morrison 1993 and Roth 1991.

10 Benjamin refers to D. W. Winnicott, "The Mirror Role of Mother and Family in Child Development"; Heinz Kohut, *The Restoration of the Self*; feminist criticism of the mirror metaphor in Carol Gilligan, "Remapping the Moral Domain"; and criticism in terms of infancy research in Daniel Stern, *The Interpersonal World of the Infant*. See Benjamin, 252–53 n. 27.

11 I refer both to the death of the author, and to de Man's suggestion that language cannot refer effectively to lived experience, that the figure determines the referent, that subject and object are congruent only by means of the illusion of the mirror.

12 Mary G. Mason concluded from her survey of women's autobiographies that "the self-discovery of female identity seems to acknowledge the real presence and recognition of another consciousness, and the disclosure of female self is linked to the identification of some 'other'" (210). Susan Friedman extended this finding to suggest that the female identifies herself not just in relation to a single other but to a community of others. Sidonie Smith raises the question whether "female preoccupation with the other [is] an essential dynamic of female psychobiography or a culturally conditioned manifestation of the ideology of gender that associates female difference with attentiveness to the other? Or does all autobiographical practice proceed by means of a self/other intersubjectivity and intertextuality?" (1987, 18). In their introduction to *Feminism and the Politics of Difference*, Sneja Gunew and Anna Yeatman discuss difference "not simply as the self-confirming other, but as the admission and recognition of incommensurabilities" (xiv).

13 The work of Carol Gilligan and Nancy Chodorow preceded that of Jessica Benjamin.

14 See Donna Perreault on the subject of autobiography as interrogative: "So a question is speaker-referential even while it addresses an external state of affairs and solicits another subject's response" (131).

15 See Christian Metz's "The Imaginary Signifier," in which he discusses cinema in association with Lacan's mirror stage.

16 I do not see these terms as interchangeable, the latter being both less technical and more open to inequities of representation than the former; it suggests a mode of positioning the self rather than an interactive mode of self-production.

17 Chambers also connects this observation to oppositional constructions of identity. When the oppositional subject transforms itself from narratee to narrator, or interpretive subject, its new "position . . . manifests the dependence of identity on otherness" (17).

18 Olney is surely referring to Philippe Lejeune with his reference to pacts, but it is worth noting, as Eakin does, that Lejeune himself, originally among the most legalistic of theorists, has dramatically expanded his range of

reference: "In *Je est un autre* and related pieces, which expand the frontiers of the study of autobiography from a narrowly literary to a broadly social and cultural context, Lejeune explodes the structures of medium and person that have traditionally defined the genre" (Eakin 1989, xix).

19 As these various technologies are available to laypeople who recognize the therapeutic value of reviewing a life near its close, strategists can help with the recording of family lives. See, for example, Rosenbluth 1997.

20 Cleve Jones began a panel for his friend Marvin Feldman, who died of AIDS in October 1986. A storefront operation opened in San Francisco in 1987, beginning a process whereby tens of thousands of people across the continent could make their own panels. David Bergman describes the NAMES quilt in Washington, October 1987: "Stretched out between the rows of autumnal trees, the Quilt turned Washington into both a bed and a grave" (185). By October 1988, almost 9,000 squares were spread on the White House lawn. In September 1990, Jones wrote of 12,000 panels. (See Elsley, 41 and 45.)

21 See Eakin's introduction to *Touching the World* for an extended discussion of Barthes on language and photography. See also Marianne Hirsch, who writes of texts and images in *Camera Lucida* as placed in "several different types of relationship: opposition, collaboration, parallelism" (9).

22 For some important new studies of visual representation in autobiography, see Adams 1999, Hirsch 1997, and Rugg 1997.

23 I am grateful to my son, David Egan, whose graduating essay for the International Baccalaureate, on comics as a distinct and literary genre, first persuaded me to read comics. His help as I did so has also been invaluable.

24 Hirsch comments on Spiegelman's inclusion of three actual photographs in the comics, suggesting that they "protrude from the narrative like unassimilated and unassimilable memories" (29).

25 Miller reads Anja Spiegelman, like St. Augustine's mother Monica, as generating this autobiography (1994, 1–27). For Hirsch, the father-son collaboration is a "masculine, Orphic creation" which "can bring Eurydice out of Hades, even as it actually needs to leave her behind" (34–35). See Charlotte Salomon for a different combination of language and pictures. Her third-person narrative, as in a child's story, is illustrated with large and colorful paintings. These are entirely flat, devoid of perspective, and frequently charged with a number of scenes, or with multiple versions of one scene (the child getting up frequently in the night). They become spare, stark, dramatic, the colors flat and drab as the war closes in. Salomon was taken to Auschwitz in September 1943.

26 Sidonie Smith and Julia Watson, in their introduction to *Getting a Life*, respond to the myth of autobiography as singular, coherent, and monologic: "But autobiographical storytelling, and by this we mean broadly the practices through which people assemble narratives out of their own experiential histories, cannot escape being dialogical, although its central myths resist that recognition" (19).

27 See, in particular, Françoise Lionnet's *Autobiographical Voices*, chap. 4, for its extended discussion of the work of Maya Angelou.

CHAPTER TWO

1 See Miller 1994 on rereading Saint Augustine or Eakin's unraveling of traditional formulations of individualism: "Do they, we need to ask, accurately
describe Rousseau's self-representation in *The Confessions?*" (1998, 66).

2 Adapted and reprinted from *a/b: Auto/Biography Studies* 9 (Spring 1994).
Copyright (c) 1994 by the Hall Center for the Humanities, University of
Kansas. Used by permission of the publisher. I am also grateful to The
Ernest Hemingway Foundation for permission to quote from unpublished
materials and from manuscript drafts for *A Moveable Feast*. I have incorporated only those deletions and emendations of the draft that could affect
our understanding of the development of the text. I have retained the *x* that
Hemingway tends to use as a period in order to convey some sense of his
hasty-looking manuscript.

3 Hemingway was indignant about the nastiness of Mizener's article on
Fitzgerald in *Life*. He called it grave robbing to sell the body. Later he
himself wrote a piece on Fitzgerald for the *Atlantic* and told Harvey Breit
he was pleased with it: "[I]t was tough to write and easy to remember and
I thought it was very interesting." But he withdrew it and sent them a story
instead. See Tavernier-Courbin 1980 (290–303).

4 Brenner makes the excellent point that *remate*, the technical term for deflection in *jai alai*, signifies a "kill-shot" (218). Working from Hemingway's
style, Brenner proceeds to demonstrate that Hemingway "usually slays his
victims by letting them die of self-exposure" (219). I suggest that Fitzgerald's self-exposure exposes Hemingway as well, and that both are vulnerable to this violent game of self- and other-de(con)struction.

5 Edmund Wilson drew Fitzgerald's attention to *in our time*, published by
the Three Mountains Press in 1924. Fitzgerald then recommended Hemingway enthusiastically to Maxwell Perkins of Scribner's and was active in
getting Hemingway onto Scribner's list.

6 Bruccoli points out that Hemingway is inaccurate here; this dust jacket,
which "has been greatly admired as an example of dust-jacket art," has "a
woman's face over an amusement park night scene" (20).

7 This kind of deflection parallels that used in his discussion of Stein; from
her he seems to learn only about homosexuality. Again, what reads at the
literal level as Hemingway's nastiness toward a former friend reads also as a
textual diversion from the central issues of the autobiographer's activity.

8 Bruccoli describes this tie as legitimate garb only in the Brigade of Guards,
"which consists of the five regiments of Foot Guards as well as the Household cavalry" (17).

9 Referred to in Wickes 1974. This pointed lapse of memory compares with
that at the opening of *The Sun Also Rises*, when no one at Princeton remembers Robert Cohn.

10 Adapted and reprinted by permission from *Prose Studies* 14 (1991), published by Frank Cass & Co. Ltd, 900 Eastern Avenue, Ilford IG2 7HH,
Essex, England.

11 Meigs's strategy is comparable to that of Lillian Hellman in *Pentimento*;

portraits of significant people in her life allow glimpses of her but only in relationship.

12 See Callaghan for a third eye perceiving Hemingway and Fitzgerald together.

13 See Kennard 1984 for a discussion of reading what one is not that enables formulation of the self, precisely because it involves full recognition of what is *other*.

14 Christina Rossetti may have felt the same as she sat for her brother's paintings. Margaret Homans discusses unpublished work by Sandra Ludig on Rossetti's angel Gabriel pointing his lily like a paintbrush at the womb of the terrified virgin (310n). H.D.'s Her reacts in ways Meigs could identify with; when George Lowndes tells her that she is a poem but her poetry is naught, she finds herself a female lover.

15 See Homans 1986 for the pre-symbolic, literal, or non-representational language of presence. She focuses on Mrs. Ramsay talking to her son and her daughter in distinctive languages (17–18).

16 Adapted and reprinted by permission from the *Journal of Narrative Technique* 18.2 (Spring 1988).

17 Jacobo Timerman writes, as a journalist and after the event, about his imprisonment in Argentina. His present-tense vignettes lack the surreal fantasy that informs Breytenbach's work but suggest equivalent and alarming times of total dislocation and disconnection. He adumbrates an exclusive and absorbing world that "is real, that corresponds to the inscriptions on the wall, the odor of the latrine matching that emitted by my skin and clothes, and those drab colors, the sounds of metal and violence, the harsh, shrill, hysterical voices" (85).

18 Gloucester at the cliffs of Dover provides a powerful sequence in Ondaatje's *Running in the Family*; it could be interesting to examine the very different uses these two writers make of this scene of testing and revelation that so entirely lacks human interaction.

19 See Primo Levi's essay, "The Dispute among German Historians" (1990), which appeared in Italian as "Buco nero di Auschwitz." The image of the Black Hole into which the autobiographer has disappeared and from which he may not be recovered is vivid for the prisoner of extreme circumstances.

20 See Eakin, especially 1999.

CHAPTER THREE

1 Peter Friedman, personal correspondence, March 27, 1994.

2 I am grateful to Jim Lane, who allowed me to watch his personal copies of these films.

3 *Life Lived Like a Story* is Julie Cruikshank's title for the autobiographies of three Yukon elders whose narration escaped the framework of her expectations.

4 This concept of subjective experience as spatial, or to be defined in terms of space, becomes important for discussion of diasporic autobiographies in

Chapter 4. Geographical relations, distances, and specific terrain interact with the linear procedures of language to complicate time sequence and to indicate the tenuous, indeed critical way in which subjective experience of the present moment, like Breytenbach's cubic chessboard, contains lost worlds and opportunities.

5 Expanded with permission from *Canadian Literature* 144 (Spring 1995).

6 See Murray 1999 for discussion of gift exchange and problematic treaties between Native or Métis and white settlers.

7 Fortunately, these situations keep evolving. In December 1997, the Supreme Court of Canada reversed Chief Justice Allan McEachern's finding. It did not suggest that he had misapplied the law as it existed in 1991. "Rather, it was introducing a new, more relaxed rule respecting the use of hearsay evidence in aboriginal rights cases and making it apply retroactively. . . . Chief Justice Lamer asserted that 'the laws of evidence must be adapted in order that (aboriginal oral histories) can be accommodated and placed on an equal footing with the types of historical evidence that courts are familiar with, which largely consists of historical documents.' In his view, the failure to consider such evidence when no written history exists would impose an impossible burden of proof on aboriginal peoples" (*Vancouver Sun*, Thursday, December 18, 1997, A19).

8 Terry Goldie has referred to the indigene as a "semiotic pawn on a chessboard under the control of the white signmaker" (70). Griffiths's recognition of the ideologies controlling her perception of what Marcia Crosby has called "the imaginary Indian," and of herself as also semiotically controlled, is important for the "exchange."

9 Penny van Toorn has drawn my attention to Joan Crate's poem (in Petrone, 161), from *Pale as Real Ladies*, to which Griffiths's situation seems to be responding; here, little half-Native girls

> . . . curl [their] hair and dust talcum powder
> over cheeks and eyelids,
> turn pale as real ladies.

10 Arnold Krupat tells me: "One reason there aren't autobiographical documents in Native cultures is demographic: no small scale society, in which everybody knows everybody else and their business would *need* to hear people tell of their lives. They know their lives and know their own lives are known. The other reason, more complicated, is that narratives ostensibly about other people, 'mythic' or 'historical' are also taken as bearing on one's own life history" (letter dated November 25, 1993). In a letter of June 9, 1998, Krupat adds that the Osage poet Carter Revard suggested the first point to him. The second he derives from his reading of Cruikshank. Krupat's comments on my writing on *The Book of Jessica* were generous and constructive but did not support my reading.

11 The indeterminacy that Lionnet describes as *métissage* appears also in *Jessica*, the play; transformations blur the boundaries established in traditional theater by scenes. Jerry Wasserman has pointed out in conversation that *Princess Pocahontas and the Blue Spots*, by Monique Mojica, another Métis writer, also uses such transformations.

1 Autobiographies of diaspora are particularly comparable to aboriginal autobiographies for their incorporation of oral narrative. Authenticating their "voices" in nonliterary languages, or with vocabulary that is not English, or from oral histories and family narratives, the Native and the diasporic both challenge cultural hierarchies by destabilizing the literary.

2 Pointing out the centrality of memory to ethnicity and to autobiography, Jennifer Browdy de Hernandez suggests that one useful concept for ethnicity is that of dialogue between ethnic and dominant cultures. She quotes Dan Aronson's definition of ethnicity as "an ideology of and for value dissensus and disengagement from an inclusive sociopolitical arena" (58) — a definition, she feels, that adds an important political dimension to ethnicity while eliminating essentialism. For sustained and valuable work on ethnicity in women's autobiography, see Lionnet 1995 and Smith and Watson 1992.

3 Autobiographers of diaspora do not seem concerned with replacing the center but with destabilizing its claims to universality, with upsetting the very concepts of center and peripheries. For example, Maxine Hong Kingston's question in *China Men* is "to find out how we landed in a country where we are eccentric people" (15).

4 See Sau-ling Cynthia Wong (1992) for a detailed discussion of Chinese American responses to *The Woman Warrior*. In general terms, Chinese Americans object to the liberties Kingston takes with traditional stories and suggest she should be a more responsible cultural interpreter of the Chinese for the white reader.

5 Commenting on Edward Said's "Reflections on Exile," Sneja Gunew describes "a productive tension resulting from a type of double vision" (38). Like the autobiographer, the critic and theorist is working with geography rather than history, identifying overlapping and contested terrains.

6 Near the middle of *China Men*, Kingston inserts a chapter called "The Laws," which details the punitive Exclusion Acts and attendant legislation directed against Chinese immigration. Not until 1952 were Chinese women allowed to immigrate under the same conditions as men. Clearly, Kingston's family took advantage of the 1898 Supreme Court decision that "stated that a person born in the United States to Chinese parents is an American" (1977, 155–56).

7 Quite apart from concerns that terminology could oversimplify relations between colonial and postcolonial, theorists also try not to elide or ignore the neocolonialism currently practiced by international corporations in the presumably postcolonial era. Lionnet, for instance, suggests "postcontact" as a more precise term that allows for simultaneity among forms of experience (1995, 4).

8 Lionnet borrows the term "transculturation" from the Cuban poet Nancy Morejón because it indicates the cultural interaction that takes place between dominant and minority cultures. As a spatial concept, furthermore, it frees the minority to describe appropriation — of language, for instance — rather than victimization by it. See Beth Cuthand's comments on Native uses of English quoted in Chapter 3.

9 David Malouf captures an extraordinary image of the liminal, transitional figure with his Gemmy, who shouts from the top rail of the fence, "arms outflung as if preparing for flight . . . 'Do not shoot. . . . I am a B-b-british object!'" (3).

10 Resistance to definition by the dominant culture forming a significant component of diasporic autobiography, Ruth Frankenberg and Lata Mani contribute to this discussion with their understanding of the struggle of African Americans in the United States as a "political resource for forging imagined diasporic communities" (285).

11 Eakin suggests that Rodriguez's "sense of the costs of acculturation distinguishes [him] from the expansive, upbeat hymns to the process of Americanization that we find in Jacob Riis, Mary Antin, and many another ethnic autobiographer" (1992, 119). Distinguishing Rodriguez within this particular tradition also suggests his being born out of time.

12 Rodriguez's deracination is distinct among those considered here because it is so largely a matter of class. Gayatri Spivak suggests the artificial separation of public and private "is, strictly speaking, a cultural class-separation" (1996, 239). Also, Rodriguez's self-identification with Richard Hoggart's "scholarship boy" associates the Mexican working-class boy growing up in the States with the working-class English boy, both of them "upwardly" mobile by virtue of education.

13 The risk identified here is not for everyone; Rodriguez's pellucid prose positions him without apology in the Eurocentric tradition of the formally literate.

14 The role playing in this film is worth comparing with that in *The Company of Strangers* and in the play, *Jessica*. The interview techniques, while necessarily resulting from significant editing, appear to be more free-standing than those in the other filmed interviews I have discussed: *Talk 16, Talk 19,* and *35 Up*.

15 While English may be a powerful tool for the autobiographer who uses it as a second language, the English-speaking reader might need to listen to Homi K. Bhabha's warning about the will to power inherent in cultural and discursive systems: "[I]n failing to specify the limits of their own field of enunciation and effectivity, [they] proceed to individualize otherness as the discovery of their own assumptions" (154).

16 Trinh explains that the title of the film "is taken from a recent socialist tradition. When a man encounters a woman, feels drawn to her, and wants to flirt with her, he teasingly asks, 'Young woman, are you married yet?' If the answer is negative, instead of saying no, she will reciprocate, 'Yes, his surname is Viet and his given name is Nam'" (142). The title, accordingly, comments on the conditions of marriage and single women and on cultural affiliations across the history of foreign dominations and the move to the States. Not surprisingly, and in keeping with the rest of the film, "[a] slight mutation of meaning occurs in that affirmation as it gets transferred from one context to another" (142).

17 "[W]hen I hunted for the magic place during geography lessons or in free library time, I never found it, and came to believe my mother's geography was a fantasy. . . . But underneath it all as I was growing up, *home* was still a

sweet place somewhere else which they had not managed to capture yet on paper, nor to throttle and bind up between the pages of a schoolbook" (14).

18 Lorde was active in collaborative, feminist publishing, working in particular to create openings for women of color. Later in life, she achieved mainstream recognition for her own work; just as she spoke on "The Transformation of Silence into Language and Action" at the Modern Language Association in 1977 (a talk published in *The Cancer Journals*), so her poetry is also now available from W. W. Norton.

19 "Zami" is a derogatory term in French patois used in the West Indies to describe lesbians as "les amies."

20 In an entirely different context, Spivak observes that "*Bharati*, all complexities of history and geography forgotten, can be taken as identical with the contemporary (Hindi) name for India" (1996, 240).

21 Mukherjee's early immersion in a liminal consciousness is wonderfully manifest in her later hurling of Vishnu novenas at her uncle's ghost (294).

22 In Mukherjee's *Wife*, Dimple Dasgupta is isolated in a marriage whose reality conflicts disastrously with her expectations, which had been conditioned by films, magazines, and television. When she murders her husband, her violent anger, suppressed but apparent in her relations with the widely varied Hindu society of New York, is Dimple's most convincing response to her impossible situation.

23 Writing in *Mother Jones* in 1997, Mukherjee describes "'America,' which to [her] is the stage for the drama of self-transformation" (32). She is, nonetheless, indignant at the Eurocentric exclusions increasingly practiced in the States that hyphenate the "American" of immigrants of color. "Multiculturalism, as it has been practiced in the United States in the past 10 years, implies the existence of a central culture, ringed by peripheral cultures" (34). She, like Maxine Hong Kingston, argues for no hyphenation; they are Americans of particular descent.

24 Kingston writes of wearing dog tags for the Korean War, the identification they provided suggesting a comparable but subtler form of erasure. "We had to fill out a form for what to engrave on the dog tags. I looked up 'religion' in the *American-Chinese Dictionary* and asked my mother what religion we were. 'Our religion is Chinese,' she said. 'But that's not a religion,' I said. 'Yes it is,' she said. 'We believe in the Chinese religion.' 'Chinese is our race,' I said. 'Well, tell the teacher demon it's Kung Fu Tse, then,' she said. The kids at school said, 'Are you Catholic?' 'No.' 'Then you're a Protestant.' So our dog tags had *O* for religion and *O* for race because neither black nor white. Mine also had *O* for blood type. Some kids said *O* was for 'Oriental,' but I knew it was for 'Other' because the Filipinos, the Gypsies, and the Hawaiian boy were *O*'s" (1977, 276).

25 Gross discrepancies between foreign schooling and domestic experience contribute significantly to the sense these autobiographers express of a divided self. In *Surname Viet Given Name Nam*, Trinh writes: "*For years we learnt about 'our ancestors, the Gauls,' we learnt that 'French Indochina' was situated in Asia under a hot and humid climate*" (89). Where Rodriguez chooses the world offered by his schooling, Lim, like Kingston and Mu-

kherjee, develops a critical sense of both worlds. Mukherjee, for example, tells the story of one woman, educated in the mission school curriculum, in which ancient Indian history was unimportant, who becomes an active feminist and fulminates against Manu the Lawgiver (ca. 500 B.C.) for his role in the suppression of Indian women (236).

26 I have been reluctant throughout this work to exercise value judgments, which apart from risking what Caren Kaplan has called the "postcolonial forms of cultural domination" (116), surely reduce the scope of my research into what kinds of autobiography come into being from what kinds of lived experience. Smadar Lavie and Ted Swedenburg also call to account such presumption of judgment. They identify "[a] new hierarchy of cultural practices . . . in the making, in which the hybrid replaces the old category of the exotic, and the Other, now hybrid, is once again reinscribed by the Eurocenter" (8).

27 Their literary pyrotechnics satisfy Avtar Brah's call for "theoretical creolisation" (210). Concluding her discussion of postcolonial representations, Lionnet finds that "the subject projects herself in the fictitious and the fabulous, thereby authorizing herself to assume her own destiny through utterances that allow her to construct her own symbolic context. . . . There is . . . an endless reproblematization of time and space with respect to a relational, hybrid context, always fluid and mobile. Movement . . . does not lead to a point of origin (geographic or mythic) but allows one to reconnect the severed ties of the colonial diaspora, following a model and a logic that deal in fruitful pluralities rather than sterile particularisms" (1995, 175–76).

28 Kingston herself has described this work emphatically as not Chinese: " 'Don't you hear the American slang? Don't you see the American settings? Don't you see the way the Chinese myths have been transmuted by America?' " (1982, 58). Lim describes Kingston's "flamboyant use of the first person" as distinctively American (1992a, 257). But the narrator's struggle to translate the crucial words "I" and "here" from Chinese ideographs into American self-presence represents the painful acquisition of an American identity, comparable to Rodriguez's reidentification of himself as a "*Rich-heard*," who speaks up, in English, in class. The activity of translation remains central.

29 Kingston describes the pirated Hong Kong edition of *China Men*, which has very wide margins. She has donated to the Bancroft Library the copy of this edition in which her father entered his own commentary, in a beautiful calligraphic hand, in these wide margins. Such commentary is part of the religious and poetic tradition informing Chinese literature. " 'I' am nothing," she writes, "but who 'I' am in relation to other people" (quoted in Lim 1991, 23).

30 In this sense, *The Woman Warrior* bears comparison with a growing body of parent/child relational (auto)biographies. See, for example, Blaise 1993, Karpf 1996, Miller 1996, Ondaatje 1989, Roth 1991, Spiegelman 1986 and 1991, and Steedman 1987.

31 See also Amy Tan's essay, "Mother Tongue," about imagining her mother as her reader. She herself has grown up speaking many Englishes and has

learned to recognize her mother's English less as "broken" or "fractured" than as vivid, intimate, and distinct.

32 In *China Men*, Kingston describes how "[t]he villagers unfolded their maps of the known world, which differed: turtles and elephants supported the continents, which were islands on their backs; in other cartographies, the continents were mountains with China the middle mountain, Han Mountain or Tang Mountain or the Wah Republic, a Gold Mountain to its west on some maps and to its east on others. Yet the explorers who had plotted routes to avoid sea monsters and those who had gone in the direction the yarrow fell had found gold as surely as the ones with more scientific worlds. They had met one another as planned in Paris or Johannesburg or San Francisco" (47).

33 See Phelan 1995 on cinematic time and space: "Vertov, and Joslin after him, discover that the problem of cinematic memory (a problem of time) enables the production of an architectural interiority within the screen itself (a resolution in space). Behind the image the spectator sees is a camera, and behind that, another camera. Behind the present image then, a past, and behind that, another past. The *mise-en-abîme* of spatial and temporal regression that Vertov exposes leads to a dizzying transfer between time and space more generally" (384).

CHAPTER FIVE

1 In an interesting paper on memorial projects for the camp at Fossoli, from which Primo Levi and other Italian Jews were sent to Auschwitz, Giovanni Leoni discusses the difficulties attending expression of the Holocaust in architectural design. Three projects were being considered at his time of writing: "Though the three solutions use different means of expression, they are at one in their effort to represent a pain that cannot be recreated, to give a sort of visibility to it. In the first case, by reconstructing the trauma through an architectural setting that is used as a supportive frame for the narrative. In the second case, by venturing into the realm of the indescribable by allusion and poetic means. And in the third, by walking among the ruins, seeing the traces and voices of those who suffered there" (214).

2 One of the English voices in Trinh's film *Surname Viet Given Name Nam* comments on the Vietnamese experience of these lethal distortions of meaning: "Reeducation camps, rehabilitation camps, concentration camps, annihilation camps. All the distinctive features of a civilization are laid bare. The slogans continue to read: 'Work liberates,' 'Rehabilitation through work.' Here, work is a process whereby the worker no longer takes power, 'for work has ceased to be his way of living and has become his way of dying' (Maurice Blanchot). Work and death are equivalents" (89).

3 Levi's discussion of Améry's responses to the Lager, and his later suicide in particular, highlights the contrasts between Améry and himself. Numerous commentators, however, now see the parallels completed in Levi's own death, which is widely assumed to have been a suicide also. See, in particular, Cynthia Ozick's essay on *The Drowned and the Saved* as Primo

Levi's "suicide note": "What was withheld before is now imploded in these pages" (41).

4 Levi suggests that people with faith fared better on the whole than people without: "[T]he nonagnostic, the believers in any belief whatsoever, better resisted the seduction of power, provided, of course, they were not believers in the National Socialist doctrine" (1989a, 145). Or again, he writes of believers: "Their universe was vaster than ours, more extended in space and time, above all more comprehensible: they had a key and a point of leverage" (1989a, 146). The religious, however, were also reduced to despair. Wiesel writes of cracks in faith as a prologue to death (83), but also of his own experience of the void where God had been: "I had ceased to plead. I was no longer capable of lamentation. . . . I was the accuser, God the accused" (75).

5 Levi uses Dante's term "sommersi" for the title of a chapter in *If This Is a Man* and for the title of his later work, *The Drowned and the Saved*. Risa Sodi suggests that Levi owes the very term "sommersi," "submerged" or "drowned," to the opening of Canto 20 of the *Inferno* and that characters in the *Inferno* are constantly submerged in one form of torture or another (1990, 44). Certainly, Levi found the image central to this thinking and used it repeatedly.

6 trovai di voi un tal, che per sua opra
in anima in Cocito già si bagna
ed in corpo par vivo ancor di sopra.
(*Inferno* 33.155–57)

Levi's poem is dedicated to a "frate" in experience; B.V. is Bruno Vasari, a partisan and survivor of Mauthausen. Levi uses this poem as the frontispiece to *Moments of Reprieve*.

7 Lev. 19:28. The deliberate nature of such offense is repeated in many forms. Writing of the kind of abuse his father had suffered as a schoolboy, Levi refers to the vilification of prayer shawls, which is "as old as anti-Semitism — from those shawls, taken from deportees, the SS would make underwear which was then distributed to the Jews imprisoned in the Lager" (1985, 5). Similarly, Levi calls the yellow star, imposed on Jews throughout the Reich, "an impious parody of ritual norms" usurping the place of the tefillin (1987, 130). Impious parody emerges also among the faithful, when faith involves self-service with no sense of community; Levi "spits" on Kuhn's prayer of thanksgiving that he has been spared selection but the young Greek, Beppo, has not (1979, 135–36).

8 See Sander Gilman 1989 on Levi's inability to speak Yiddish and his sense that he, as an Italian Jew, had been separated from the strong Judaic traditions of Eastern Europe. He actually studied Yiddish in order to write *If Not Now, When?* (Sodi 1988, 44), in which, however, he suggests that Hebrew will be the language of future Jewry because it has not been contaminated by the camps.

9 Levi began writing poetry immediately on his return to Italy in 1945. His first telling of the Lager experience was published by De Silva in 1947 but received little attention. A revised edition was published by Einaudi in 1958, has been translated into many languages, and has not been out of

print. His last book, *The Drowned and the Saved*, appeared in Italian in 1986. Primo Levi died in Turin in 1987. In a recent review of Marco Belpoliti's three volumes published to coincide with the tenth anniversary of Levi's death, Robert Gordon writes: "[Levi] was always at work on one story or another from 1946 until 1987, at times bringing texts to fruition and integrating them with others to create books only decades after their conception" (*Times Literary Supplement*, October 9, 1998: 4).

10 Levi's Italian title, *Se questo è un uomo*, was published in French by Buchet-Castel in 1961 as *J'etais un homme* (Tarrow 1994, 107), indicating a failure in comprehension that justified Levi in pulling it from circulation. It now appears in French as *Si C'est un Homme*. He himself supervised the German translation very closely. "Experience," he writes, had taught him "that translation and compromise are synonymous" (1989a, 172). For discussion of the translation into German, see Gilliland's excellent article and Levi himself in *The Drowned and the Saved*, 170–75. Levi insisted on retaining "'il 'suo' tedesco," the crude and vulgar German he had learned at Auschwitz, turning it, Gilliland suggests, to excellent purpose: "[I]n positioning himself (through a language that is 'unfamiliar' or 'strange' to the German Self) as the continuing Other in 'his' German translation, [Levi] forces the German reader to respond to this Other in the text" (196). The German publication in 1960, however, turned the meditation of Levi's title into a direct question: *Ist das ein Mensch?* (Gilliland, 201). The American title, *Survival in Auschwitz*, is also inadequate, suggesting that appeal to the buying public took precedence over Levi's own appeal for moral examination. For this discussion, accordingly, I have stayed with the English title, *If This Is a Man*, which is more faithful to the Italian.

11 Wiesel's writing restates in many forms the character of the beggar or the madman, the vagrant or the outsider, who has a tale to tell. He could be a prophet in disguise, so one should attend carefully. He appears in such an unlikely form, however, that he is rarely taken seriously. Moché the Beadle, in *Night*, comes back to the village of Sighet literally from the edge of the grave, to warn the Jews of their danger, but nobody listens; they consider him mad. Similarly, Mme. Schächter screams about fire in the crowded cattle car. Her neighbors bind and gag her to control the fear she arouses, but no one else sees the flames until the train arrives at Birkenau. "They expect the worst," Delbo writes. "[T]hey do not expect the unthinkable" (6).

12 Levi's essay, "The Dispute among German Historians" (1990, 163–66), appeared in *La Stampa* on January 22, 1987, less than three months before he died, under the title "Buco nero di Auschwitz." I am grateful to Jonathan Druker for highlighting the allusive nature of the original title. "The Black Hole of Auschwitz" refers, as he puts it, "to those anomalous places in the cosmos from which nothing escapes, not even light" (Druker, 58). Levi's alarm at revisionists and Holocaust deniers, and his sense that even publicity simplified the nature of the death camps and reduced their significance, complicated his task of reporting what he knew.

13 Similarly, Ozick points out that Levi is being anti-metaphorical in his use of Coleridge's lines from "The Ancient Mariner":

> Since then, at an uncertain hour,
> That agony returns,
> And till my ghastly tale is told
> This heart within me burns.

She calls Levi's use of these lines "newly startling to a merely literary reader, for whom the words of Coleridge's poem have never before rung out with such an anti-metaphorical contemporary demand, or seemed so cruel" (34).

14 Studying what he called the prevailing *Untergang der Sprache*, or undermining of language, Karl Kraus described Nazi-Deutsch as literalizing metaphors, restoring content to violent phrases that had been for a long time empty (Rosenfeld, 134–35). Steiner has proved controversial with his suggestion that German was irreparably polluted during the Third Reich, but Rosenfeld cites Victor Klemperer: "Nazi language . . . saturates words, phrases, and sentences with its poison" (132).

15 The lyrical romances of Levi's *Periodic Table* indicate, of course, that he combined the talents of artist and scientist to a remarkable degree. He frequently cites his training as a chemist, however, to explain his methodology for understanding the complex forces at work in Auschwitz.

16 "Shema" means "Hear," the opening word of God's injunction to the children of Israel (Deut. 6:4–9). "Hear, O Israel, the Lord is our God, one Lord, and you must love the Lord your God with all your heart and soul and strength. These commandments which I give you this day are to be kept in your heart; you shall repeat them to your sons, and speak of them indoors and out of doors, when you lie down and when you rise. Bind them as a sign on the hand and wear them as a phylactery on the forehead; write them up on the doorposts of your houses and on your gates."

17 Sodi (1995) makes the nice point that, insofar as *If This Is a Man* represents the new Bible, it begins with the making not of light but of night.

18 Just as Levi's *Shema* is spoken not by God to His chosen people but by the poet to his fellow human beings, I wonder whether this Metamir does not attach to the forehead as a secular tefillin, not God's ordinances worn faithfully as visible witness of a man's relation to God, but part of human interaction to enlighten and guide conduct, part of a man's relation to other people.

19 I am indebted to Cicioni (53 n. 29) and Gunzberg (28 n. 23) for my interpretation of Null Achtzehn's "name."

20 The Italian reads "Compagni, io sono l'ultimo!" (1968, 188), which suggests "Letzte" (rather than "Letz") more precisely as "the last man."

21 Wiesel says he witnessed many hangings but speaks of God hanging dead on the gallows at the execution of a small child (70–72).

22 "Especially during the last years of the war, the Lagers constituted an extensive and complex system which profoundly compenetrated the daily life of the country; one has with good reason spoken of the *univers con-centrationnaire*, but it was not a closed universe" (1989a, 15).

23 "Améry called me 'the forgiver.' I consider this neither insult nor praise but imprecision. I am not inclined to forgive our enemies of that time, nor do I feel I can forgive their imitators in Algeria, Vietnam, the Soviet Union,

Chile, Argentina, Cambodia, or South Africa, because I know no human act that can erase a crime; I demand justice" (1989a, 137).

24 See "A Mystery in the *Lager*" in *The Mirror Maker* (66–70).

25 Levi's "holy tongue" provides the language for his new *Shema* but also shares with other writers of diaspora that juxtaposition and combination of relatively pure cultures which create an original blend expressing the writer's perspective. See, in particular, Kingston or Ondaatje.

26 It is also true that partisans were generally shot, whereas Jews were sent to Italian holding camps.

27 Levi apparently wrote this poem three months after his return to Turin on October 14, 1945. Calling it "If This Is a Man," he used it as the frontispiece for his first autobiography of Auschwitz. He retitled it "Shema" when it appeared in 1975 in the Ruth Feldman and Brian Swann translation, which I am using here.

28 I am also grateful to Marguerite Chiarenza, from Hispanic and Italian Studies at the University of British Columbia, who provided valuable insights when she spoke to one of my classes on Primo Levi's use of Dante.

29 In "The Intellectual in Auschwitz," Levi writes: "[W]here I wrote 'I would give today's soup . . ?' I had neither lied nor exaggerated. I would really have given bread and soup, that is, blood, to save from nothingness those memories. . . . They made it possible for me to reestablish a link with the past, saving it from oblivion and reinforcing my identity" (1989a, 139).

30 Marginal note on my draft for this chapter.

31 Jean Samuel told Tarrow that, just as Levi had exchanged bread for German lessons, he had exchanged bread for math books. He describes walking on the first night of the death march with Jacques Feldbau, who talked all night of Fermat's theorem, helping Samuel "to forget the pain and the cold of that endless night" (Tarrow, 105). Similarly, in *Night of the Mist*, Eugene Heimler tells of an animated discussion about Hungarian poetry and the crucial question whether it was authentic or whether it borrowed too much from the West (137).

CHAPTER SIX

1 Because they are neither life stories brought to a narrative conclusion nor memoirs of the illnesses and deaths of other people, but self-life-writing about subjective experiences of the processes of dying, I propose to distinguish the texts considered here with Nancy K. Miller's vivid term, "autothanatography" (1994, 12). Robert Kastenbaum, in *The Psychology of Death*, credits Elie Metchnikoff with coining the term "thanatology" in *The Nature of Man* (1903). Kastenbaum himself dislikes the misplaced authority implicit in the term "thanatology," until he realizes that "thanatology is simply the study of death with life left in" (233). I believe Kastenbaum may himself be responsible for coining the term "deathniks," a nudge of humor for those of us who become immersed in death studies.

2 Writing of "death memoirs," in which the narrator has been close to the dying parent/lover/friend, Nancy K. Miller describes the turn that a focus

on death gives to life writing. "We have tended to think of autobiography as the history of an isolate becoming — attaining freedom, finding a voice, getting published — and often an overcoming of obstacles, crises, incapacities. Here the autobiographical narrative, by its focus on the failing other, provides the account of an undoing, an unbecoming" (1992a, 13).

3 Eakin suggests that "the concepts of self and death, which pair so largely in the theory and practice of autobiographical discourse . . . [are] linked in Popper's view of human evolution, determined alike by the exercise of man's capacity for language" (1985, 194). Paul de Man's ironic twist concludes his essay "Autobiography as De-facement": "Death is a displaced name for a linguistic predicament, and the restoration of mortality by autobiography . . . deprives and disfigures to the precise extent that it restores. Autobiography veils a defacement of the mind of which it is itself the cause" (930). In a different vein, "Every autobiography, we might say, is also an autothanatography" (Miller 1994, 12).

4 Peter Noll's title for his autothanatography. See also Harold Brodkey: "Much of the time I do nothing. I lie in bed or on the porch. I stare at death, and death stares at me" (111).

5 Miller reopens *The Confessions of Saint Augustine* by reading it in terms of feminist self-construction and identity through alterity, and she concludes that "autobiography — identity through alterity — is also writing against death twice: the other's and one's own" (1994, 12). Appreciating her radical work on Saint Augustine, I depart from her in my understanding of double- or even multiple-voiced autothanatographies. Where Saint Augustine may define himself by means of his mother, Monica, or his life and his death in relation to her life and death, I am concerned with writing not "against" but "into" death, and with writing, furthermore, as a transaction between people who remain their own subjects, who do not become objects to each other. These terms refer primarily, of course, to textual positioning rather than to moral values.

6 See Stewart Alsop's early work in this genre; *Stay of Execution* is a moving account of Alsop's struggle with leukemia, during which he comes to welcome what he calls "Uncle Thanatos."

7 I part company here with G. Thomas Couser, who describes autopathography as a subgenre; despite his association of breast cancer with body-identity, for example, he believes that "autopathography becomes autobiography" either by integrating the illness into distinctive and ongoing life narrative or by using the illness to explore the issues it raises, transcending ready-made pathology formulas in order to become "the story of a life" (1997, 43–44).

8 Emily Carr's little volume, *Pause*, containing drawings and episodes from her extended stay in a hospital in England, is based on the premise that illness requires time out from life and is not, therefore, part of the real business of life. Alice James might have argued otherwise, and, quite clearly, so do many autobiographers today, who seem to feel that serious illness focuses the understanding in hard but rewarding ways.

9 See Blaise 1993, Karpf 1996, Miller 1996, Blake Morrison 1993, Roth 1991, Schreiber 1990, Steedman 1987, and Terry Tempest Williams 1991.

10 Focusing on traditional forms of autobiography, Couser felt at that point that "barring some sort of miracle, the narrative cannot include an account of the writer's death" (52).

11 See Egan 1984 for discussion of the personal values inherent in mythic paradigms.

12 Panourgiá attributes the term "auto-anthropology" to Strathern (1987, 7). As with autothanatography and autopathography, the timing of such coinage indicates a new development that needs to be distinguished from what has gone before.

13 See Nuland 1994: "Everybody is required to die of a named entity. . . . Everywhere in the world, it is illegal to die of old age" (43).

14 Repeatedly, the healthy intrude with unsolicited judgments or advice. "You have to ask yourselves why Harvey chose to have cancer," says one well-wisher in Pekar, Brabner, and Stack's *Our Cancer Year*. Responding to many such directives, Treya Wilber says: "Pain is not punishment, death is not a failure, life is not a reward" (279).

15 See Park, 232–53, and Sontag 1990.

16 I am grateful to my son, Michael Egan, for introducing me to *Doonesbury* and guiding me through its complex and interconnected cast and subject matter.

17 This discussion has been adapted with permission from *Modern Fiction Studies* 40 (Fall 1994).

18 Peter Friedman, personal correspondence, March 27, 1994.

19 See Bruss 1980, which identifies the apparent disjunction in film of subjectivity and subject matter (296–320).

20 Paul Monette discusses the artist's need to leave a record, "to say we have been here" (152).

21 I am indebted to many conversations with my daughter, Catherine Egan, whose readings of contemporary women writers have affected my own.

22 See Jeanne Perreault's discussion of Lorde's "real me." Couser makes the point that she reconstructs herself as a warrior to deal with her predicament (1997, 52).

23 Christina Middlebrook, for example, develops a boy soldier as her Jungian animus, recognizing stages of her own "battle" in terms of his struggles before battle, on beaches, and in jungle and arid desert. Pekar, Brabner, and Stack narrate their experience of Harvey Pekar's cancer in juxtaposition with the Gulf War and the traumas of young peace activists from war-torn countries.

24 Consider Meigs creating her lesbian body through the layers of literature and art with which she identifies, or Breytenbach playing hide-and-seek with his identity; his series of smoke-and-mirrors effects allow only pieces to emerge and only for passing moments. Surface and depth, physical manifestation of psychological presence, do not depend on the visual arts.

25 Couser calls the Butler and Rosenblum book collaborative and makes the point that such collaboration is a major coping strategy. He comments also on the simultaneous engagement and distance between the two writers, and the closure in death that "is somewhat compensated for by the reader's access to a grieving consciousness" (1997, 61).

26 This mirroring and interchangeability are particularly apparent in Lucy Massie Phenix's "film of the book." Posture, movements, and attention to each other speaking all suggest very sensitive levels of reciprocity.

27 Reviewing Humphrey Carpenter's authorized biography of Dennis Potter (1998), Sean O'Brien describes this interview. "Even this event seems ambiguous in retrospect—an authentic utterance stage-managed for maximum effect. It was beyond criticism but not entirely above suspicion—a combination Potter had long been happy to exploit" (*Times Literary Supplement*, September 25, 1998: 36).

28 Couser vividly describes how "[i]nsofar as one equates the remaining pages, consciously or not, with the subject's remaining lifetime, one may feel complicit in the shortening of the narrator's life as one reads, for the reader controls the rate of the consumption of the written life" (1997, 55).

CODA

1 See Chapter 6, note 3.

2 I am grateful to Angela Szeto, former student, for this elegant phrasing.

Works Cited

Abbott, H. Porter. 1988. "Autobiography, Autography, Fiction: Groundwork for a Taxonomy of Textual Categories." *New Literary History* 19:597–615.

Adams, Timothy Dow. 1999. *Light Writing and Life Writing: Photography in Autobiography*. Chapel Hill: University of North Carolina Press.

———. 1990. *Telling Lies in Modern American Autobiography*. Chapel Hill: University of North Carolina Press.

Alsop, Stewart. 1973. *Stay of Execution: A Sort of Memoir*. Philadelphia and New York: J. B. Lippincott Co.

Andrews, Jennifer. 1996. "Framing *The Book of Jessica*: Transformation and the Collaborative Process in Canadian Theatre." *English Studies in Canada* 22:297–313.

Anzaldúa, Gloria. 1987. *Borderlands/La Frontera: The New Mestiza*. San Francisco: Spinsters/aunt lute.

Apted, Michael, dir. 1991. *35 Up*. Granada TV.

Arendt, Hannah. 1964. *Eichmann in Jerusalem: A Report on the Banality of Evil*. Revised and enlarged edition. New York: Penguin.

Ariès, Philippe. 1981. *The Hour of Our Death*. Translated by Helen Weaver. New York: Alfred A. Knopf.

Armstrong, Jeannette C. 1990. "Panel One: Audience Discussion." In *Telling It: Women and Language across Cultures: The Transformation of a Conference*, edited by The Telling It Book Collective. Vancouver: Press Gang Publishers. 43–52.

———. 1985. "Writing from a Native Woman's Perspective." In *in the feminine: women and words/les femmes et les mots: Conference Proceedings 1983*, edited by Ann Dybikowski et al. Edmonton: Longspoon. 55–57.

Arnott, Brian. 1978. "The Passe-Muraille Alternative." In *The Human Elements: Critical Essays*, edited by David Helwig. Ottawa: Oberon. 97–111.

Bakhtin, M. M. 1986. *The Problem of Speech Genres and Other Late Essays*. Translated by Vern W. McGee. Edited by Caryl Emerson and Michael Holquist. Austin: University of Texas Press.

Barnouw, Erik. 1974. *Documentary: A History of the Non-Fiction Film*. New York: Oxford University Press.

Barros, Carolyn A. 1992. "Figura, Persona, Dynamis: Autobiography and Change." *biography* 15:1–28.

Barthes, Roland. 1981. *Camera Lucida: Reflections on Photography*. Translated by Richard Howard. New York: Hill and Wang.

———. 1977. *Image, Music, Text*. Selected and translated by Stephen Heath. New York: Hill and Wang.

Bauman, Zygmunt. 1992. *Mortality, Immortality and Other Life Strategies*. Oxford: Polity.

Baumgarten, Murray. 1982. *City Scriptures: Modern Jewish Writing*. Cambridge: Harvard University Press.

Beaujour, Michel. 1991. *Poetics of the Literary Self-Portrait*. Translated by Yara Milos. New York: New York University Press.

Beauvoir, Simone de. 1966. *A Very Easy Death*. Translated by Patrick O'Brian. Harmondsworth: Penguin.

Bell, Quentin. 1972. *Virginia Woolf: A Biography*. London: Hogarth.

Belpoliti, Marco, ed. 1997a. *Conversazione e Interviste 1963–1987*. Turin: Einaudi.

———. 1997b. *Primo Levi*. Milan: Marcos y Marcos / Riga 13.

———. 1997c. *Primo Levi: Opere*. 2 vols. Turin: Einaudi.

Benjamin, Jessica. 1988. *The Bonds of Love: Psychoanalysis, Feminism, and the Problem of Domination*. New York: Pantheon.

Berger, John. 1972. *Ways of Seeing*. London and Harmondsworth: BBC and Penguin.

Bergland, Betty. 1994. "Postmodernism and the Autobiographical Subject: Reconstructing the 'Other.'" In *Autobiography and Postmodernism*, edited by Kathleen Ashley, Leigh Gilmore, and Gerald Peters. Amherst: University of Massachusetts Press. 130–66.

Bergman, David. 1992. "Larry Kramer and the Rhetoric of AIDS." In *AIDS: The Literary Response*, edited by Emmanuel S. Nelson. Toronto: Maxwell Macmillan Canada. 175–86.

Bersani, Leo. 1993. "Is the Rectum a Grave?" In *media spectacles*, edited by Jann Matlock, Marjorie Garber, and Rebecca Walkowitz. London: Routledge. 197–222.

Bessai, Diane. 1992. *Playwrights of Collective Creation*. Vol. 2 of *The Canadian Dramatist*. Toronto: Simon and Pierre.

Bhabha, Homi K. 1986. "The other question: difference, discrimination and the discourse of colonialism." In *Literature, Politics and Theory: Papers from the Essex Conference 1976–84*, edited by Francis Barker, Peter Hulme, Margaret Iverson, and Diana Loxley. London: Methuen. 148–72.

Blaise, Clark, and Bharati Mukherjee. 1995. *Days and Nights in Calcutta*. St. Paul: Hungry Mind Press.

Blaise, Clark. 1993. *I Had a Father: A Post-Modern Autobiography*. Toronto: HarperCollins.

Bowie, Malcolm. 1979. "Jacques Lacan." In *Structuralism and Since: From Lévi-Strauss to Derrida*, edited by John Sturrock. Oxford: Oxford University Press. 116–53.

Brah, Avtar. 1996. *Cartographies of Diaspora: Contesting Identities*. London: Routledge.

Brenner, Gerry. 1983. *Concealment in Hemingway's Works*. Columbus: Ohio State University Press.

Breytenbach, Breyten. 1984. *Mouroir: Mirrornotes of a Novel*. New York: Farrar, Straus, Giroux.

———. 1983. *The True Confessions of an Albino Terrorist*. New York: Farrar, Straus, Giroux.

Brodkey, Harold. 1996. *This Wild Darkness: The Story of My Death*. New York: Metropolitan Books.

Browdy de Hernandez, Jennifer. 1996. "The Plural Self: The Politicization of Memory and Form in Three American Ethnic Autobiographies." In *Memory and Cultural Politics: New Approaches to American Ethnic Literatures*, edited by Amritjit Singh, Joseph Skerrett, Jr., and Robert E. Hogan. Boston: Northeastern University Press. 41–59.

Bruccoli, Matthew J. 1978. *Scott and Ernest: The Authority of Failure and the Authority of Success*. New York: Random House.

Bruss, Elizabeth. 1980. "Eye for I: Making and Unmaking Autobiography in Film." In *Autobiography: Essays Theoretical and Critical*, edited by James Olney. Princeton: Princeton University Press. 296–320.

———. 1976. *Autobiographical Acts: The Changing Situation of a Literary Genre*. Baltimore: Johns Hopkins University Press.

Buss, Helen M. 1991. "Reading for the Doubled Discourse of American Women's Autobiography." *a/b: Auto/Biography Studies* 6:95–108.

Butler, Sandra, and Barbara Rosenblum. 1996. *Cancer in Two Voices*. 2d ed. Duluth: Spinsters Ink.

Callaghan, Morley. 1963. *That Summer in Paris*. Toronto: Macmillan.

Campbell, Maria. 1973. *Halfbreed*. Toronto: McClelland and Stewart.

Carpenter, Humphrey. 1998. *Dennis Potter: The Authorized Biography*. London: Faber.

Carr, David. 1986. *Time, Narrative, and History*. Bloomington: Indiana University Press.

Carr, Emily. 1953. *Pause: A Sketch Book*. Toronto: Clarke, Irwin.

Chambers, Ross. 1996. "The Suicide Experiment: Hervé Guibert's AIDS Video, *La pudeur ou l'impudeur*." Talk given at Green College, University of British Columbia, May 10.

———. 1991. *Room for Maneuver: Reading the Oppositional (in) Narrative*. Chicago: University of Chicago Press.

Cheung, King-Kok. 1990. "Self-Fulfilling Visions in *The Woman Warrior* and *Thousand Pieces of Gold*." *biography* 13:143–53.

Chodorow, Nancy. 1978. *The Reproduction of Mothering*. Berkeley: University of California Press.

Chow, Rey. 1993. *Writing Diaspora: Tactics of Intervention in Contemporary Cultural Studies*. Bloomington: Indiana University Press.

Cicioni, Mirna. 1995. *Primo Levi: Bridges of Knowledge*. Oxford and Washington, D.C.: Berg.

Clifford, James, and George E. Marcus, eds. 1986. *Writing Culture: The Poetics and Politics of Ethnography*. Berkeley: University of California Press.

Cohen, Anthony P. 1994. *Self-Consciousness: An Alternative Anthropology of Identity*. London and New York: Routledge.

Couser, G. Thomas. 1997. *Recovering Bodies: Illness, Disability, and Lifewriting*. Madison: University of Wisconsin Press.

———. 1989. "Maxine Hong Kingston: The Auto/biographer as Ghost-Writer." In *Biography East and West: Selected Conference Papers*, edited by Carol Ramelb. Honolulu: College of Languages, Linguistics and Literature, University of Hawaii and the East-West Center. 231–37.

———. 1978. "The Shape of Death in American Autobiography." *Hudson Review* 31:53–66.

———, ed. 1991. Special Issue: Illness, Disability, and Lifewriting: *a/b: Auto/Biography Studies*.

Crosby, Marcia. 1991. "Construction of the Imaginary Indian." In *Vancouver Anthology: The Institutional Politics of Art*, edited by Stan Douglas. Vancouver: Talonbooks. 267–91.

Cruikshank, Julie. 1990. *Life Lived Like a Story*. Lincoln: University of Nebraska Press.

Cuthand, Beth. 1985. "Transmitting Our Identity as Indian Writers." In *in the feminine: women and words/les femmes et les mots: Conference Proceedings 1983*, edited by Ann Dibykowski et al. Edmonton: Longspoon. 53–54.

Dante, Alighieri. 1969. *Inferno*. Translated by Allan Gilbert. Durham: Duke University Press.

De Lauretis, Teresa. 1984. *Alice Doesn't: Feminism, Semiotics, Cinema*. Bloomington: Indiana University Press.

Delbo, Charlotte. 1968. *None of Us Will Return*. Translated by John Githens. Boston: Beacon Press.

De Man, Paul. 1979. "Autobiography as De-facement." *Modern Language Notes* 94/5:919–30.

Dickinson, Peter. 1995. " 'Go-go Dancing on the Brink of the Apocalypse': Representing AIDS: An Essay in Seven Epigraphs." In *Postmodern Apocalypse: Theory and Cultural Practice at the End*, edited by Richard Dellamora. Philadelphia: University of Pennsylvania Press. 219–40.

Druker, Jonathan. 1994. "Primo Levi's *Survival in Auschwitz* and *The Drowned and the Saved*: From Testimony to Historical Judgment." *Shofar: An Interdisciplinary Journal of Jewish Studies* 12:47–58.

Eakin, Paul John. 1999. *How Our Lives Become Stories: Making Selves*. Ithaca: Cornell University Press.

———. 1998. "Relational Selves, Relational Lives: The Story of the Story." In *True Relations: Essays on Autobiography and the Postmodern*, edited by G. Thomas Couser and Joseph Fichtelberg. Westport, Conn.: Hofstra University and Greenwood Press. 63–81.

———. 1992. *Touching the World: Reference in Autobiography*. Princeton: Princeton University Press.

———. 1989. Foreword to *On Autobiography*, by Philippe Lejeune. Translated by Katherine Leary. Edited by Paul John Eakin. Minneapolis: University of Minnesota Press. vii–xxviii.

———. 1985. *Fictions in Autobiography: Studies in the Art of Self-Invention*. Princeton: Princeton University Press.

Egan, Susanna. 1987. "Changing Faces of Heroism: Some Questions Raised by Contemporary Autobiography." *biography* 10:20–38.

———. 1984. *Patterns of Experience in Autobiography*. Chapel Hill: University of North Carolina Press.

Elias, Norbert. 1985. *The Loneliness of the Dying*. Translated by Edmund Jephcott. Oxford: Basil Blackwell.

Elsley, Judy. 1996. *Quilts as Text(iles): The Semiotics of Quilting*. New York: Peter Lang.

Epstein, Adam. 1987. "Primo Levi and the Language of Atrocity." *Bulletin of the Society for Italian Studies* 20:31–38.

Epstein, Robert, and Jeffrey Friedman, dirs. 1989. *Common Threads: Stories from the Quilt*. Distributed by Home Box Office (HBO).

Fee, Margery. 1990. "Upsetting Fake Ideas: Jeannette Armstrong's 'Slash' and Beatrice Culleton's 'April Raintree.'" In *Native Writers and Canadian Writing: Canadian Literature Special Issue*, edited by W. H. New. Vancouver: University of British Columbia Press. 168–80.

Fischer, Michael M. J. 1994. "Autobiographical Voices (1, 2, 3) and Mosaic Memory: Experimental Sondages in the (Post)modern World." In *Autobiography and Postmodernism*, edited by Kathleen Ashley, Leigh Gilmore, and Gerald Peters. Amherst: University of Massachusetts Press. 79–129.

Fleishman, Avrom. 1983. *Figures of Autobiography: The Language of Self-Writing in Victorian and Modern England*. Berkeley: University of California Press.

Fong, Bobby. 1989. "Maxine Hong Kingston's Autobiographical Strategy in *The Woman Warrior*." *biography* 12:116–26.

Frank, Arthur W. 1995. *The Wounded Storyteller: Body, Illness, and Ethics*. Chicago: University of Chicago Press.

Frankenberg, Ruth, and Lata Mani. 1996. "Crosscurrents, Crosstalk: Race, 'Postcoloniality,' and the Politics of Location." In *Displacement, Diaspora, and Geographies of Identity*, edited by Smadar Lavie and Ted Swedenburg. Durham: Duke University Press. 273–93.

Frankl, Viktor. 1963. *Man's Search for Meaning: An Introduction to Logotherapy*. Translated by Ilse Lasch. New York: Washington Square Press.

Franklin, John Hope. 1985. *George Washington Williams: A Biography*. Chicago: University of Chicago Press.

Fraser, Ronald. 1984. *In Search of a Past: The Rearing of an English Gentleman, 1933–45*. New York: Atheneum.

Freedman, Diane P., Olivia Frey, and Frances Murphy Zauhar, eds. 1993. *The Intimate Critique: Autobiographical Literary Criticism*. Durham: Duke University Press.

Freud, Sigmund. 1957. "Thoughts for the Times on War and Death." In *The Standard Edition of the Complete Psychological Works of Sigmund Freud*, translated and edited by James Strachey in collaboration with Anna Freud, assisted by Alix Strachey and Alan Tyson. London: Hogarth Press and the Institute of Psycho-Analysis. 275–300.

Friedman, Susan Stanford. 1988. "Women's Autobiographical Selves: Theory and Practice." In *The Private Self: Theory and Practice of Women's Autobiographical Writings*, edited by Shari Benstock. Chapel Hill: University of North Carolina Press. 34–62.

Fulton, Robert, ed. 1965. *Death and Identity*. New York: John Wiley.

Gates, Henry Louis, Jr. 1994. *Colored People: A Memoir*. New York: Alfred A. Knopf.

———. 1988. *The Signifying Monkey: A Theory of Afro-American Literary Criticism*. New York: Oxford University Press.

Gavin, William Joseph. 1995. *Cuttin' the Body Loose: Historical, Biological, and*

Personal Approaches to Death and Dying. Philadelphia: Temple University Press.

Geertz, Clifford. 1973. *The Interpretation of Cultures*. New York: Basic Books.

Gilligan, Carol. 1982. *In a Different Voice: Psychological Theory and Women's Development*. Cambridge: Harvard University Press.

Gilliland, Gail. 1992. "Self and Other: Christa Wolf's *Patterns of Childhood* and Primo Levi's *Se questo è un uomo* as Dialogic Texts." *Comparative Literature Studies* 29:183–209.

Gilman, Sander L. 1989. "To Quote Primo Levi: 'Redest keyn jiddisch, bist nit kejn jid' ['If you don't speak Yiddish, you're not a Jew']." *Prooftexts: A Journal of Jewish Literary History* 9:139–60.

———. 1988. *Disease and Representation: Images of Illness from Madness to AIDS*. Ithaca: Cornell University Press.

———. 1987. "Aids and Syphilis: The Iconography of Disease." *October* 43:87–107.

Gilmore, Leigh. 1994a. *Autobiographics: A Feminist Theory of Women's Self-Representation*. Ithaca: Cornell University Press.

———. 1994b. "The Mark of Autobiography: Postmodernism, Autobiography, and Genre." In *Autobiography and Postmodernism*, edited by Kathleen Ashley, Leigh Gilmore, and Gerald Peters. Amherst: University of Massachusetts Press. 3–18.

Girelli-Carasi, Fabio. 1990. "The Anti-Linguistic Nature of the Lager in the Language of Primo Levi's *Se questo è un uomo*." In *Reason and Light: Essays on Primo Levi*, edited by Susan R. Tarrow. Ithaca: Center for International Studies, Cornell University. 40–59.

Godard, Barbara. 1990. "The Politics of Representation: Some Native Canadian Women Writers." In *Native Writers and Canadian Writing: Canadian Literature Special Issue*, edited by W. H. New. Vancouver: University of British Columbia Press. 183–225.

Goffman, Erving. 1986. *Stigma: Notes on the Management of Spoiled Identity*. New York: Simon and Schuster.

Goldie, Terry. 1987. "Fear and Temptation: Images of Indigenous Peoples in Australian, Canadian, and New Zealand Literature." In *The Native in Literature*, edited by Thomas King, Cheryl Calver, and Helen Hoy. Toronto: ECW. 67–79.

Griffin, Ada, and Michelle Parkerson, dirs. 1995. *A Litany for Survival: The Life and Work of Audre Lorde*. Distributed by Third World Newsreel.

Griffin, Susan. 1992. *A Chorus of Stones: The Private Life of War*. New York: Doubleday.

Griffiths, Linda, and Maria Campbell. 1989. *The Book of Jessica: A Theatrical Transformation*. Toronto: Coach House.

Grosz, Elizabeth. 1994. *Volatile Bodies: Toward a Corporeal Feminism*. Bloomington: Indiana University Press.

Gunew, Sneja, and Anna Yeatman, eds. 1993. *Feminism and the Politics of Difference*. Halifax: Fernwood Press.

Gunn, Janet Varner. 1982. *Autobiography: Toward a Poetics of Experience*. Philadelphia: University of Pennsylvania Press.

Gunzberg, Lynn M. 1986. "Down among the Dead Men: Levi and Dante in Hell." *Modern Language Studies* 16:10–28.

Gusdorf, Georges. 1956/1980. "Conditions and Limits of Autobiography." In *Autobiography: Essays Theoretical and Critical*, edited by James Olney. Princeton: Princeton University Press. 24–48.

Hall, Stuart. 1990. "Cultural Identity and Diaspora." In *Identity: Community, Culture, Difference*, edited by Jonathan Rutherford. London: Lawrence and Wishart. 222–37.

Halpern, Daniel, ed. 1993. *Dante's Inferno: Translations by Twenty Contemporary Poets*. Hopewell, N.J.: Ecco Press.

Hanlan, Archie J. 1979. *Autobiography of Dying*. New York: Doubleday.

Harasym, Sarah, ed. 1990. *The Postcolonial Critic: Interviews, Strategies, Dialogues*. New York: Routledge.

Hart, Kitty. 1983. *Return to Auschwitz*. London: Granada.

Harty, Kevin J. 1992. "'All the Elements of a Good Movie': Cinematic Responses to the AIDS Pandemic." In *AIDS: The Literary Response*, edited by Emmanuel S. Nelson. New York and Toronto: Twayne/Maxwell Macmillan Canada. 114–30.

Hawkins, Anne Hunsaker. 1993. *Reconstructing Illness: Studies in Pathography*. West Lafayette, Ind.: Purdue University Press.

H.D. 1984. *Her*. London: Virago.

Heimler, Eugene. 1959. *Night of the Mist*. New York: Vanguard.

Hellman, Lillian. 1973. *Pentimento*. Boston: Little, Brown.

Hemingway, Ernest. 1964. *A Moveable Feast*. New York: Macmillan.

Hemingway, Mary. 1964. "The Making of the Book: A Chronicle and a Memoir." *New York Times Book Review*, May 10. 26–27.

Hillis, Doris. 1988. "'You Have to Own Yourself': An Interview with Maria Campbell." *Prairie Fire* 9:44–58.

Hinz, Evelyn. 1992. "Mimesis: The Dramatic Lineage of Auto/Biography." In *Essays on Life Writing: From Genre to Critical Practice*, edited by Marlene Kadar. Toronto: Toronto University Press. 195–212.

Hirsch, Marianne. 1997. *Family Frames: Photography Narrative and Postmemory*. Cambridge: Harvard University Press.

Homans, Margaret. 1986. *Bearing the Word: Language and Female Experience in Nineteenth-Century Women's Writing*. Chicago: University of Chicago Press.

hooks, bell. 1996. *Bone Black: memories of girlhood*. New York: Henry Holt and Co.

———. 1989. *Talking Back: thinking feminist, thinking black*. Boston: South End Press.

Howe, Irving. 1985. "How to Write about the Holocaust." *New York Review*, March 28: 14–17.

Hoy, Helen. 1993. "'When You Admit You're a Thief, Then You Can Be Honourable': Native/Non-Native Collaboration in *The Book of Jessica*." *Canadian Literature* 136:24–39.

Hutcheon, Linda. 1989. *The Politics of Postmodernism*. London: Routledge.

Jagendorf, Zvi. 1993. "Primo Levi Goes for Soup and Remembers Dante." *Raritan: A Quarterly Review* 12:31–51.

James, Alice. 1964. *The Diary of Alice James*. Harmondsworth: Penguin.

James, Clive. 1988. "Last Will and Testament." *New Yorker*, May 23: 86–92.

Jarman, Derek, dir. 1993. *Blue*. Distributed by Basilisk Communications/ Uplink.

Jay, Paul. 1984. *Being in the Text: Self-Representation from Wordsworth to Roland Barthes*. Ithaca: Cornell University Press.

Johnson, Barbara. 1986. "Thresholds of Difference: Structures of Address in Zora Neale Hurston." In *"Race," Writing, and Difference*, edited by Henry Louis Gates, Jr. Chicago: University of Chicago Press. 317–28.

Johnston, Denis W. 1990. "Lines and Circles: The 'Rez' Plays of Tomson Highway." In *Native Writers and Canadian Writing*, edited by W. H. New. Vancouver: University of British Columbia Press. 254–64.

Joslin, Tom, dir. 1993. *Silverlake Life: The View from Here*. Distributed by Zeitgeist.

———. 1976. *Blackstar*. No distributor.

Jouve, Nicole Ward. 1991. *White Woman Speaks with Forked Tongue: Criticism as Autobiography*. New York: Routledge.

Kadar, Marlene, ed. 1992. *Essays on Life Writing: From Genre to Critical Practice*. Toronto: University of Toronto Press.

Kamenetz, Rodger. 1985. *Terra Infirma*. Fayetteville: University of Arkansas Press.

Kaplan, Caren. 1992. "Resisting Autobiography: Out-Law Genres and Transnational Feminist Subjects." In *De/Colonizing the Subject: The Politics of Gender in Women's Autobiography*, edited by Sidonie Smith and Julia Watson. Minneapolis: University of Minnesota Press. 115–38.

Kaplan, Chaim A. 1965. *Scroll of Agony: The Warsaw Diary of Chaim A. Kaplan*. Translated by Abraham I. Katsch. New York: Macmillan.

Karpf, Anne. 1996. *The War After: Living with the Holocaust*. London: Heinemann.

Kastenbaum, Robert. 1992. *The Psychology of Death*. 2d ed. New York: Springer Publishing Co.

Kaysen, Susanna. *Girl, Interrupted*. 1993. New York: Turtle Bay Books.

Keeshig-Tobias, Lenore. 1990. "The Magic of Others." In *Language in Her Eye: Views on Writing and Gender by Canadian Women Writing in English*, edited by Libby Scheier, Sarah Sheard, and Eleanor Wachtel. Toronto: Coach House. 173–77.

Kennard, Jean E. 1984. "Ourself Behind Ourself: A Theory for Lesbian Readers." *Signs* 9:647–62.

Kerby, Anthony Paul. 1991. *Narrative and the Self*. Bloomington: Indiana University Press.

Kermode, Frank. 1972. *The Art of Telling: Essays on Fiction*. Cambridge: Harvard University Press.

———. 1966. *The Sense of an Ending: Studies in the Theory of Fiction*. New York: Oxford University Press.

Keyssar, Helene. 1991. "Drama and the Dialogic Imagination: *The Heidi Chronicles* and *Fefu and Her Friends*." *Modern Drama* 34:88–106.

———. 1985. *Feminist Theatre: An Introduction to Plays of Contemporary British and American Women*. New York: Grove Press.

Kingston, Maxine Hong. 1983. "Maxine Hong Kingston: From an Interview between Kingston and Arturo Islas, Professor of English, Stanford

University, October 1, 1980, Berkeley, California." In *Women Writers of the West Coast: Speaking of Their Lives and Careers*, edited by Marilyn Yalom. Santa Barbara: Capra Press. 11–19.

——. 1982. "Cultural Mis-readings by American Reviewers." In *Asian and Western Writers in Dialogue*, edited by Guy Amirthanayagam. London: Basingstoke. 55–65.

——. *China Men*. 1977. New York: Random House.

——. 1975. *The Woman Warrior: Memoirs of a Girlhood among Ghosts*. New York: Random House.

Kleinman, Arthur. 1988. *The Illness Narratives: Suffering, Healing, and the Human Condition*. New York: Basic Books.

Krupat, Arnold. 1991. "Native American Autobiography and the Synecdochic Self." In *American Autobiography: Retrospect and Prospect*, edited by Paul John Eakin. Madison: University of Wisconsin Press. 171–94.

——. 1989. *The Voice in the Margin: Native American Literature and the Canon*. Berkeley: University of California Press.

——. 1985. *For Those Who Come After: A Study of Native American Autobiography*. Berkeley: University of California Press.

Kübler-Ross, Elisabeth. 1969. *On Death and Dying*. New York: Macmillan.

Kuper, Jack. 1967. *Child of the Holocaust*. Toronto: General Publishing Co.

Lacey, Liam. 1986. "Fascinating Jessica Works on Several Different Levels." *Globe and Mail*, March 27. D1.

Lane, Jim, dir. 1986. *East Meets West: A Video Diary*. No distributor.

——. 1981. *Long Time No See*. No distributor.

Langer, Lawrence L. 1975. *The Holocaust and the Literary Imagination*. New Haven: Yale University Press.

Lavie, Smadar, and Ted Swedenburg, eds. 1996. *Displacement, Diaspora, and Geographies of Identity*. Durham: Duke University Press.

Lee, Robert G. 1991. "*The Woman Warrior* as an Intervention in Asian American Historiography." In *Approaches to Teaching Kingston's "The Woman Warrior,"* edited by Shirley Geok-lin Lim. New York: Modern Language Association. 52–63.

Leitner, Isabella. 1978. *Fragments of Isabella: A Memoir of Auschwitz*. New York: Thomas Y. Crowell.

Lejeune, Philippe. 1991. "The Genetic Study of Autobiographical Texts." *biography* 14:1–11.

——. 1989. *On Autobiography*. Translated by Katherine Leary. Edited by Paul John Eakin. Minneapolis: University of Minnesota Press.

Leoni, Giovanni. 1994. "'The First Blow': Projects for the Camp at Fossoli." In *Holocaust Remembrance: The Shapes of Memory*, edited by Geoffrey H. Hartman. Oxford: Blackwell. 204–14.

Lerner, Gerda. 1978. *A Death of One's Own*. New York: Simon and Schuster.

Levi, Primo. 1992. *Collected Poems*. Translated by Ruth Feldman and Brian Swann. London: Faber and Faber.

——. 1990. *The Mirror Maker*. Translated by Raymond Rosenthal. London: Methuen.

——. 1989a. *The Drowned and the Saved*. Translated by Raymond Rosenthal. New York: Vintage Books.

——. 1989b. *Other People's Trades*. Translated by Raymond Rosenthal. London: Michael Joseph.

——. 1987a. *If Not Now, When?* Translated by William Weaver. London: Abacus.

——. 1987b. *Moments of Reprieve*. Translated by Ruth Feldman. New York: Viking Penguin.

——. 1986. "Questions with and without Answers." *New Republic*, February 17: 28.

——. 1985. *The Periodic Table*. Translated by Raymond Rosenthal. London: Michael Joseph.

——. 1984. "Beyond Survival." *Prooftexts: A Journal of Jewish Literary History* 4:9–21.

——. 1979. *"If This Is a Man" and "The Truce."* Translated by Stuart Woolf. London: Abacus.

——. 1968. *Se questo è un uomo*. Turin: Einaudi.

Lim, Shirley Geok-lin. 1996. *Among the White Moon Faces: An Asian-American Memoir of Homelands*. New York: Feminist Press.

——. 1992a. "The Ambivalent American: Asian American Literature on the Cusp." In *Reading the Literatures of Asian America*, edited by Shirley Geok-lin Lim and Amy Ling. Philadelphia: Temple University Press. 13–32.

——. 1992b. "The Tradition of Chinese American Women's Life Stories: Thematics of Race and Gender in Jade Snow Wong's *Fifth Chinese Daughter* and Maxine Hong Kingston's *The Woman Warrior*." In *American Women's Autobiography: Fea(s)ts of Memory*, edited by Margo Culley. Madison: University of Wisconsin Press. 252–67.

——, ed. 1991. *Approaches to Teaching Kingston's "The Woman Warrior."* New York: Modern Language Association.

Lionnet, Françoise. 1995. *Postcolonial Representations: Women, Literature, Identity*. Ithaca: Cornell University Press.

——. 1989. *Autobiographical Voices: Race, Gender, Self-Portraiture*. Ithaca: Cornell University Press.

Lorde, Audre. 1988. *a burst of light*. Toronto: Women's Press.

——. 1982. *Zami: A New Spelling of My Name*. Freedom, Calif.: Crossing Press.

——. 1980. *The Cancer Journals*. San Francisco: aunt lute books.

Lorenz, Clarissa M. 1983. *Lorelei Two: My Life with Conrad Aiken*. Athens: University of Georgia Press.

Lundman, Janis, and Adrienne Mitchell, dirs. 1993. *Talk 19*. Distributed by Back Alley Film Productions.

——. 1991. *Talk 16*. Distributed by National Film Board of Canada (NFB).

McCarthy, Mary. 1955/1995. *A Charmed Life*. San Diego: Harcourt Brace Jovanovich.

McClintock, Anne. 1993. "The Angel of Progress: Pitfalls of the Term 'Post-Colonialism.'" In *Colonial Discourse and Post-Colonial Theory: A Reader*, edited by Patrick Williams and Laura Chrisman. New York: Harvester. 291–304.

Malouf, David. 1993. *Remembering Babylon*. Toronto: Random House.

Mason, Mary G. 1980. "The Other Voice: Autobiographies of Women

Writers." In *Autobiography: Essays Theoretical and Critical*, edited by James Olney. Princeton: Princeton University Press. 207–35.

Meigs, Mary. 1997. *The Time Being*. Vancouver: Talonbooks.

———. 1991. *In the Company of Strangers*. Vancouver: Talonbooks.

———. 1987. *The Box Closet*. Vancouver: Talonbooks.

———. 1983. *The Medusa Head*. Vancouver: Talonbooks.

———. 1981. *Lily Briscoe a Self-Portrait: An Autobiography by Mary Meigs*. Vancouver: Talonbooks.

Mellard, James. 1991. *Using Lacan: Reading Fiction*. Urbana and Chicago: University of Illinois Press.

Mercer, Kobena. 1988. "Diaspora Culture and the Dialogic Imagination: The Aesthetics of Black Independent Film in Britain." In *Blackframes: Critical Perspectives on Black Independent Cinema*, edited by Mbye B. Cham and Claire Andrade-Watkins. Cambridge: MIT Press. 50–61.

Metz, Christian. 1975. "The Imaginary Signifier." *Screen* 16:14–76.

Middlebrook, Christina. 1996. *Seeing the Crab: A Memoir of Dying*. New York: Basic Books.

Miller, Nancy K. 1996. *Bequest and Betrayal: Memoirs of a Parent's Death*. New York: Oxford.

———. 1994. "Representing Others: Gender and the Subjects of Autobiography." *differences: A Journal of Feminist Cultural Studies* 6:1–27.

———. 1992a. "Autobiographical Deaths." *MR: The Massachusetts Review* 33:19–47.

———. 1992b. "Facts, Pacts, Acts." *Profession*, 10–14.

Moi, Toril. 1985. *Sexual/Textual Politics: Feminist Literary Theory*. London: Methuen.

Mojica, Monique. 1991. *Princess Pocahontas and the Blue Spots*. Toronto: Women's Press.

Momeyer, Richard W. 1982. "Death Mystiques: Denial, Acceptance, Rebellion." *Mosaic* 15:1–12.

Monette, Paul. 1988. *Borrowed Time: An AIDS Memoir*. New York: Avon Books.

Morrison, Blake. 1993. *And when did you last see your father?* London: Granta Books.

Morrison, James. 1992. "The Repression of the Returned: AIDS and Allegory." In *AIDS: The Literary Response*, edited by Emmanuel S. Nelson. New York and Toronto: Twayne / Maxwell Macmillan Canada. 167–74.

Moses, Daniel David, and Terry Goldie, eds. 1992. *An Anthology of Canadian Native Literature in English*. Toronto: Oxford University Press.

Mukherjee, Bharati. 1997. "American Dreamer." *Mother Jones*, January / February: 32–35.

———. 1975. *Wife*. New York: Fawcett Crest.

Murphy, Robert F. 1978. *The Body Silent*. New York: Henry Holt and Co.

Murray, Laura J. 1999. "The Economics of Experience in *The Book of Jessica*." *Tulsa Studies in Women's Literature* (forthcoming, Fall).

Neuman, Shirley. 1992. "Autobiography: From Different Poetics to a Poetics of Difference." In *Essays on Life Writing: From Genre to Critical Practice*, edited by Marlene Kadar. Toronto: University of Toronto Press. 213–30.

———. 1990. "Life Writing." In *Canadian Literature in English*. Vol. 4 of *Literary History of Canada*, edited by W. H. New. 2d ed. Toronto: University of Toronto Press. 333–70.

———. 1989. "'An appearance walking in a forest the sexes burn':
Autobiography and the Construction of the Feminine Body." *Signature* 2:1–26.

———. 1986. "Importing difference." In *A/mazing Space: Writing Canadian Women Writing*, edited by Shirley Neuman and Smaro Kamboureli. Edmonton: Longspoon/NeWest. 392–405.

———. 1981. "The Observer Observed: Distancing the Self in Autobiography." *Prose Studies* 4:317–36.

New, W. H., ed. 1990. *Native Writers and Canadian Writing: Canadian Literature Special Issue*. Vancouver: University of British Columbia Press.

Nichols, Bill. 1991. *Representing Reality: Issues and Concepts in Documentary*. Bloomington: Indiana University Press.

Nolan, Christopher. 1987. *Under the Eye of the Clock: The Life Story of Christopher Nolan*. London: Weidenfeld and Nicolson.

Noll, Peter. 1989. *In the Face of Death*. Translated by Hans Noll. New York: Viking.

Nuland, Sherwin B. 1994. *How We Die: Reflections on Life's Final Chapter*. New York: Knopf.

Olney, James. 1986. "(Auto)biography." *Southern Review* 22:428–41.

———. 1980. "Autobiography and the Cultural Moment: A Thematic, Historical, and Bibliographical Introduction." In *Autobiography: Essays Theoretical and Critical*, edited by James Olney. Princeton: Princeton University Press. 4–27.

———. 1972. *Metaphors of Self: The Meaning of Autobiography*. Princeton: Princeton University Press.

Ondaatje, Michael. 1989. *Running in the Family*. Toronto: McClelland and Stewart.

Ong, Walter J. 1982. *Orality and Literacy: The Technologizing of the Word*. New York: Methuen.

Ozick, Cynthia. 1989. *Metaphor and Memory: Essays*. New York: Alfred A. Knopf.

Panourgiá, Neni. 1995. *Fragments of Death, Fables of Identity: An Athenian Anthropography*. Madison: University of Wisconsin Press.

Park, Katharine. 1993. "Kimberly Bergalis, AIDS, and the Plague Metaphor." In *media spectacles*, edited by Jann Matlock, Marjorie Garber, and Rebecca Walkowitz. London: Routledge. 235–53.

Pascal, Roy. 1960. *Design and Truth in Autobiography*. Cambridge: Harvard University Press.

Patruno, Nicholas. 1995. *Understanding Primo Levi*. Columbia: University of South Carolina Press.

Pekar, Harvey, Joyce Brabner, and Art Stack. 1994. *Our Cancer Year*. New York and London: Four Walls Eight Windows.

Perreault, Donna. 1990. "What Makes Autobiography Interrogative?" *biography* 13:130–42.

Perreault, Jeanne. 1995. *Writing Selves: Contemporary Feminist Autography*. Minneapolis: University of Minnesota Press.

Petrone, Penny. 1990. *Native Literature in Canada: From the Oral Tradition to the Present*. Toronto: Oxford University Press.

Phelan, Peggy. 1995. "Dying Man with a Movie Camera: *Silverlake Life: The View from Here.*" *GLQ: Journal of Lesbian and Gay Studies* 2:380–98.

Phenix, Lucy Massie. 1993. *Cancer in Two Voices*. Distributed by Video Arts.

Porter, Roger J. 1996. "Self and Other Is One Flesh: Double Voicing in Recent Autobiographical Writing." Paper presented at "All by Myself" Autobiography Conference, November 14, at the University of Gröningen.

Portugues, Catherine. 1988. "Seeing Subjects: Women Directors and Cinematic Autobiography." In *Life/Lines: Theorizing Women's Autobiography*, edited by Bella Brodzki and Celeste Schenck. Ithaca: Cornell University Press. 338–50.

Potter, Dennis. 1994. *Seeing the Blossom: Two Interviews, a Lecture and a Story*. London: Faber and Faber.

Price, Reynolds. 1994. *A Whole New Life: An Illness and a Healing*. New York: Atheneum.

Profeit-LeBlanc, Louise. 1990. "Ancient Stories, Spiritual Legacies." In *Telling It: Women and Language across Cultures: The Transformation of a Conference*, edited by The Telling It Book Collective. Vancouver: Press Gang Publishers. 111–16.

Reichek, Morton A. 1991. "Elie Wiesel." In *Jewish Profiles: Great Jewish Personalities and Institutions of the Twentieth Century*, edited by Murray Polner. Northvale, N.J.: Jason Aronson.

Ricoeur, Paul. 1992. *Oneself as Another*. Translated by Kathleen Blamey. Chicago: University of Chicago Press.

Ridington, Robin. 1988. *Trail to Heaven: Knowledge and Narrative in a Northern Native Community*. Vancouver: Douglas and McIntyre.

Ringelblum, Emmanuel. 1974. *Notes from the Warsaw Ghetto*. Translated by Jacob Sloan. New York: Schocken Books.

Rodriguez, Richard. 1983. *Hunger of Memory: The Education of Richard Rodriguez*. Toronto: Bantam Books.

Rosenbluth, Vera. 1997. *Keeping Family Stories Alive: A Creative Guide to Taping Your Family Life and Lore*. 2d ed. Point Roberts, Wash.: Hartley and Marks.

Rosenfeld, Alvin H. 1980. *A Double Dying: Reflections on Holocaust Literature*. Bloomington: Indiana University Press.

Roth, Philip. 1991. *Patrimony: A True Story*. New York: Simon and Schuster.

Ruby, Jay. 1988. "The Image Mirrored: Reflexivity in the Documentary Film." In *New Challenges for Documentary*, edited by Alan Rosenthal. Berkeley: University of California Press. 64–77.

Rugg, Linda Haverty. 1997. *Picturing Ourselves: Photography and Autobiography*. Chicago: University of Chicago Press.

Rushdie, Salman. 1991. *Imaginary Homelands: Essays and Criticism 1981–1991*. London: Granta Books.

Ryan, Judith. 1992. *The Vanishing Subject: Early Psychology and Literary Modernism*. Chicago: University of Chicago Press.

Sacks, Oliver. 1984. *A Leg to Stand On*. New York: Summit.

Salomon, Charlotte. 1963. *Charlotte: A Diary in Pictures*. London: Collins.

Sarraute, Nathalie. 1984. *Childhood*. Translated by Barbara Wright. New York: G. Braziller.

Scarry, Elaine. 1985. *The Body in Pain: The Making and Unmaking of the World*. New York: Oxford University Press.

Schlueter, June. 1987. "*Keep Tightly Closed in a Cool Dry Place*: Megan Terry's Transformational Drama and the Possibilities of Self." *Studies in American Drama 1945–Present* 2:59–69.

Scholes, Robert. 1982. *Semiotics and Interpretation*. New Haven: Yale University Press.

Schreiber, LeAnne. 1990. *Midstream*. New York: Viking.

Schueller, Malini. 1989. "Questioning Race and Gender Definitions: Dialogic Subversions in *The Woman Warrior*." *Criticism* 31:421–37.

Scott, Cynthia, dir. 1991. *The Company of Strangers*. Distributed by National Film Board of Canada (NFB).

Smith, Paul. 1988. *Discerning the Subject*. Minneapolis: University of Minnesota Press.

Smith, Sidonie. 1993. *Subjectivity, Identity, and the Body: Women's Autobiographical Practices in the Twentieth Century*. Bloomington: Indiana University Press.

———. 1987. *A Poetics of Women's Autobiography: Marginality and the Fictions of Self-Representation*. Bloomington: Indiana University Press.

Smith, Sidonie, and Julia Watson, eds. 1996. *Getting a Life: Everyday Uses of Autobiography*. Minneapolis: University of Minnesota Press.

———. 1992. *De/Colonizing the Subject: The Politics of Gender in Women's Autobiography*. Minneapolis: University of Minnesota Press.

Sobchack, Vivian. 1984. "Inscribing Ethical Space: Ten Propositions on Death Representation and Documentary." *Quarterly Review of Film Studies* 9:283–300.

Sodi, Risa. 1995. "The Rhetoric of the Univers Concentrationnaire." Paper presented at the Primo Levi Conference, November 5, at the Holocaust Centre in Vancouver.

———. 1990. *A Dante of Our Time: Primo Levi and Auschwitz*. New York: Peter Lang.

———. 1988. "Primo Levi: A Last Talk." *Present Tense* 15:40–45.

———. 1987. "An Interview with Primo Levi." *Partisan Review* 54:355–66.

Sommer, Doris. 1988. "'Not Just a Personal Story': Women's Testimonies and the Plural Self." In *Life/Lines: Theorizing Women's Autobiography*, edited by Bella Brodzki and Celeste Schenck. Ithaca: Cornell University Press. 107–30.

Sontag, Susan. 1990. *Illness and Metaphor and AIDS and Its Metaphors*. New York: Farrar, Straus, Giroux.

———. 1973/1977. *On Photography*. New York: Farrar, Straus, Giroux.

Spence, Jo. 1988. *Putting Myself in the Picture: A Political, Personal and Photographic Autobiography*. Seattle: Real Comet Press.

Spiegelman, Art. 1991. *Maus: A Survivor's Tale II: And Here My Troubles Began*. New York: Pantheon.

———. 1986. *Maus: A Survivor's Tale: My Father Bleeds History*. New York: Pantheon.

Spivak, Gayatri Chakravorty. 1996. "How to Teach a Culturally Different Book." In *The Spivak Reader: Selected Works of Gayatri Chakravorty Spivak*, edited by Donna Landry and Gerald MacLean. New York: Routledge. 237–66.

———. 1990. "Strategy, Identity, Writing." In *The Postcolonial Critic: Interviews, Strategies, Dialogues*, edited by Sarah Harasym. New York: Routledge. 35–49.

Stanton, Domna. 1987. "Autogynography: Is the Subject Different?" In *The Female Autograph*, edited by Domna Stanton. New York: University of Chicago Press. 3–20.

Starobinski, Jean. 1971 / 1980. "The Style of Autobiography." In *Autobiography: Essays Theoretical and Critical*, edited by James Olney. Princeton: Princeton University Press. 73–83.

Steedman, Carolyn Kay. 1987. *Landscape for a Good Woman: A Story of Two Lives*. New Brunswick, N.J.: Rutgers University Press.

Stein, Gertrude. 1966. *The Autobiography of Alice B. Toklas*. Harmondsworth: Penguin.

Steiner, George. 1967. *Language and Silence: Essays on Language, Literature, and the Inhuman*. New York: Atheneum.

Stone, Albert E. 1982. *Autobiographical Occasions and Original Acts: Versions of American Identity from Henry Adams to Nate Shaw*. Philadelphia: University of Pennsylvania Press.

Strathern, Marilyn. 1987. "The Limits of Auto-Anthropology." In *Anthropology at Home*, edited by Anthony Jackson. London: Tavistock. ASA Publications 25:16–37.

Styron, William. 1991. *Darkness Visible: A Memoir of Madness*. New York: Vintage.

Tan, Amy. 1995. "Mother Tongue." In *Under Western Eyes*, edited by Garrett Hongo. New York: Doubleday. 315–20.

Tarrow, Susan R. 1994. "Remembering Primo Levi: A Conversation with 'Il Pikolo del Kommando 98.'" *Forum Italicum* 28:101–10.

———, ed. 1990. *Reason and Light: Essays on Primo Levi*. Ithaca: Center for International Studies, Cornell University.

Tavernier-Courbin, Jacqueline. 1980. "The Mystery of the Ritz-Hotel Papers." *College Literature* 7:289–303.

Terdiman, Richard. 1985. *Discourse/Counter-Discourse: The Theory and Practice of Symbolic Resistance in Nineteenth-Century France*. Ithaca: Cornell University Press.

Thomson, Ian. 1987. "Primo Levi in Conversation with Ian Thomson." *PN Review* 14:15–19.

Timerman, Jacobo. 1981. *Prisoner Without a Name, Cell Without a Number*. Translated by Toby Talbot. New York: Knopf.

Treichler, Paula A. 1993. "AIDS, Homophobia, and Biomedical Discourse: An Epidemic of Signification." In *media spectacles*, edited by Jann Matlock, Marjorie Garber, and Rebecca Walkowitz. London: Routledge. 31–70.

Trinh, T. Minh-ha. 1992. *Framer Framed*. New York: Routledge.

———, dir. 1989. *Surname Viet Given Name Nam*. Distributed by Women Make Movies, New York; Museum of Modern Art, New York; Cinenova,

London; Idera, Vancouver; Image Forum, Tokyo; National Library of
Australia, Canberra.

Trudeau, G. B. 1995. *Flashbacks: Twenty-five Years of Doonesbury*. Kansas City:
Andrews and McMeel.

———. 1993. *The Portable Doonesbury*. Kansas City: Andrews and McMeel.

Turner, Victor. 1985. *On the Edge of the Bush: Anthropology as Experience.*
Tucson: University of Arizona Press.

Van Toorn, Penny. 1990. "Discourse/Patron Discourse: How Minority Texts
Command the Attention of Majority Audiences." In *A Sense of Audience:
Essays in Post-Colonial Literatures*, edited by William McGaw. SPAN
30:102–15.

Veeser, H. Aram. 1996. *Confessions of the Critics: North American Critics'
Autobiographical Moves.* New York: Routledge.

Verdecchia, Guillermo. 1993. *Fronteras Americanas: (American Borders).*
Toronto: Coach House Press.

Waskow, Howard, and Arthur Waskow. 1993. *Becoming Brothers.* New York:
Free Press.

Wasserman, Jerry, ed. 1985. *Modern Canadian Plays.* Vancouver: Talonbooks.

Wasson, Kirsten. 1994. "A Geography of Conversion: Dialogical Boundaries
of Self in Antin's *Promised Land.*" In *Autobiography and Postmodernism*,
edited by Kathleen Ashley, Leigh Gilmore, and Gerald Peters. Amherst:
University of Massachusetts Press. 167–87.

Watson, Julia. 1992. "Unspeakable Differences: The Politics of Gender in
Lesbian and Heterosexual Women's Autobiographies." In *De/Colonizing
the Subject: The Politics of Gender in Women's Autobiography*, edited by
Sidonie Smith and Julia Watson. Minneapolis: University of Minnesota
Press. 139–68.

Wickes, George. 1974. "Sketches of the Author's Life in Paris in the Twenties."
In *Hemingway in Our Time*, edited by Richard Astro and Jackson J.
Benson. Corvallis: Oregon State University Press. 25–38.

Wiesel, Elie. 1987. *The Night Trilogy: "Night," "Dawn," "The Accident."* New
York: Hill and Wang.

Wilber, Ken. 1991. *Grace and Grit: Spirituality and Healing in the Life and
Death of Treya Killam Wilber.* Boston: Shambhala.

Williams, Donna. 1992. *Nobody Nowhere: The Extraordinary Autobiography of
an Autistic.* Toronto: Doubleday Canada.

Williams, Terry Tempest. 1991. *Refuge: An Unnatural History of Family and
Place.* New York: Pantheon Books.

Wolff, Charlotte. 1972. *Love between Women.* New York: Harper.

Wollen, Peter. 1969. *Signs and Meaning in the Cinema.* Bloomington: Indiana
University Press.

Wong, Hertha D. 1994. "Plains Indian Names and 'the Autobiographical
Act.'" In *Autobiography and Postmodernism*, edited by Kathleen Ashley,
Leigh Gilmore, and Gerald Peters. Amherst: University of Massachusetts
Press. 212–39.

Wong, Sau-ling Cynthia. 1992. "Autobiography as Guided Chinatown Tour?
Maxine Hong Kingston's *The Woman Warrior* and the Chinese-American
Autobiographical Controversy." In *Multicultural Autobiography: American*

Lives, edited by James Robert Payne. Knoxville: University of Tennessee Press. 248–79.

———. 1991. "Kingston's Handling of Traditional Chinese Sources." In *Approaches to Teaching Kingston's "The Woman Warrior,"* edited by Shirley Geok-lin Lim. New York: Modern Language Association. 26–36.

Woods, Gregory. 1992. "AIDS to Remembrance: The Uses of Elegy." In *AIDS: The Literary Response*, edited by Emmanuel S. Nelson. New York and Toronto: Twayne/Maxwell Macmillan Canada. 155–66.

Woolf, Virginia. 1960. *To the Lighthouse*. London: Hogarth.

York, Lorraine M. 1994. "'The things that are seen in the flashes': Timothy Findley's *Inside Memory* as Photographic Life Writing." *Modern Fiction Studies* 40:643–56.

———. 1988. *"The Other Side of Dailiness": Photography in the Works of Alice Munro, Timothy Findley, Michael Ondaatje, and Margaret Laurence*. Toronto: Essays on Canadian Writing.

Young, David. 1986. *Incognito: A Collection by David Young*. Toronto: Coach House.

Zola, Irving. 1982. *Missing Pieces: A Chronicle of Living with a Disability*. Philadelphia: Temple University Press.

Index

Abbott, H. Porter, 15
ACT-UP, 211
Adams, Timothy Dow: on lying, 35, 36
Adorno, Theodor, 186
AIDS, 207–15; and death, 97, 201; and film, 18, 87; and literature, 196; and politics, 226; quilt, 17–19, 233 (n. 20). *See also* Death and dying; Film: *Silverlake Life*
Améry, Jean, 164, 179, 241 (n. 3), 244 (n. 23)
Andrews, Jennifer, 105
Anthropology, 10–11, 202, 228
Anzaldúa, Gloria, 120, 124
Appropriation, 26, 28, 105, 109, 128, 144, 237 (n. 8); in *The Book of Jessica*, 101, 110–11; colonial, 102, 114; in dialogic genres, 85, 86, 101; and exchange, 103; in literature, 117; resistance to, 112, 124; in treaties, 108
Apted, Michael, 26, 86, 91–96
Ariès, Philippe, 197, 201
Arlen, Michael, 40
Armstrong, Jeannette C., 106, 118
Arnott, Brian, 103
Auschwitz, 5, 27, 35, 81, 159, 233 (n. 25), 244 (n. 15); death camps, 241 (n. 2), 243 (n. 12); death march, 181; death of idea of human beings, 162, 164; death of Italians, 164
Auto-anthropology, 247 (n. 12)
Autobiographics, 14, 15
(Auto)biography, 1, 2, 3, 7, 10, 16, 17, 18, 19, 21, 214, 240 (n. 30)
Autoethnography, 15
Autography, 15

Autogynography, 14
Autopathography, 15, 201, 246 (n. 7), 247 (n. 12)
Autoportrait, 15
Autothanatography, 6, 195–224 passim, 246 (n. 4); AIDS-related, 207–15; central to autobiography, 200, 202; dialogic forms in, 198, 199, 203, 246 (n. 5); making meaning in, 205, 206, 225; as Miller's coinage, 15, 245 (n. 1); politics of, 226. *See also* Body; Death and dying

Babel, 169, 170, 171, 189
Bakhtin, Mikhail, 24, 104, 108, 228
Barnouw, Erik, 91
Barros, Carolyn A., 231
Barthes, Roland, 20, 89
Bauman, Zygmunt, 196, 204
Bazin, André, 89
Beaujour, Michel, 15
Beauvoir, Simone de, 130, 201
Bell, Quentin, 52, 53
Bell, Vanessa, 52
Benjamin, Jessica, 8. *See also* Intersubjectivity
Berger, John, 21
Bergland, Betty, 24
Bergman, David, 211, 233
Bersani, Leo, 207
Bessai, Diane, 105
Bhabha, Homi K., 238 (n. 15)
Biography, 1, 2, 7, 10
Biomythography, 15, 132, 134
Blackstar. See Film: *Blackstar*
Blais, Marie-Claire, 27, 54, 56, 59–60

	DATE DUE		